D1557540

Conversations with Chinua Achebe

Literary Conversations Series

Peggy Whitman Prenshaw
General Editor

© Dan Hamerman

Conversations with Chinua Achebe

Edited by
Bernth Lindfors

University Press of Mississippi
Jackson

Copyright © 1997 by University Press of Mississippi
All rights reserved
Manufactured in the United States of America

00 99 98 97   4 3 2 1

The paper in this book meets the guidelines for permanence and durability of the Committee on
Production Guidelines for Book Longevity of the Council on Library Resources.

Library of Congress Cataloging-in-Publication Data

Achebe, Chinua.
      Conversations with Chinua Achebe / edited by Bernth Lindfors.
          p.   cm—(Literary conversations series)
      Includes index.
      ISBN 0-87805-929-6 (cloth : alk. paper).—ISBN 0-87805-999-7
(paper : alk. paper)
      1. Achebe, Chinua—Interviews.   2. Authors, Nigerian—20th
century—Biography.   I. Lindfors, Bernth.   II. Title.   III. Series.
PR9387.9.A3Z58   1997
823—dc21
[B]   97-6953
                                                                                      CIP

British Library Cataloging-in-Publication data available

Books by Chinua Achebe

Things Fall Apart. London: Heinemann, 1958; New York: McDowell, Obolensky, 1959.
No Longer at Ease. London: Heinemann, 1960; New York: Obolensky, 1961.
The Sacrificial Egg, and Other Stories. Onitsha, Nigeria: Etudo, 1962.
Arrow of God. London: Heinemann, 1964; New York: Day, 1967; revised, London: Heinemann, 1974.
Chike and the River. Cambridge: Cambridge University Press, 1966.
A Man of the People. London: Heinemann, 1966; New York: Day, 1966.
Beware, Soul Brother, and Other Poems. Enugu, Nigeria: Nwankwo-Ifejika, 1971; revised and enlarged edition, London: Heinemann, 1972; republished as *Christmas in Biafra and Other Poems.* Garden City, NY: Anchor/Doubleday, 1973.
Girls at War and Other Stories. London: Heinemann, 1972; Garden City, NY: Doubleday, 1973.
(with John Iroaganachi). *How the Leopard Got His Claws.* Enugu, Nigeria: Nwamife, 1972; New York: Third Press, 1973; Nairobi: East African Publishing House, 1976.
Morning Yet on Creation Day: Essays. London: Heinemann, 1975; enlarged edition, Garden City, NY: Anchor/Doubleday, 1975.
The Drum: A Children's Story. Enugu, Nigeria: Fourth Dimension, 1977.
The Flute: A Children's Story. Enugu, Nigeria: Fourth Dimension, 1979.
The Trouble with Nigeria. Enugu, Nigeria: Fourth Dimension, 1983; London and Exeter, NH: Heinemann, 1984.
What Has Literature Got to Do with It? [Lagos, Nigeria]: Federal Republic of Nigeria, 1986.
Anthills of the Savannah. London: Heinemann, 1987; New York: Anchor/Doubleday, 1988; Ibadan: Heinemann Educational Books (Nigeria), 1988.
Hopes and Impediments: Selected Essays, 1965–1987. London: Heinemann, 1988; New York: Doubleday, 1989.
The University and the Leadership Factor in Nigerian Politics. Enugu, Nigeria: Abic, 1988.
The African Trilogy: Things Fall Apart; No Longer at Ease; Arrow of God. London: Picador, 1988.
The Voter. Johannesburg: ViVa Books, 1994.

Books Edited

(with Arthur Nwankwo, Samuel Ifejika, and Flora Nwapa). *The Insider: Stories of War and Peace from Nigeria.* Enugu, Nigeria: Nwankwo-Ifejika, 1971.
(with Dubem Okafor). *Don't Let Him Die: an Anthology of Memorial Poems for Christopher Okigbo (1932–1967).* Enugu, Nigeria: Fourth Dimension, 1978.
(with Obiora Udechukwu). *Aka Weta: Egwu aguluagu Egwu edeluede.* Nsukka, Nigeria: Okike, 1982.
(with C.L. Innes). *African Short Stories.* London and Portsmouth, NH: Heinemann, 1985.
(with C.L. Innes). *The Heinemann Book of Contemporary African Short Stories.* Oxford and Portsmouth, NH: Heinemann, 1992.

Contents

Introduction

Chinua Achebe is Africa's most important novelist. His books are read throughout the English-speaking world and have been translated into more than fifty languages. His publishers estimate that over eight million copies of his first novel *Things Fall Apart* (1958) have been sold; indeed, it has outsold all the rest of the three hundred titles in Heinemann's African Writers Series combined. One reason this novel became such a runaway bestseller is that it was quickly adopted for use as a textbook in highschool and university English classes, particularly in Africa and most notably in Nigeria. As far back as 1965 the *Times Literary Supplement* could report that "already *Things Fall Apart* is as big a factor in the formation of a young West African's picture of his past, and of his relation to it, as any of the still rather distorted teachings of the pulpit and the primary school" (16 September 1965, p. 791). Achebe's other novels have also been extremely influential and commercially successful. They too are studied widely, as are his short stories, poetry and essays. As a consequence, a large and vigorous critical industry has grown up around his work. More books, articles, study guides, doctoral dissertations and master's theses have been produced on his writings than on those of any other African novelist.

It is therefore not surprising that he frequently has been sought out by interviewers who have wanted to know more about the man behind these marvelous books. How did he get started? What kind of upbringing and education did he have? Which writers influenced him? Were there any teachers or mentors who encouraged and guided him? What prompted him to write fiction when few other Nigerians were doing so? How did his first manuscript find its way into print? Sheer biographical curiosity has been one of the principal motives behind these persistent questions. Interviewers have been seeking solutions to a puzzling riddle: how does one explain a rare phenomenon like Chinua Achebe? How does he explain himself?

According to Achebe, it all began with his love for stories, especially oral stories. He told Jerome Brooks that it was this interest in narratives that initially pointed him in the direction of writing: "I knew I loved stories, stories told in our home, first by my mother, then by my elder sister—such as the story of the tortoise—whatever scraps of stories I could gather from conversations, just hanging around, sitting around when my father had visitors. When I began going to school, I loved the stories I read. They were different, but I loved them too" (*Paris Review,* Winter 1994, p. 145). This interest grew and developed as he matured and gained a fuller exposure to the world through his formal education—first at mission primary schools, then at an elite boys' boarding school, and finally at Nigeria's first university. It was during his university years that his reading of racially biased British novels— particularly Joyce Cary's *Mister Johnson* and Conrad's *Heart of Darkness*— led him to contemplate writing a novel of his own. As he explained to Lewis Nkosi and Wole Soyinka, "I said to myself, this is absurd. If somebody without any inside knowledge of the people he is trying to describe can get away with it, perhaps I ought to try my hand at it."

The consequences of that decision have been enormous, not just for Achebe himself but also for all those who followed him and were inspired by his example. He often has been called the inventor of the African novel, and though he modestly denies the title, it is true that modern African literature would not have flowered so rapidly and spectacularly had he not led the way by telling Africa's story from a distinctively African point of view. Almost single-handedly he helped Africa to find its own voice and to speak so eloquently that its message could resonate both locally and throughout the rest of the world.

This has been a message with a pronounced moral. Achebe believes that literature should serve a useful social purpose, should aim to enlighten and instruct. The novelist should be a teacher who helps others to understand their human predicament. In a conversation with Charles H. Rowell he emphasized that in Africa "People are expecting from literature serious comment on their lives. They are not expecting frivolity. They are expecting literature to say something important to help them in their struggle with life. This is what literature, what art, is supposed to do: to give us a second handle on reality so that when it becomes necessary to do so, we can turn to art and find a way out. So it is a serious matter." It is this kind of socially supportive literature that Achebe has been intent on producing. He has not been creating art solely for art's sake.

Unlike some Western writers, Achebe believes that good literature can change the world. Stories, he told Jonathan Cott, "are the very center, the very heart of our civilization and culture." He elaborated on this point when speaking to Chris Searle: "It is the story that conveys all our gains, all our failures, all we hold dear and all we condemn. To convey this to the next generation is the only way we can keep going and keep alive as a people. Therefore the story is like the genes that are transferred to create the new being. It is far more important than anything else." In his fifth novel *Anthills of the Savannah* (1987) Achebe had one of his characters, a wise old man, insist that storytelling is far more important to a community than drumming or fighting a war. "Why? Because it is only the story can continue beyond the war and the warrior. It is the story that outlives the sound of war-drums and the exploits of brave fighters. It is the story, not the others, that saves our progeny from blundering like blind beggars into the spikes of the cactus fence. The story is our escort; without it, we are blind. Does the blind man own his escort? No, neither do we the story; rather it is the story that owns us and directs us." Over the last century Africa has experienced a great deal of turmoil, has heard many war-drums and seen lots of battles. Initially these were colonial conflicts; today they tend to be civil wars or struggles between unelected leaders and the peoples they misrule. The full story of these turbulent years has not been an easy one to tell, but many writers have taken a stab at it, putting on record at least a small portion of Africa's contemporary history in instructive fictional terms.

Of these storytellers no one has been more successful than Chinua Achebe. His novels have offered us lucid lessons and profound enlightenment, enabling us to see more clearly what has happened in Africa and why. His stories have been our escort, our most reliable guide to that continent's troubled past and troubling present. He has made it impossible for us to remain blind to African realities.

Throughout his career Achebe has kept pace with the times by responding to the changing preoccupations of his society. Forty years ago, when he wrote *Things Fall Apart* at the end of the colonial era, he was a reconstructionist dedicated to creating a dignified image of the African past; today he is an angry reformer crusading against the immorality and injustices of the African present. His novels thus not only chronicle one hundred years of Nigerian history but also reflect the dominant African intellectual concerns of the past four decades.

For this reason one suspects his works will have enduring significance. Later generations of readers will find in them an interpretation of African experience that is characteristic of its time. The compassionate evocations of Ibo village life, the graphic depictions of modern city life, the brilliantly drawn characters will probably speak with as much power then as they do today, evocatively reconstructing crucial moments in that confused era in Nigeria's past which began with the arrival of the first white men and ended with the imposition and perpetuation of indigenous military rule. Tomorrow as well as today Achebe's novels will continue to guide us to a better understanding of an eventful century in African history.

Achebe will also be remembered for his short stories, his children's books, his prize-winning poetry, and his incisive essays on literary, political and cultural matters. Indeed, he has emerged as one of Africa's most articulate literary critics, and his insightful interventions in debates on African literature, collected in *Morning Yet on Creation Day* and *Hopes and Impediments,* are frequently quoted and cited by other scholars. In the interviews printed here he is sounded out on some of the provocative ideas he has put forward in various essays and speeches. His remarks on these issues, as well as on his own writings, will fascinate those who have closely followed his career and will also interest those who are coming to his work for the first time. Achebe's thoughts on literature have been shaped by a lifetime of commitment to important causes, so they are firmly grounded in a set of stern ethical principles, but over the years he has responded imaginatively to new challenges by refusing to be rigidly dogmatic or doctrinaire and by granting the legitimacy of seeing matters a different way. This makes him a formidable opponent in debate, for he invariably argues from the vantage point of a cogently reasoned position, not one based on simplistic absolutes.

Achebe also is an impressive speaker, and those who have had an opportunity to hear him lecture will never forget the fluency and force with which he expresses his ideas, presenting them in language that is simple yet pungent, moderate yet peppered with colorful images and illustrations. This appears to be an inborn gift, for it is evident in his conversation too. In speech as well as writing Achebe demonstrates the skills of an expert rhetorician, one who chooses his words with care in order to convince or persuade an audience.

It is this talent for deep and meaningful communication, this intimate way with words, that makes Achebe's interviews a delight to read. He has a facility for penetrating to the essence of a question and framing a response that addresses the concerns of the questioner yet sometimes goes beyond those concerns to matters of more general interest. Indeed, the answers he gives are apt to be much better than the questions he gets, for he quickly perceives what lies beneath a question and speaks directly to that underlying issue as well.

The interviews collected here span more than thirty years of Achebe's writing career. The earliest was recorded in 1962, the latest in 1995. Achebe has been interviewed frequently, and it has been possible to reprint here only a representative sample of what has appeared in newspapers, journals and books in many different countries. One early interview, originally published in the French journal *Afrique,* is reproduced here in translation; another conducted in 1981 by postgraduate students in India and a third recorded in 1995 by Gordon Lewis in the United States are appearing in print for the first time. An effort has been made to select interviews from different points in Achebe's career and to present his thoughts on a variety of issues, but since the original transcripts have not been cut or condensed, occasionally one may find some repetition in the nature of the questions asked and the responses given. Interviews rich in biographical information, in analysis of specific texts, and in opinions on more general literary or cultural matters have been preferred over those concerned with the nitty-gritty of Nigerian politics. The focus throughout has been on Achebe as a man of letters, a man of ideas, a man of words.

Chronology

1930   Born, 16 November in Ogidi, a small town near Onitsha, Nigeria; fifth child of Isaiah Okafo Achebe, a catechist for the Church Missionary Society, and Janet N. Iloegbunam Achebe.

1936–42 Attends Ogidi CMS Central School

1943   Attends CMS Central School, Nekede, Owerri

1944–48 Attends Government College, Umuahia

1948–53 Attends University College, Ibadan; B.A. (London) 1953

1953–54 Teaches for eight months at Merchant of Light School, Oba

1954   Talks Producer, Nigerian Broadcasting Corporation

1955   Begins writing *Things Fall Apart*

1956   Attends BBC staff training school, London

1957   Head of Talks Department, NBC; completes *Things Fall Apart*.

1958   Controller, NBC Eastern Region; *Things Fall Apart* published.

1959   Wins Margaret Wrong Memorial Prize for African literature

1960   Nigeria attains independence; *No Longer at Ease* published; travels in East and Central Africa on a Rockefeller Fellowship (1960–61).

1961   Director of External Broadcasting, NBC; wins Nigerian National Trophy for Literature; marries Christie Chinweifenu Okoli.

1962   Birth of daughter Chinelo; assumes editorship of Heinemann African Writers Series.

1963   Travels in the United States, Brazil and Britain on a UNESCO Fellowship

1964   *Arrow of God* published; birth of son Ikechukwu.

1966   *A Man of the People* and *Chike and the River* published; Nigeria experiences first military coup in January, counter-coup in July; moves with family to Eastern Nigeria; *Arrow of God* wins Jock Campbell-*New Statesman* Award for Literature.

1967   Birth of son Chidi; Biafra secedes from Nigeria, and civil war begins; appointed Senior Research Fellow, University of Nigeria, Nsukka (1967–72); establishes Citadel Press in Enugu with Christopher Okigbo; travels to parts of Africa, Europe and the United States on behalf of Biafra.

1969   Chairman of National Guidance Council, Biafra

1970   Biafra surrenders unconditionally to Nigeria; birth of daughter Nwando Chioma.

1971   *Beware, Soul Brother* published; founds *Okike: an African Journal of New Writing;* edits *Nsukkascope,* a campus magazine; edits (with others) *The Insider: Stories of War and Peace from Nigeria.*

1972   *Girls at War and Other Stories* and *How the Leopard Got His Claws* (co-authored with John Iroaganachi) published; joint-winner of first (British) Commonwealth Poetry Prize; accepts position as Visiting Professor of English at University of Massachusetts at Amherst (1972–75); resigns editorship of Heinemann African Writers Series; awarded honorary doctorate by Dartmouth College.

1973   Appointed Professor of English, University of Nigeria, Nsukka

1974   Awarded honorary doctorate by Southampton University, England

1975   *Morning Yet on Creation Day: Essays* published; accepts appointment as University Professor of English at University of Connecticut (1975–76); named Honorary Fellow of the Modern Language Association of America and Neil Gunn Fellow of the Scottish Arts Council; awarded honorary doctorate by Stirling University, Scotland

1976   Resumes position at University of Nigeria, Nsukka, as Professor of Literature (1976–81); awarded honorary doctorate by Prince Edward Island University, Canada.

1977   *The Drum: A Children's Story* published

1978   Edits (with Dubem Okafor) *Don't Let Him Die: An Anthology of Memorial Poems for Christopher Okigbo (1932–1967)*

1979   Accepts first Nigerian National Merit Award and appointment as
            Officer of the Order of the Federal Republic (OFR), another na-
            tional honor; *The Flute: A Children's Story* published; awarded
            honorary doctorates by University of Massachusetts at Amherst
            and University of Ife, Nigeria.

1981   Forms Association of Nigerian Authors and is elected its first
            President; takes early retirement from University of Nigeria,
            Nsukka; made Fellow of the Royal Society of Literature (Lon-
            don); awarded honorary doctorates by University of Kent, En-
            gland, and University of Nigeria, Nsukka.

1982   Edits (with Obiora Udechukwu) *Aka Weta: Egwu aguluagu Egwu
            edeluede,* a collection of poems in Igbo

1983   *The Trouble with Nigeria* published; appointed Deputy National
            Chairman of People's Redemption Party; made Honorary Fellow
            of the American Academy of Arts and Letters.

1984   Visiting Professor of English at University of Guelph, Ontario,
            and Regents Professor of English at University of California at
            Los Angeles; awarded honorary doctorates by University of
            Guelph and Mount Allison University, Canada; founds *Uwa ndi
            Igbo,* a bilingual journal of Igbo life and culture.

1985   Awarded honorary doctorate by Franklin Pierce College, New
            Hampshire; appointed Professor Emeritus at the University of Ni-
            geria, Nsukka; edits (with C.L. Innes) *African Short Stories.*

1986   Steps down as President of Association of Nigerian Authors; ap-
            pointed Pro-Chancellor and Chairman of Council of Anambra
            State University of Technology at Enugu, Nigeria; elected Presi-
            dent-General of Ogidi Union Nigeria (a town council).

1987   *Anthills of the Savannah* published and shortlisted for Booker
            Prize; Fulbright Professor of African Studies at University of
            Massachusetts, Amherst (1987–88).

1988   *Hopes and Impediments* and *The University and the Leadership
            Factor in Nigerian Politics* published.

1989   Visiting Distinguished Professor of English, City College of the
            City University of New York; 25 May proclaimed Chinua Achebe
            Day by the Borough of Manhattan; founds *African Commentary,*
            a magazine for people of African descent; elected first President
            of Nigerian chapter of PEN; re-elected President-General of Ogidi

Union Nigeria; appointed by Indian Government to an International Jury to award the annual Indira Gandhi Prize for Peace, Disarmament and Development (1989–92); awarded honorary doctorates by Westfield College (Massachusetts), the Open University (England), and the University of Ibadan.

1990   Montgomery Fellow and Visiting Professor of English at Dartmouth College; symposium held at the University of Nigeria, Nsukka, honoring him on his sixtieth birthday; receives citation from the USSR Academy of Sciences; receives Triple Eminence Award from the Association of Nigerian Authors; partially paralyzed in an automobile accident and convalesces in England; awarded honorary doctorate by Georgetown University; accepts Charles P. Stevenson, Jr., Chair in Literature at Bard College (1990–98).

1991   Receives Langston Hughes Award from Lincoln University; awarded honorary doctorates by Skidmore College, the New School for Social Research, Hobart and William Smith Colleges, Marymount Manhattan College, and the University of Port Harcourt, Nigeria.

1992   Edits (with C.L. Innes) *The Heinemann Book of Contemporary African Short Stories;* awarded honorary doctorate by City College of the City University of New York.

1993   Appointed Visiting Fellow and Ashby Lecturer, Clare Hall, Cambridge University; awarded honorary doctorate by Colgate University.

1994   Awarded honorary doctorate by Fitchburg State College, Massachusetts

1996   Awarded honorary doctorates by State University of New York at Binghamton, Bates College, and Harvard University; receives Campion Medal and Order of Kilimanjaro Award.

Conversations with Chinua Achebe

Chinua Achebe

Lewis Nkosi / 1962

From *African Writers Talking: A Collection of Radio Interviews*, edited by Cosmo Pieterse and Dennis Duerden (London: Heinemann Educational Books, 1972), 3–6. Reprinted by permission of Heinemann Educational Books and Dennis Duerden of the Transcription Centre.

At the time of recording this interview Chinua Achebe was Director of the External Service of the Nigerian Broadcasting Corporation. He had already published with Heinemann *Things Fall Apart* (1958) and *No Longer at Ease* (1960), and was working on *Arrow of God* which was published in 1964. A fourth novel *A Man of the People* (1966) was to be followed by the publication of his short stories under the title *Girls at War, and Other Stories* (Heinemann 1972). Achebe has published some children's books, as well as *The Sacrificial Egg, and Other Stories* (Etudo, Onitsha 1962).

Chinua Achebe was educated at Government College, Umuahia, and at University College, Ibadan, where he was one of the first graduates to take a full degree course. In 1954 he joined the Nigerian Broadcasting Corporation, and was Director of External Broadcasting until 1966. His first two novels—*Things Fall Apart* (1958) and *No Longer at Ease* (1960)—have been published in many countries; *Arrow of God* (1964) was awarded the first Jock Campbell/*New Statesman* Award; and *A Man of the People* aroused widespread interest on its first publication in January 1966. In 1970 he became a Senior Research Fellow in the Institute of African Studies at Nsukka.

Nkosi: Well, Chinua Achebe, you are one of the leading novelists in Nigeria, you're famous in America, and England, as well as Europe. When did you really begin to write?

Achebe: I wrote *Things Fall Apart* in 1958, or rather it was published in '58—I started work on it around '56—towards the end of '56. But the story itself had been sort of maturing in my mind for about two years previously.

Nkosi: When did you really become interested in writing as an art, something that you might use throughout your life? Did you start this at school?

Achebe: Well, I think at the university at Ibadan—I can't say definitely when it was but I know around '51, '52—I was quite certain that I was going to try my hand at writing, and one of the things that set me thinking was Joyce Cary's novel set in Nigeria, *Mr. Johnson*, which was praised so much, and it was clear to me that this was a most superficial picture of—not only of the country, but even of the Nigerian character, and so I thought if this was famous, then perhaps someone ought to try and look at this from the inside.

Nkosi: Yes; well, according to the blurb in one of your books, you had been sent to the university to study medicine, is that correct?

Achebe: Yes, that's right, it's just one of those things: you see, when I left school I didn't really know what I wanted to do and medicine was very glamorous—it was either medicine or engineering—but I soon discovered that it wasn't really my cup of tea, so I changed.

Nkosi: Of the two books you have written, which gives you the greatest satisfaction?

Achebe: That's very difficult—it's really quite impossible to say, it depends on when I am asked this question: some days I feel happier with *Things Fall Apart*, some days with the other one. They are so different, you see; I think it's rather like one's children, perhaps—you know, you like one for certain things and the other for other things. *Things Fall Apart* I wrote with more affection, but that doesn't mean I prefer it; I wrestled a lot more with *No Longer At Ease*, and so I think that probably *No Longer at Ease* is better technically, but that's as far as I can go.

Nkosi: Yes; well, most of us would probably differ with the author himself since lots of us like the first one very much; the texture of the writing seems to be so much more finished and syntactically finished. What are you working on at the moment?

Achebe: I'm trying to, you see, what I've decided to do really is to oscillate between the past—the immediate past—and the present: *Things Fall Apart* is about a hundred years ago; *No Longer at Ease* is today; and I want to go back now to not quite the time of *Things Fall Apart*, but a little later, because I think there's a lot of interesting material there; and the fourth one would be present day. And that's the way I intend to work.

Nkosi: There is quite a community of writers in Nigeria. Could you tell us something about this, whether there is any social intercourse between you and the younger writers writing at the moment or do you lead an isolated life?

Achebe: Well, you see, there are so few—that's the thing, so it's quite easy to get to know one another and I think most of the younger writers have been students at the University College, Ibadan—so it's a community. In Lagos here we are trying to start a writers' club, well, a society of authors really, but it's not so that we can get acquainted but to have a platform, you know, to do battle if necessary.

Nkosi: Yes; now, as a professional broadcaster do you find much time to do your own writing, and what hours do you use for writing?

Achebe: Well, I find that if I have a story that I badly want to tell, I can always find the time. Of course, it is becoming increasingly difficult for me to write as quickly as I would want. The novel on which I am working now is taking me much longer than I had thought. But it doesn't matter: I don't think the speed is all that important.

Nkosi: Is this latest novel that you are working on centred around Lagos or does it deal with the urban community?

Achebe: No, it goes back to the village. You see, it goes back to what I've said before: if I want to write about Nigeria, say a hundred years ago, seventy-five years ago, it has to be the village society. The present day would be Lagos and the towns.

Nkosi: Yes. It is very interesting how well you are able to capture the nuances of tribal life. Have you lived in the rural areas yourself?

Achebe: Yes. I was brought up in a village, went to school there; I didn't really get into any big town until I went to Ibadan, and you see, in the villages in Nigeria—well, where I come from in the Eastern Region, life is still—well, things are changing very fast but if one is interested, one can still see signs of what life used to look like.

Nkosi: Do you yourself find this ambivalent? Did you, at the time when you were growing up, have the feeling that you were no longer at ease with the rural scene and at the same time find that you had a tremendous affection for the life of your people in the rural setting. How did you reconcile this within yourself?

Achebe: Well, as a little boy it didn't worry me at all. I took most of these things for granted. I was born into a Christian family; you see, my father was a missionary and that was the life of the . . . You know, the sort of civilized life of the village was us, but it was only later—even though I was brought up as a Christian, the life of the village was there for you to see—it as only later that I began to evaluate, so to speak.

Nkosi: Yes. Were you overseas very long?

Achebe: No, I've only been out once to Britain in '56 for a short period at the BBC.

Nkosi: What would you say are the main influences on your life, say, from the point of view of literature? Whom do you admire most amongst writers?

Achebe: That again is very difficult. I don't really think that there's any one I can say I admire all that much. I used to like Hemingway; and I used to like Conrad, I used to like Conrad particularly; and I like Graham Greene, I find him a bit heavy going now and again but I do like him; and some of the younger people like Kingsley Amis and—well, I don't have any special favourites.

Nkosi: Now, if we may just ask this rather peculiar question, just how much power does a professional artist, a professional writer, have in a society like Lagos or the Nigerian society as a whole?

Achebe: Not much, because writing is so new and we are only just beginning to be known but I think by power you don't mean—

Nkosi: I mean influence.

Achebe: Influence, yes, well I think that will come; if one writes good novels or writes good poetry, he's bound to have an influence but I don't see much of it at present, only the beginnings, you see, in the schools and that sort of thing, which shows that perhaps the next generation will be influenced by what we write today.

Nkosi: Yes. Do you set yourself any particular time schedule for your writing: how many novels, for instance, you have to do within a year, you know, that sort of thing?

Achebe: No, no, I don't; you see, I think writing is such a serious thing that one ought to take it fairly easily and slowly, you know, at its own pace. I don't like forcing a story. Some days, weeks even, I can't write anything, and I don't want to go to the table and start scribbling, you see, I feel it's—it is an important thing and ought to be taken seriously.

An Interview with Chinua Achebe

Afrique / 1962

From *Afrique* (Paris), 27 (1963), 41–42, and translated by Judith E. McDowell. Reprinted by permission of Judith E. McDowell.

Interviewer: If, outside the continent, Amos Tutuola is the best known Nigerian writer, and if, in Lagos, Cyprian Ekwensi is the most popular novelist, in the whole of Nigeria Chinua Achebe is considered by those who know as the greatest hope for Nigerian literature.

This slender young man with a bearing both hesitant and determined, the director of the external service of Radio Nigeria, is part of that new generation (he was born in 1930, while Ekwensi was born in 1921) which, reaching manhood at the time of Independence, examines social and political events with an eye at once lucid and objective and which, especially in Nigeria, does not allow itself to be impressed by former greatness. Like his friends the poets Christopher Okigbo and John Pepper Clark, the novelist Gabriel Okara, the novelist Wole Soyinka, as well as several more young artists and television producers in Nigeria, he likes to go sometimes to the Mbari Club, a kind of picture gallery/café/club in the middle of old Ibadan where expositions, shows, or open-air meetings take place by turns. There, if they aren't rebuilding Africa every fifteen minutes, they are at least creating an intellectual center, rather new in Africa, over which the critic Ulli Beier keeps jealous watch.

At the moment, Chinua Achebe is discreetly seated behind his little desk in Lagos and is talking in a sedate and calm manner, which now and then reveals much sensitivity.

C.A.: I have written only two novels since 1958. In reality, they will eventually constitute only one, a kind of trilogy, when I have written the third. I wanted to write it, in fact, ever since I was very young, since 1953. I had been impressed by the works of Joyce Cary and especially by one of his books, *Mister Johnson*, in which he shows Nigerian characters. He is an excellent English writer who has lived here, for he resided in Northern Nigeria during his youth, but he cannot see the Hausa like a proper Nigerian and, in fact, what results is more of a caricature than a true description. Also, reading Cary impelled me to show what was false in him and brought forth

7

a desire to write that I've had for a long time. I really wanted to write a long novel, the action of which would take place over a hundred years. I divided it into three parts. But when I got to the second panel of the triptych, I had to abandon it for the time being.

Interviewer: But surely your second book, *No Longer at Ease*, is the sequel to your first, *Things Fall Apart*?

C.A.: Yes and no, since in *No Longer at Ease* the story is about the grandson of the hero of the first book. The books are, in fact, the story of the country of my birth, Ogidi, in eastern Nigeria. In the first, I tell of the village traditions and the hopes and fears of all the inhabitants at the time when the first contacts with Europeans are taking place. In the second book, which is in fact the third of the trilogy, the story is about my generation. In the missing book, the story will be about my father's generation, those who were Christianized. The theme of it will be the conflict of the head priest with the rest of the village during the 1920's. But I can't write it yet, because I haven't yet got far enough back into the problems of that period. It is too easy to discredit the former generation. In reality, that generation is very important and I must still pay attention to it.

Interviewer: Recently, the South African writer Ezekiel Mphahlele, who elsewhere considered you the best Nigerian writer at the moment, said that your second novel is rather pessimistic with regard to the conflict between the diverse African and European cultures: a young man returns home from England; he goes to work in Lagos, moves up to a good position, but succumbs to the temptations of corruption. He is arrested and ends up in prison. On the way he even clashes with his own family's beliefs when he wants to marry a young Ibo girl of another class.

C.A.: This is not pessimism but rather casting a cold eye on things. It is only one man's story, and I think that things will go better, but difficulties exist and nothing is served by hiding them under a poetic veil or under a lyricism of the past. I am against slogans. I don't think, for example, that "negritude" has any meaning whatsoever. Pan-Africanism? Perhaps. Negritude, no. I can't understand why a large number of African writers, notably those who write in French, have such a nostalgia for the past.

Interviewer: Do you believe that a novel should be essentially social? Realistic?

C.A.: No, I am not a poet and up to now I have never had the desire to write poetry. But I don't think that the novel should be specifically social. A writer must not be limited. It is true that here the social surrounds us so much that it cannot help but come out in our work despite us. As for being realistic, I try to be so, depending on the reality: I mean, for example, in the first book which describes a society still homogeneous, in which each person has his well-determined place, it was normal to use a more lyrical manner, for the events themselves were in some ways lyrical. Today everything is mixed up, and so it was necessary to convey that former charm in a more direct style. I don't hesitate to make my characters speak "pidgin English" in a very direct and very popular style of conversation. It is difficult to express the reality of Ibo society in classical English.

Interviewer: Isn't this different from numerous black authors who write in French and who use a very pure French, preferring to save their efforts, especially in poetry, for searching for rhythms and new words?

C.A.: Perhaps. But it is precisely those I often find too sweet, a little syrupy. Besides, I can't understand this nostalgia for the golden age that one finds in most of them, notably in Senghor, in Mongo Beti, and even in Camara Laye, whom I still like very much, especially in his second book. Here in Nigeria, we don't pretend that formerly life was nice and easy. The stories of Amos Tutuola appear to strangers far away as a little exotic, a kind of dream about tradition, they are not very popular here. As for Cyprian Ekwensi, his popular stories, not to mention his novels, are very close to life, to the swarming city or the bush where one must fight thieves every day.

Interviewer: Can one speak, then, of a Nigerian style?

C.A.: No, but I think that there exists among us a way of viewing life, African problems, and literature which is perhaps right for Nigeria.

Interviewer: Do you have much contact among yourselves?

C.A.: Relatively, for Ibadan is not far away; it is not possible, as in Europe, to see each other very often in places "where the mind is inspired." Okigbo is in Ibadan at the office of the Cambridge University Press; Soyinka is a professor at the University; Nzekwu is the editor-in-chief of *Nigeria Magazine*; Clark is at present in the United States; Aluko is working daily. But we all know each other personally, and, living in the same country, often in the same town or in nearby towns, we can compare our opinions, something which I think is not the case with black authors who write in French and who are today separated by borders. Also, we have been students, often together in the same university.

Interviewer: Has there been a possibility for writers to make a living entirely by their works?

C.A.: No, not yet. Ekwensi does articles and film scripts. But for each of us the editions of our works are still small, especially for poetry. Thus, *Things Fall Apart* has been published in Great Britain and in the U.S.A. and has been translated into Italian, German, and Spanish, but the world editions don't actually go beyond 15,000 copies, split among several editions, especially in England. Likewise, *No Longer at Ease*, which has been translated into Czechoslovakian, had a first edition of 4000 copies, of which 3000 were immediately sold. Even so, you see, that is not enough to live on. Yet I can't complain since Heinemann just brought both books out in 1962, in its series of educational texts for Africa, which puts them among the first Nigerian books directly studied or read in schools. But the Nigerian public, properly so called, still prefers to buy books "in order to learn"—history, biographies, political essays—and after all, that is normal. There are few libraries here and their clientele is not so much interested in novels. Until the present there weren't even any publishing houses except in Onitsha, where very tiny firms publish pamphlets or love stories. Now the first real Nigerian publishing house has just been established, African University Press, for which, moreover, I am preparing a series of biographies.

Interviewer: All the same you have been able to make an immediate start in literature; can't one speak of a new generation of writers "coming out of the universities"?

C.A.: That is so; by comparison with writers like Ekwensi, who began as a pharmacist, or Tutuola, we are "ex-students" coming directly from the university. But like many others, after my "general degree" and my Bachelor of Arts from Ibadan I taught in a secondary school. I wanted to go to Cambridge. But that didn't work out. Today I'm happy not to have gone there, because I definitely would not like to remain in an academic framework: the academic life is in fact terribly sterilizing for the creative mind. The most curious thing is that at the beginning I wanted to study medicine. Fortunately I got into radio!

Interviewer: Have you written for the radio?

C.A.: Paradoxically, no. Yet I think that radio could have had an influence on me, notably in regard to dialogue, for the radio style is very close to conversation. But I have thought of the theater. Perhaps I'll launch into that later. At least there's an intermediary way open to me: television. Perhaps, in fact, here in Nigeria, television will be a great opportunity for creativity when there is a little more money for original programs and fewer American films.

Conversation with Chinua Achebe

Lewis Nkosi and Wole Soyinka / 1963

Filmed interview retranscribed by Bernth Lindfors and published by permission of *Africa Report* and Dennis Duerden of the Transcription Centre.

Nkosi: Here at the Museum of Nigeria in Lagos, we are sitting with Chinua Achebe, a man possessed of a startling original talent in writing. Chinua Achebe has given the world two novels, *Things Fall Apart* and *No Longer at Ease*, and all critics seem to agree that he combines a simplicity in technique and a very complex talent. Maybe Wole Soyinka would like to add a few words of introduction.

Soyinka: No, I'd like to go straight into your work, and I'd like to take as my point of reference, for a start, the last carving you showed me, the carving of Ikenga. This represents, as you said, the spirit of manhood, of strength, of real masculine energy in Ibo society. In *Things Fall Apart* Okonkwo seems to me to represent the kind of figure in society who's acted upon from within by this kind of strong spiritual quality. I'd like to know from you whether this is a conscious derivative in the creation of this character—the sense of a man in society, his religion, his beliefs.

Achebe: Well, not conscious, but Okonkwo, as you said, symbolizes strength and aggressiveness. These are some of the qualities that his people admire, and I wanted a character who could be called representative of this particular group of people. And they admired a man of strength, a man of wealth, a man who had a big compound with wives and who had many farms, that sort of thing.

Soyinka: This is a dangerous question, I know, but does it imply anything in your own personal attitude toward this society which places so much premium on what, after all, may be a kind of exhibitionist side of the masculine ego? Does it imply something of your own attitude—the fact that Okonkwo, by his very personal immersion in this kind of value, heads for a fall?

Achebe: Yes, yes, I think there is a point there. The weakness of this particular society, I think, is a lack of adaptation, not being able to bend. I can't say that this represents the Ibo people today, but I think in his time the strong men were those who did not bend, and I think this was a fault in the culture itself.

11

Nkosi: Chinua, I'm more interested in what some people have described as your deliberate attempt to avoid passing moral judgements on your characters. For instance, in *Things Fall Apart* there is this absolute cruelty. Because the tribal society sanctions the killing of a ward by his protector, this man carries it out. Although he seems to have some kind of doubt, he doesn't avoid doing so. The way you wrote that passage seemed to imply that you were not able to make any particular judgment on that action. Is this true?

Achebe: No, I don't think this is a fair assessment at all. You have to see the story as a whole. This is what I was saying to Wole earlier on, that this particular society has believed too much in manliness, and perhaps this is part of the reason why it crashed at the end. I don't think a writer should point a moral lesson on every page. I think that the total effect at the end of the story is that this is the way things went. I like my moral to be not as obvious as . . .

Nkosi: Yes, what I was getting at was whether you had some kind of moral point of view, taking the book as a whole.

Achebe: Yes, yes, I did. You see, I feel that this particular society had its good side: the poetry of the life; the simplicity, if you like; the communal way of sharing in happiness and in sorrow and in work and all that. It had all that; also it had art and music. But it also had this cruel side to it, and it is this that I think helped to bring down my hero.

Soyinka: Well, for a moment I was going to say that this sounded dangerously like the philosophy of negritude, the mythology of negritude, but I was relieved when you mentioned an extra dimension to it. But if I may pick up on something which Lewis was saying about the whole question of style, do you accept the evaluation which has been placed on your style by some critics, that there is a kind of almost precise workmanship about it, almost an unrelieved competence as opposed to genuine artistic inspiration? How do you react to this?

Achebe: You don't expect me to accept that! I don't think one could describe my method in those terms because I don't particularly spend a lot of time on polishing. As a matter of fact, *Things Fall Apart* was written straight, without any kind of draft.

Nkosi: As a South African, I am very conscious of the fact that there seems to be some kind of continuity between modern-day society in Nigeria, from which I suppose you spring, and the old, traditional society. What were the formative influences upon your life? How were you able to draw such an accurate picture of traditional society? How are these influences passed on?

Achebe: Well, I think I belong to a very fortunate generation in this respect: that the old hadn't been completely disorganized when I was growing up. I think this disorganization has gone a stage further now. But when I was growing up, it was easy, especially if you lived in a village, to see, if not in whole, at least in part, these old ways of life. I was particularly interested in listening to the way old people talked, and this was a kind of background, you see. The festivals, of course, were still observed; maybe not in the same force, but they were still there.

Soyinka: So this didn't really entail a deliberate kind of research of the adult artist into this life.

Achebe: No, no, I didn't do any research at all.

Nkosi: Chinua, when you were going to University College Ibadan and you switched off from a course in medicine to literature, did you find any precursors in the West African novel—English people who had written novels about your society which you could use as a model, or did you find nothing at all that was useful to you?

Achebe: There wasn't very much when I was at college. Joyce Cary had written some of his books. If I may say so, perhaps he helped to inspire me, but not in the usual way. I was very angry with his book *Mister Johnson*, which was set in Nigeria. I happened to read this, I think, in my second year, and I said to myself, this is absurd. If somebody without any inside knowledge of the people he is trying to describe can get away with it, perhaps I ought to try my hand at it.

Soyinka: Now that you mention *Mister Johnson*, the hero of your second book *No Longer at Ease* struck me in some way as a rather effete kind of character. You do not see any kind of equation at all between him and his particular weaknesses—I refer especially to his relationship with his European boss—and Mister Johnson?

Achebe: No, I don't. To me Mister Johnson doesn't live at all; I mean he is merely a caricature.

Soyinka: Precisely. I know Mister Johnson is a caricature, but then a caricature is really something you exaggerate. You exaggerate some factual elements. You do not think that your hero demonstrates some of the exaggerated qualities of Mister Johnson? Again, I go back to his relationship with his boss in the office, a kind of peculiar deference he had towards him, a kind of tolerance of this boss, which is exaggerated.

Achebe: If you will go back to that book, you will see that he actually didn't have much respect for his boss, but his nature was such that he was able to dismiss him as an example of this or that. There was in fact a passage when he was thinking of the Greens of this generation: they are a tragedy. His problem was that he was perhaps too civilized to shout, and this might be what you're referring to. But I don't think he's the same thing as Mister Johnson. Perhaps even caricature is not the correct word. Perhaps he's completely a puppet.

Soyinka: A complete travesty of a situation.

Nkosi: Chinua, Professor Abraham in his book, *The Mind of Africa*, selects you as one of the most original or the more African of all the African novelists that he had read in English-speaking Africa. I was just wondering whether you found that there was something to be done with this alien form, as I suspect the novel is, whether you found that you could experiment with the form, not just with the content? Is there room to turn around in this alien form at all?

Achebe: Well, I think that the novel form suits me extremely well just now. I haven't read Dr. Abraham's book, but I think I can regard myself, with justice, as very much an African writer. I think I'm basically an ancestor worshipper, if you like, but not in the same sense as my grandfather would probably do it, pouring palm wine on the floor for the ancestors. With me it takes the form of celebration, and I feel a certain compulsion to do this. It's not because I think this would appeal to my readers. I feel that this is something that has to be done before I move on to the contemporary scene; and, in fact, the reason why my third book goes back again to the past, though not as remotely as the first, is that I have come to think that my first book is no longer adequate. I've learned a lot more about these particular people, my ancestors.

Soyinka: Let's move to a more general topic. Do you agree with what Lewis said about the novel being an alien form? I have in mind when I say this the kind of idiom of storytelling which is very prevalent in the East, even much more than in the West, whereby a story can be recited with action, with demonstration, with dances, with make-up, for days and nights. Is this really a difference of material?

Achebe: I agree with you. The art of the story is the same really. I think it's not any more alien than telling a traditional story, but it is a question of writing it down. There will always be somebody who likes a good story.

Soyinka: Using a different language also.

Achebe: Yes, yes.

Nkosi: I don't want to make too tight a distinction between the story told within the tradition in Africa and the European form of the novel, but I do feel that the European novel has a certain background, a bourgeois background, and that individual authorship is another permanent feature of it, and of course the fact that it can be enjoyed by a single person by himself, without being gathered together with lots of other people. But, no matter, I want to pass on to another question I would like to put to you, and it's more a sociological question. I am interested in just how much social power a novelist in Nigeria has, how much influence he has with his society, or is the society completely indifferent to him?

Achebe: Well, the novel is comparatively young here. It's only about ten years old, and it would be impossible to state exactly what kind of influence we are going to have. All I can say is that it is growing. My books, for instance, have done extremely well in Nigeria and in other parts of Africa, and I think the same goes with the other novelists here. Whether you can call this a social influence—I think probably we ought to wait some years to see.

Nkosi: Yes, but I'm interested because there has already been a definite reaction from, say, the Federal Government of Nigeria to Cyprian Ekwensi's novel which was about to be filmed. They banned this, and they said it shouldn't be done because it doesn't accurately reflect the life of Nigeria. Are these politicians beginning to react to some kind of social criticism contained in the younger literature of Nigeria?

Achebe: I can only quote from my own experience here, and I haven't come up against any obstructions like the example you've given. Maybe when I move into the present and write a political novel, that will be the time to test. But all I can say is that I haven't yet come up against any kind of opposition.

Soyinka: In any case, I think politicians behave pretty much the same all over the world. Even Cyprian Ekwensi's book, for instance, is not really a piece of social criticism. I think it's just this problem of politicians getting nervous about a false image being presented without ever understanding the whole business of creative writing. They cannot understand that if a prostitute is written about in a book, that this isn't a kind of treatise on sociology.

But I would like to make an abrupt transition here. I know you were in the States very recently, and I'd like to know if you met any of the American novelists, particularly the Negro novelists and writers. Maybe there's something you'd like to say on this.

Achebe: Yes, I did indeed. In fact, that was the very purpose of my visit. I did meet with the Harlem group of writers: Langston Hughes and John Killens, and a whole lot of younger ones. I didn't meet Baldwin, unfortunately, because he was tied up with other duties. I also met quite a few white writers, not just novelists. I met Arthur Miller, the dramatist. But perhaps what I got most was a kind of closer relationship with the literary pulse in America. I think I'm now a lot more interested in what is being written there than I was before.

Soyinka: Did you notice any similarity of problems? For instance, I would like to know if you felt that the Negro writers were particularly interested in your work because of your orientation around the traditional African way of life and philosophy.

Achebe: Yes, yes, very much so. In fact, I remember now one Negro writer who autographed a book of hers with words something to this effect: "To Achebe, who depicted so beautifully the culture that might have been mine." This is the kind of feeling I think they have.

Nkosi: Chinua, the European critics have been most kind to your novels, at least in their appreciation and acceptance of them; but you have been the most vicious critic of the European critics. Why is this so? What do you find so objectionable in their approach to African literature?

Achebe: Well, I'm surprised to hear you think that I'm the most vicious critic of the critics. No, I don't object to critics at all. What I do object to is people preaching from a position of ignorance, and this you'll find quite a lot in the criticisms that are made of our work. Even when they are praising you, you find that this is not really for the right reasons at all. Of course I'm not saying that they should shut up, but I hate any kind of cultural or literary popes being set up who can pontificate on the "real" African literature. You'll find a lot of words like "real" or "true" or "valid." These words, I think, are almost meaningless in the context.

Soyinka: How do you react to the critic who lumped you, Cyprian Ekwensi and Onuora Nzekwu together as an unbeatable treble choice? How do you react personally to this as a writer?

Achebe: I think I know who you mean, and I don't particularly care for him as a critic. Of course, he's welcome to his opinion about us being unbeatable. I mean, I couldn't quarrel with that. But I don't care for him as a critic.

Soyinka: Yes, but can we pursue this a bit further? He also makes a statement on which I think you might like to comment. Talking about I forget whose book now, he says, "and he also writes the kind of books which his readers, his Africa people, like to read: a novel with a moral at the end." You talked earlier about one of your novels possessing some kind of moral, but do you make a distinction in the way he used this?

Achebe: Yes, I'm sure what he means is the kind of moral which you have in stories for children. This obviously is not the right approach for a novelist.

Nkosi: Chinua, you have said something about the latest novel you have written having progressed beyond the two books that you worked on the first time. Could you indicate perhaps in what direction you think you have made this advance—technically or otherwise?

Achebe: Well, it would be difficult to describe the technical superiority . . .

Nkosi: Is there a difference in subject matter?

Achebe: Yes, there is, definitely. I'm handling a whole lot of more complex themes, you see, like the relationship between a god and his priest. My chief character in this novel is a village priest, not a Christian priest—a traditional African religion. And I am interested in the whole question of who decides what shall be the wish of the gods—that kind of situation. And I've also tried to develop my treatment of character. Whether I succeed or not is still to be seen, but I think I have progressed in that direction.

Nkosi: The other question is a more general one which bothers a lot of people and has to do with the audience. Do you find that you're beginning to develop an indigenous audience in Nigeria so that you can rely less on metropolitan audiences; or to put it in another form, so that you can become less conscious of the demands of European audiences?

Achebe: Yes, I think you're right. Although, I must say that I don't think I was consciously working with an audience in mind in my first book. In fact, I remember being surprised when the first person who read it said, "Who did you have in mind?" Now, that doesn't mean I didn't have somebody in mind, but I wasn't thinking of it primarily. The second time, of course, this thought having been put into my mind, I found myself thinking about it. But now I feel I don't have to worry over-much about who understands what I am saying or who doesn't. I feel that there will always be enough people interested in a good story.

Nkosi: Well, perhaps this is a good time to stop. We are greatly privileged to have met Chinua Achebe at the Museum of Nigeria, surrounded as we are by the masks and the brooding spirit, which is about the same kind of thing that broods in the novels by Chinua Achebe—the past is very much there. Chinua Achebe, all critics agree, has great promise and promises to give us some of the best things that will be produced in African literature.

I Had to Write on the Chaos I Foresaw

Tony Hall / 1967

From *Sunday Nation* (Nairobi), 15 January 1967, 15–16. Reprinted by permission of *Sunday Nation*.

Chinua Achebe, born in Eastern Nigeria, is perhaps the most widely acclaimed of African novelists at the moment. He was one of the first graduates to take a full degree course at University College, Ibadan. From 1954 he worked for the Nigerian Broadcasting Corporation, resigned last August as Director of External Broadcasting. His first novel *Things Fall Apart* was published in 1958. Then came *No Longer at Ease* and *Arrow of God*, which won the *New Statesman*/Jock Campbell Award. Then last year came *A Man of the People*, which spelt out the corruption of Nigerian politics, foresaw a military coup—and was published in the same week as the actual coup.

I'd like to ask you first about your own background in relation to your writing—those robust, full-blooded characters in the old Ibo villages and those settings and situations which convey the vitality of African traditions—are they really part of your own early life or did you come to them from a more modern environment and study them consciously?

It's a mixture of both, really. I was brought up in a village where the old ways were still active and alive, so I could see the remains of our tradition actually operating. At the same time I brought a certain amount of detachment to it too, because my father was a Christian missionary, and we were not fully part of the "heathen" life of the village. It was divided into the people of the Church and the people of the "world." I think it was easier for me to observe. Many of my contemporaries who went to school with me and came from heathen families ask me today: "How did you manage to know all these things?" You see, for them these old ways were just part of life. I could look at them from a certain distance, and I was struck by them.

To come up to the present, you and Wole Soyinka are at the moment the most prominent figures in African literature—because of the quality of your writing and because you have both tackled real situations in independent Africa as it is right now; you have put some muscle in African literature.

Today you are lionised in intellectual circles. How does it feel to have "ar-rived" so completely?

My books have done extremely well, I know. But I don't honestly feel much different from when I began to write. I still think we have a long way to go. I suppose my name means more in Nigeria today than it did five years ago. But I feel the job that literature should do in our community has not even started. It's not yet part of the life of the nation. We are still at the beginning. It's a big beginning, because now we are catching the next genera-tion in the schools. When I was their age, I had nothing to read that had any relevance to my own environment.

What really worries me is that those who are in positions of power are not really affected by what we are writing. In the moral dialogue you want to start, you really want to involve the leaders. People ask me: "Why were you so bold as to publish *A Man of the People*? How did you think the Govern-ment was going to take it? You didn't know there was going to be a coup?" I said rather flippantly that nobody was going to read it anyway, so I wasn't likely to be fired from my official position. It's a distressing thought that we cannot engage our leaders in the kind of moral debate we need.

Yet it seems that in Africa leaders are very sensitive to the printed word. Wasn't there any reaction from the kind of politicians you were attacking?

Well, if I wrote newspaper articles, they were more likely to react immedi-ately. But a novel or a play, you see, rarely touched them. For instance, Wole Soyinka was writing skits on the current situation in Western Nigeria. For a long time it didn't really cause any trouble in high places until many people were talking about them. If he was writing a deeply involved work, I think it would almost go unnoticed.

It's not that they are indifferent. It's just that they don't read, that crowd. I mean they were not brought up with books. Until you get a society that is brought up on reading and watching plays and talking about good films and so on, it's going to be difficult. I think we'll start getting there with the next generation.

Do you see any dangers to yourself from becoming established so quickly on the international literary scene? Do you find yourself becoming too toler-ant of critics? I mean I don't think you've had a bad review from a serious critic anywhere, have you?

No, not really. I've had some bad reviews, but I regard them as coming from rather less serious critics, perhaps grinding some political axe.

Do you sometimes get an uneasy feeling that some people may be judging you as a slightly special case—as the "African Writer"—and that you are given special critical treatment?

Quite frankly, no. It doesn't worry me what goes on in the mind of the critic. I have seen a lot of strange reasons for the good comments. So I know at once that there must be very many ways of reading what I write, depending on the culture and background the reader brings to the book. But once you are writing for an international audience I think you shouldn't worry unduly about these special interpretations. And my success was not really so rapid. My first book came out eight years ago, and it was pretty slow to catch on.

Who "discovered" you?

I don't think anybody did, except in a small way. I took the manuscript of *Things Fall Apart* to London when I went on a BBC course. One of my teachers there happened to be a novelist—I think very good, but not very well-known. I rather diffidently went to him and asked him to look at my manuscript. He was very excited and passed it on to his publishers. So that was the start. They took it on.

In the magazine West Africa *there was recently a review of Soyinka's* The Lion and the Jewel. *It found the play was certainly not his best, whereas in London it was getting high praise. And this review ended on a note of warning to African writers: Beware, the cult is on display!*

Yes, I think there's an element of truth there. The point is whether or not Wole Soyinka has done anything better. Personally I prefer the earlier things. I think the reviewer is saying that the exotic quality of the play may account for all the raves. But I don't know. I think if you want an African play, then you've got to carry the African paraphernalia with it. It's just a question of people getting used to a new area of culture.

And is African literature becoming something of a cult among literati in London?

Well, I don't frequent London. I don't know what the sort of intellectual, arty-crafty crowd there are doing and thinking. But my understanding of the cult is that something from Africa must automatically be "wonderful and different," and so ordinary rules of criticism are likely to be a little lowered. But I don't think this applies to Wole Soyinka's plays.

Do you feel there is any danger of being swallowed up in activities like whizzing around the world to writers' conferences, making speeches and so forth?

Well, it is beginning to pile on. I don't think it will be difficult for me to accept a certain amount of it without letting it interfere with my work. The main consumer of my time so far was my fulltime job as director of External Broadcasting in Nigeria. I gave that up in August.

Did you give it up willingly?

I did. But it also had something to do with the political situation. Now I'll have more time, though I'm not sure that will automatically mean writing more. I have had cause to doubt this in the past. I need a stimulating situation.

Could you live off the income from your novels today?

Yes, just about. I have about 16 translations of all four books. But in terms of money you don't really get much from translations. It's in the English editions that you get most. Quite a lot of the money comes when your work becomes a school text. *Things Fall Apart* has sold 120,000 copies. It is still the biggest seller. *A Man of the People* has been very popular. The hardcover edition sold out very quickly, but I don't think it has had time to establish itself.

And now you have a reputation, even among people who don't read much African writing, as the man who predicted the army coup in Nigeria. Were you worried about people's reactions at home to this rather accurate prediction—or that it might take away from the reputation you really want?

No. You see, the situation in Nigeria exploded the same week as the book was published. There wasn't much time for speculating on this. Many of my friends did ask: "What do you think would have happened to you if the coup hadn't come along?"

It must have taken a certain amount of courage . . .

Well, I was quite determined that the thing had to be said. I felt that the worst that might have happened would be losing my job. I think the civilian regime in Nigeria was very tolerant, for all its other faults.

Do you think perhaps that the overthrow of a civil Government by the military is never worth it in the long run, that taking the political character out of Government is always a step backwards? I mean there has been a rash of troubles since the first coup, and now Nigeria may fall apart. Have you any thoughts on this?

Oh, yes. My thoughts are not fully clarified on this. It is always unfortunate when things have got to a state where military intervention has to take place—but military takeovers are not always bad in themselves. You see, the Nigerian situation left no political solution. The political machine had been so abused that whatever measures were taken, it could only produce the same results. We had got to a point where some other force had to come in.

When I was writing *A Man of the People*, it wasn't clear to me what that force was going to be—whether it would be the army, or even civil war. In fact, civil war was already developing in Western Nigeria. So I don't think one can say a military takeover is never worth it. Now the fact that it has sort of soured was rather due to a second stage. I don't think it was inevitable from the first stage. We should not ignore the idealistic character of the first revolution because it has been overtaken by a counter-revolution that has no basis other than tribalism.

Now one hears about arms going into Nigeria and the possibility of a civil war?

I don't know about arms, beyond the usual rumours, but certainly the situation in Nigeria is fraught with danger. You have the bitterness engendered by the massacre of as many as 30,000 Easterners mostly in the North, and the withdrawal of the rest back into the Eastern Region. So now you have a different Nigeria, in which the main tribes are in their home bases. What is needed is the framing of a constitution which takes this into account, and does not pretend that everything is as it was. Some form of revenge is even being called for among the people.

But the leadership is well aware that if there is any more bloodshed, then the idea of Nigeria will be finished forever. The best thing is to cut our losses now and to come to some kind of arrangement that will ensure the removal of those things that caused friction in the past: struggling for the same posts, running businesses in somebody else's territory—the kind of thing which the Easterners went in for with the conviction that Nigeria was one country, and that as a citizen of this country you could go anywhere and do business legally.

So in effect you've got to constitutionalise your tribalism?
Yes, yes . . .

This is a tremendous abdication from an ideal. How do you yourself feel about it?
Well, the point is, it is facing realities rather than an abdication. Some people perhaps lived under the illusion that if you talked enough about unity

and showed this attitude of "one country," that our problems would be solved after a period. Ironsi said just before he was overthrown that anybody who talks about tribes in Nigeria needs to have his head examined. Now this was the attitude of the Eastern Region. It was always at the forefront of the nationalist movement—pressing even for a strong unitary Government. They only accepted a federal system as a compromise. So it is really the East which has learned a very bitter lesson: that perhaps the others are right and that we should start from a certain basis and see whether after a number of years the economic factors will impose their weight and we may get closer together again.

This is rather like the way Africa as a whole has had to come to terms with itself in 1966.
That's right! It's the very problem of the OAU in 1966. And in this way Nigeria can be seen as a paradigm of Africa.

General Gowon once said he would like to be thought of as the Kennedy of Africa. Do you think there is a genuine intention in his regime to go back to the barracks eventually?
I cannot talk for them because I have no contact at all with Gowon and the powers in Lagos. I do know that in the East the average man is not anxious that the military should hand over to the politicians. There is still so much cleaning up to do. The recent upheaval has caused a tremendous setback to the clean-up of corruption. This is one of the tragedies of the July takeover: that just as we were about to embark on setting our house in order, bringing to book the worst members of the last regime, everything was upset. Now the fate of the whole country is at stake, so the clean-up has had to take second place. Now handing back to the politicians is going to be a matter of months—or years.

What is the purpose of your present visit to East Africa?
I'm going home in a roundabout way from Paris and London. Right now my interest is in politics, or rather my interest in the novel is politics. *A Man of the People* wasn't a flash in the pan. This is the beginning of a phase for me, in which I intend to take a hard look at what we in Africa are making of our independence—but using Nigeria, which I know best. So I'm seeing how things are developing in various places, including East Africa.

Are you now starting on this novel?
Well, I take a lot of time thinking about what the next book is going to be,

without writing anything, just letting the idea crystallise, and I think it is beginning to do that. I might be sitting down to write before the year is out.

How do you actually tackle your writing?

I avoid as much as possible taking down notes—only the little episodes that go to fill out the novel. I let most of it come during the writing itself, and for that reason I write slowly. I take eight months to a year to write a novel. So the details and characterisation develop during the writing itself. I don't do, as some writers, a first and second and final draft. I make changes here and there.

A British critic recently was talking about the "novel of fact"—a trend in fiction writing today which he said is boring, because writers are simply piling up evidence in a documentary fashion about all sorts of situations. And they are failing to tackle themes in terms of large ideals and strong emotions. He quoted your book A Man of the People *as worthwhile not so much because of hunger for information about Nigeria, but because the reader can take part in a moral debate between an author and his society. Do you agree with this approach to what the novel should be?*

Yes, completely. This is what the novel should be doing. In fact, people have criticised me for documentation, but I think it is people who haven't actually read the books. There is a certain amount of factual information that has to go into setting the scene, especially if you are writing about a situation that is not already well-known. This is the case where the literature is new. But the main thing is not these external things, but the characters themselves.

In your "political" phase don't you think you may get caught up in expounding a political philosophy in your books? If you go around Africa, looking at it politically, something is going to invade your mind about what the solution should be to problems, and you will expound a formula?

In fact, I don't do this. One criticism I know I have received in some quarters is that I *don't* prescribe, that I don't offer solutions. My answer is that unless I have a solution, I'm not going to offer any. If I suddenly see a solution, I would offer it for what it is worth. At the moment I am concerned with something more limited. I don't want to be dogmatic and say a writer shouldn't prescribe. If he feels strongly enough, let him do so. If he sees a solution clearly and in all honesty, he is welcome to put it forward, as long as it does not cloud his vision. At the moment I don't see myself in any danger of trying to legislate for Africa.

We have had some pretty fierce arguments going on here about the alleged poverty of African writers in East Africa. You are editor of African writings for a London publisher. What are your views about this?

Yes, I do see a lot of manuscripts. In fact, I'm not taking credit for James Ngugi, but I did see his work before he was published, and I put him in touch with my publisher. I know he has a new thing coming out. I don't think really one should worry. I think it's the difference in the level of mass education between West and East Africa. It's a matter of time—not decades, it's going to take just a few years. I mean it's only 15 years since the first Nigerian novel was published in English. Yet in that time a lot has happened. There are now a number of new and some very exciting writers coming on.

Southern Africa has produced astonishingly few novels from Africans, when you think of the situation which cries out for fiction treatment. In the last couple of years you've had only one or two. Have you any idea why?

No, I'd like someone to tell me. I believe the South Africans' theory was that the situation there was so desperate that there wasn't really time or leisure for anyone to embark on anything like a full-length novel. So the short story is the most likely form to come out of this situation. I'm not fully convinced of this myself, though it sounds reasonable. But Alex La Guma has written something between a short story and a novel which I think is very good: *A Walk in the Night.*

What about the documentary-style novel of conditions within South Africa?

Well, I don't find that very exciting any more. You can only do that sort of thing once or twice, and if the reader knows in advance the kind of thing he is going to read, there is no point. I mean the tense situation, as far as I can see, is not changing greatly, and one doesn't want to be reading this over and over again.

Do you know of any European writers in Africa really able to portray African characters, really getting under the skin of their characters?

Well, I can only talk about Nigeria. The most competent writer to try was Joyce Cary—a fine writer, but he didn't succeed. His famous novel *Mister Johnson* is highly praised, especially by Europeans, but it seems to me to portray not a character but a caricature. I mean Johnson does not begin to live for me.

What about Graham Greene? He seems in The Comedians *to have really described the putrefaction of a "developing" society, which we may be in danger of having soon in parts of Africa, and what it does to people.*

He is really good there—and he knows his limitations in advance, so he merely sets a story in a place. He set *The Heart of the Matter* in Sierra Leone, and he uses the heat and humidity and the landscape very well. His main characters are washed-out Europeans acting out their lives. He is not out of his depth. I like *The Comedians* very much. It is better than the one set in the Congo, *A Burnt-Out Case*.

Lately one sees a number of film companies coming particularly into East Africa, with a lot of money and enterprise—and all this is being used up on White Hunter stories, wildlife epics, and the rest of it. Now you have written a novel which is the first of its kind about independent Africa. Do you think in the next few years maybe somebody will film your book?

Well, you really got to me on this one! I think there is more interest in wildlife than in human life here. In fact, a film company established itself in the United States to film *Things Fall Apart* and *No Longer at Ease*. And they got a really good script. But, oh, one thing and another, when they do get backing, there is political trouble somewhere in Africa and those who put money in it shy away.

But I hope one day we'll catch the attention of the filmmakers. I think West Africa is really excellent film country, and when it does start, it will really catch on. We in Africa, with the backing of our governments, must do all we can to start our own film industries.

Interview with Chinua Achebe

Bernth Lindfors, Ian Munro, Richard Priebe,
and Reinhard Sander / 1969

From *Palaver: Interviews with Five African Writers in Texas*, edited
by Lindfors, Munro, Priebe and Sander (Austin: African and Afro-
American Research Institute, University of Texas at Austin, 1972),
5–12. Reprinted by permission of the African and African American
Studies Center, University of Texas at Austin.

When Chinua Achebe visited The University of Texas at Austin in
November 1969 on the final leg of a month-long American speaking
tour, he was very tired but more than willing to undergo another hectic
round of interviews, speeches and discussions. Within the space of
twenty-four hours he gave a press conference, conducted two university classes, taped a half-hour television interview, delivered a public
lecture, and met with numerous students, faculty and townspeople at
an informal reception held in his honor. He spoke mostly about the
Nigerian/Biafran conflict but also about the role of the writer in modern Africa. When questioned about his own writing, he frequently tried
to relate his answers to the larger themes and issues that preoccupied
him. What follows is an edited transcript of some of his remarks on
the African writer and then some questions and answers.

When people talk about African culture, they quite often mean an assortment
of old customs. The reason for this is quite clear. When Europe came to
Africa and said, "You have no culture, no civilization, no religion, no history," Africa was bound sooner or later to reply by displaying her own ac-
complishments. To do this, her spokesmen—her writers and intellectuals—
stepped back into the past into what you might call the "era of purity," before
the coming of Europe. What they uncovered there they put into their books
and poems, and this became known as their culture, their answer to Europe's
arrogance. They spoke of civilizations that were satisfying to those born into
them and of gods with whom they were at ease; they wept over the death of
these gods, over the destruction of these civilizations.

But the culture of a people is more than books and poems. It is their
cooperative effort to make a clearing in the jungle and build on it a place of
human habitation. If this place is disturbed or despoiled, these people will
move to another spot, make another clearing, and begin to build on it another

home. So while the African intellectual was busy displaying the past culture
of Africa, the troubled peoples of Africa were already creating new revolutionary cultures which took into account their present conditions. As long as
people are changing, their culture will be changing. The only place where
culture is static, and exists independently of people, is the museum, and this
is not an African institution. Even there it is doubtful whether culture really
exists. To my mind it is already dead. Of course, a good curator can display
the artifacts so skillfully that an impression of completeness or even of life
can be given, but it is no more than the complete skin which a snake has
discarded before going its way.

This has been the problem of the African artist: he has been left far behind
by the people who make culture, and he must now hurry and catch up with
them—to borrow the beautiful expression of Fanon—in that zone of occult
instability where the people dwell. It is there that customs die and cultures
are born. It is there that the regenerative powers of the people are most potent.
These powers are manifest today in the African revolution, a revolution that
aims toward true independence, that moves toward the creation of modern
states in place of the new colonial enclaves we have today, a revolution that
is informed with African ideologies.

What is the place of the writer in this movement? I suggest that his place
is right in the thick of it—if possible, at the head of it. Some of my friends
say, "No, it's too rough there. A writer has no business being where it is so
rough. He should be on the sidelines with his note-paper and pencil where he
can observe with objectivity." I say that a writer in the African revolution
who steps aside can only write footnotes or a glossary when the event is over.
He will become like the contemporary intellectual of futility in many other
places, asking questions like: "Who am I? What's the meaning of my existence? Does this place belong to me or to somebody else? Does my life
belong to me or to some other person?"—questions that no one can answer.

What are you doing in the United States?
I'm here on a program arranged by the Committee for Biafran Writers and
Artists. This is an American committee which is trying to bring over Biafran
artists and writers to show that Biafra is all kinds of people and not only
starving children, though that is a part of it. The Committee is also trying to
send American writers into Biafra to see things for themselves.

What is your position in Biafra?
It's difficult to say. If things were normal I would be at the University of
Biafra, but the university is not functioning.

As a professor?
Well, as some kind of writer in residence.

Can we talk a bit about your past writing? In the four novels you have written do you try to bring out one message, one theme, or do you give each book a different theme?
I like to make each book I write different; otherwise, to my mind, there wouldn't be any point in writing another.

Do you believe literature should carry a social or political message?
Yes, I believe it's impossible to write anything in Africa without some kind of commitment, some kind of message, some kind of protest. Even those early novels that look like very gentle recreations of the past—what they were saying, in effect, was that we had a past. That was protest, because there were people who thought we didn't have a past. What we were doing was to say politely that we *did*—here it is. So commitment is nothing new. Commitment runs right through our work. In fact, I should say all our writers, whether they're aware of it or not, are committed writers. The whole pattern of life demanded that you should protest, that you should put in a word for your history, your traditions, your religion, and so on.

One big message, of the many that I try to put across, is that Africa was not a vacuum before the coming of Europe, that culture was not unknown in Africa, that culture was not brought to Africa by the white world. You would have thought it was obvious that everybody had a past, but there were people who came to Africa and said, "You have no history, you have no civilization, you have no culture, you have no religion. You are lucky we are here. Now you are hearing about these things from us for the first time." Well, you know, we didn't just drop from the sky. We too had our own history, traditions, cultures, civilizations. It is not possible for one culture to come to another and say, "I am the way, the truth, and the life; there is nothing else but me." If you say this, you are guilty of irreverence or arrogance. You are also stupid. And this is really my concern.

Some literary critics, however, don't regard you as a protest writer because you write with such restraint.
Well, according to my own definition of protest, I *am* a protest writer. Restraint—well, that's my style, you see.

But you don't picture the Europeans who came to Iboland as blackhearted villains.

No, I don't think that is necessary. I think they were very ignorant. And that's very bad, you know, when you are trying to civilize other people. But you don't really need to be blackhearted to do all kinds of wrong things. Those who have the best intentions sometimes commit the worst crimes. I think it's not my business to present villains without any redeeming features. This would be untrue. I think what's more likely to be true is somebody coming with the best of intentions, really believing that there is nothing here, and that he is bringing civilization. He's wrong, of course. He's completely wrong and misguided. But that's the man that interests me because he has potentialities for doing great harm.

Would you say that the focus of your protest has changed considerably over the years?

Well, my role has been changing. And I think this is true of all the other writers in one way or another. We started off—and this was necessary—showing that there was something here—a civilization, a religion, a history. Then we had to move on to the era of independence. Having fought with the nationalist movements and been on the side of the politicians, I realized after independence that they and I were now on different sides, because they were not doing what we had agreed they should do. So I had to become a critic. I found myself on the side of the people against their leaders—leaders this time being black people. I was still doing my job as a writer, but one aspect of the job had changed. I think what you do as a writer depends on the state of your society.

Ezeulu, the hero of your third novel Arrow of God, *is a chief priest who tries to manipulate another religion—Christianity—for political reasons. What do you think of his behavior?*

Well, he was a man I have a lot of respect for, a great intellectual. He saw what was happening; he saw that change was inevitable—unlike the intellectual today who perhaps doesn't see that the change has in fact happened—he saw this and he asked himself, "How do I use this new force, while still retaining my position, and make it my own?" That was good. He failed, unfortunately, but he saw clearly what was happening, unlike my character in *Things Fall Apart* who was not an intellectual and did not see what was going on. Okonkwo just saw his duty to protect his own and stand against the assault. So he failed. Ezeulu said, "Right, I've seen this thing; these people are powerful but that doesn't mean they are superior to me. I'll make use of them." But he failed too, and that's a pity.

So Ezeulu didn't really believe that Christianity was better simply because it was more powerful.

No, he didn't believe it was right. He didn't accept it. He was concerned with tactics, with basic realities, and he recognized the need to make temporary alliances. He said, "This thing is coming. I'll send someone to go and make an alliance with them, but the assumption is that I will remain in power—that the religion, the civilization, the tradition I embody will still remain in power. Let us absorb this thing that is coming; let's arrest it before it ruins or breaks us."

But Ezeulu's opponent Nwaka charged that he was trying to become more than a chief priest, that he wanted to become a king as well. Do you think this was true?

What that man was saying in reality was that Ezeulu was getting too powerful. You see, the idea of kings really was not accepted among the Ibos. We did not go in for kings. So the word "king" was used here to describe someone who was trying to become too powerful. And this runs against the Ibo belief in the complete integration of life, against their concept of an individual versus society. I think Nwaka was reacting as people normally do whenever they see the possibility of someone becoming too strong in the society.

You think Ezeulu might have had a tendency to try and assume too much power?

I think he had enough priestly arrogance to attempt it. This shows from time to time, like when he's confusing his thinking with the thinking of the god. These are natural feelings for a man who is a priest. Every priest, I think, can fall into that danger.

Our class has just finished reading A Man of the People *and we wondered what your outlook on Odili was. Did you picture him as being naive and idealistic or did you intend him as an object of satire, even burlesque?*

My picture of him is there. What you are asking me is what your picture of him should be, which is not really fair. Well, I like that young man. He was idealistic, he was naive, he was this and he was that, but I think he was also basically honest, which makes a difference. He was very honest. He knew his own shortcomings; he even knew when his motives were not very pure, and he admitted that these motives were not very pure. This puts him in a class worthy of attention, as far as I'm concerned. And I think he probably would return to do a better job next time. He suffered in this kind of

society because it was very cruel, very ruthless. But he was learning very
fast, and at the end I think he had improved his chances of being of service,
of doing the things he thought should be done. He'd improved those chances.

What is the significance of the sex in A Man of the People*?*
What a question! Well, I don't know what the significance is. It's a part of
life. More particularly, it's an aspect of this young man's attitude. At the
beginning, when he was just floating like anybody else, like a lot of young
people, wondering what his role should be, he uses sex in a way that is
appropriate in that kind of situation. Later on, when he gets involved in politics, his attitude changes quite considerably. The sex is not there just for
titillation, if that's what you're worrying about. I think it plays an important
part in the development of this character.

*But how seriously should we take the revenge idea? Was Odili's sexual
failure an isolating factor which led him into politics?*
Well, people stumble into right causes in all kinds of ways. It seems to me
perfectly legitimate to stumble into politics through failure in a love affair. If
you take the view that politics is so important that one should only approach
it through training in a monastery or something, then that's not really life.
It's not necessary to judge a man's action simply in terms of "well, he's only
seeking revenge." He himself was honest enough to know that there was that
element in his motivation, but soon there were other more worthwhile reasons. And I think I wouldn't quarrel with him at all for that.

Is Nanga characteristic of political leaders in Africa?
He was characteristic of the leadership just before the military came into
politics in Nigeria and characteristic of leadership in other places where the
military did not come into politics. I would give you names, but I think I had
better not. But if you look at the politics of Africa today, I think you'll find
other countries where everything will be quite parallel to this book except
the very end. In fact, two years ago a friend in an East African country I shall
not name [Kenya] bought copies of this book and gave one to each government minister for Christmas.

What factors caused the emergence of politicians like Nanga?
Well, the colonial departure from the scene was not really a departure. I
mean independence was unreal, and people like Nanga were actually used as
front men, as puppets, by the former colonial power. As long as they could
go about saying they were ministers, as long as they enriched themselves,

they were happy, and they would leave the real exploiter at his work. So I think in a very basic sense, characters like Nanga flourished because the colonial situation leading to the independence period in Africa made it possible. And it still happens; it's not a thing of the past.

Was it from the events in the Western Region of Nigeria prior to 1966 that you drew the political action of the novel? Or was it an anticipation of something that had not yet happened?

The novel was completed at least two years before January 1966. It was completed in '64. And the indication as to how politics was going to develop in Nigeria was there already. If you cared to look, I think the signs were everywhere, not only in the West. There were parallel events all over. The worst no doubt was in the West because that was the seat of the crisis. That was where the manipulation was the most blatant. But I think you could see signs elsewhere.

Although there has been trouble in Nigeria between ethnic groups, you don't seem to make reference to any kind of tribal antagonism in your novels, particularly A Man of the People *where one might expect to see this portrayed.*

I hate the word tribe. Tribes were not really all that important, you know, in the past. However, it is not quite correct to say that I don't make reference to these antagonisms because I do. I can even refer to places were somebody loses a job or doesn't get a job and blames it on somebody from another tribe. But it was at that level; this didn't really become a terribly dangerous and explosive issue until it became a subject for political manipulation, especially since independence. There were rumbles before, but they were not more than you'd find anywhere else. It really got out of hand when you had politicians exploiting it to win elections. It's very easy for resentments to be exploited, and so we had explosions.

In addition to recording the past and current revolutions and changes that are going on, do African writers have any influence in determining Africa's future?

Yes, I think by recording what had gone on before, they were in a way helping to set the tone of what was going to happen. And this is important because at this stage it seems to me that the writer's role is more in determining than merely in reporting. In other words, his role is to act rather than to react. Today we are saying, "Well, let's not waste too much time explaining what we were and pleading with some people and telling them we are also human. Let us forget that; let us map out what we are going to be tomorrow." I think our most meaningful job today should be to determine what kind of society we want, how we are going to get there, what values we can take from the past, if we can, as we move along.

Are you doing any writing now?

Yes, but not novels. I do articles and some poetry, but I can't do more than that. I started a novel just before the war which seemed to me at the time terribly important—I already had the idea for it as far back as '66—but I finally gave it up because it later seemed to me completely unimportant.

Often we think of creativity as something that has to come from a kind of contemplation, quiet or repose. How can you keep the artistic integrity of your writing while being so totally involved in the political situation?

I think there is a myth about creativity being something apart from life, but this is only a half truth. I can create, but of course not the kind of thing I created when I was at ease. I can't write a novel now; I wouldn't want to. And even if I wanted to, I couldn't. So that particular artistic form is out for me at the moment. I can write poetry—something short, intense, more in keeping with my mood. I can write essays. I can even lecture. All this is creating in the context of our struggle. At home I do a lot of writing, but not fiction, something more concrete, more directly related to what's going on. What I'm saying is that there are forms of creativity which suit different moments. I wouldn't consider writing a poem on daffodils particularly creative in my situation now. It would be foolish; I couldn't do it.

Are most of the writers in Biafra young writers?

Yes. I'm supposed to be a sort of "elder statesman."

Do you foresee a time when you will go back to writing novels?

Oh yes, it's always possible, if one survives. There's always time. But these are not normal times, not for me. These are not normal times at all.

Achebe: Accountable to Our Society

Ernest and Pat Emenyonu / 1972

From *Africa Report*, May 1972, 21+. Reprinted by permission of *Africa Report*.

The well-known Nigerian novelist Chinua Achebe, whose first novel, *Things Fall Apart* (1958), is today one of the most widely read African novels, seems to have been removed from the world of literature since 1966. That year marked the publication of his fourth novel, *A Man of the People*, which prophesied the Nigerian civil war that broke out in July 1967. Since the end of the civil war in January 1970, Achebe has been at the Institute of African Studies of the University of Nigeria, Nsukka, as a senior research fellow. He has not done any major work but has not ceased writing. He co-authored a collection entitled *The Insider* and has also brought out a collection of poems, *Beware, Soul Brother*. Yet another collection of short stories of his, *Girls at War*, has come out. He is co-author of a modern African fable *How the Leopard Got His Claws*, soon to be published, which is about a modern Africa nation that lost its unity. He also edits *Okike*, a new literary journal.

Emenyonu: You once said that you regard what you write as applied art. Can you talk more about this?

Achebe: What I was saying was that there is so much crank in the talk of an artist who says, "My work is not didactic, I am not a teacher. I have no ideas. I just write my poetry and it is self-sufficient." It is this type of attitude that I was trying to confront by saying that I don't believe that art is useless or can be useless. I believe that art has some use—and drawing from our own experience, the African experience, I don't see any example of the uselessness of art or its being independent of man. This thing can be carried to an absurd extent.

I was at a conference some years ago at Makerere. One poet from Rhodesia, white, came up with the idea that a good poem writes itself. That kind of idea, that art is autonomous and that it happens by itself, is simply madness. What we say, what we write or what we paint is as human beings who live in society and are accountable to that society.

Emenyonu: Should a writer's philosophy or beliefs be taken into account in assessing his work?

Achebe: No, I don't think so. A work of art does not have to have an appendix where a writer's point of view and philosophy are stated. If his philosophy is relevant to the story, then it will be in the story. Take folktales, for instance. We don't know who created them, or what they thought, but we can tell from the story the kind of view they took of the world generally. This is all that one requires, and not a tight philosophy. We are not philosophers in that sense.

The folktales have their moral lessons, sometimes directly, at other times not so directly. There is the story about the chicken that declined to attend a meeting of all the animals and told them that any decision reached by the majority would be all right with him. So at the meeting they decided that henceforth the chicken would be the sacrificial animal, and this was carried by acclamation.

Now this is really a serious political statement. The discussion of public affairs is the business of all, and if you neglect your responsibility in this way you may suffer the fate of the fowl. This kind of thing should be there in any important story in one form or the other; otherwise I don't see how you can call it important at all. Many people don't like the word moral or didactic, but it is an important element in any story.

Emenyonu: You often talk about your African experiences and what you personally learned from your Ibo village as bearing direct influence on your art. Does this entirely exclude any political influences or foreign ideologies—Négritude or Marxism, for example.

Achebe: I had already decided to write before I knew about these ideologies that you mention. But very often people object to foreign ideologies, not because they are genuinely concerned about local and indigenous ideologies but because they resent any type of change. If someone comes here and says that Marxism is the only form of economic system that will work here, we ought to look at it and not reject it just because its origin is foreign to us. At the same time, if somebody comes and says that in the past we had an economic system that is likely to work better than Marxism and then shows in concrete terms the way it was, and also how the amenities, the fruits, or the national cake was shared in the past, we should not overlook him.

People who talk about foreign ideologies in an exclusive way are often merely saying "don't upset the system we have got now," which is the system of "grab and keep." That I will not accept. In any society you have to work out a system in which people are treated as fairly as possible. If Marxism is going to provide it, then we ought to try it. If, on the other hand, some other system has been proved to be able to solve the problem, then we should look at that. I am not really a politician and I keep an open mind.

As for Négritude, that has been flogged too much. It was a good war cry once upon a time. It no longer is—and one good pointer to the fact that it is no longer is Senegal, which to my mind is one of the seats of neocolonialism. If this is a result of Négritude, and one of its archpriests is, in fact, running the affairs of Senegal, then obviously that thing no longer works.

But there isn't such a thing as "we have the truth and everything else is falsehood," or "we are right and everybody else is wrong." From the African standpoint, what I am saying is that there may be something in what these foreigners are saying, or there may be some faults in our own system.

There were certainly faults in the Ibo system that was depicted in *Things Fall Apart*. There is no reason, for instance, for twins to be thrown away. But if you take a position for or against, then you find yourself defending the throwing away of twins, or else you say that everything in Africa is barbarism, which appears to be the new trend today among some black writers, and they are immediately applauded by whites because it gives them an easy conscience again after all this period of doubt. Now I don't want to take either position. For every proverb you produce I can give you one that says the opposite. This is the way it seems to me that the world is made to run.

Emenyonu: Yet wouldn't many black people who read your works think you are stopping short of saying something that could be relevant to this age of black power?

Achebe: I don't know if they think so; but if they do, that doesn't worry me.

I am not saying that there are no issues on which people can go to war—but when they do, let them understand that there is something on the other side that makes you have an opponent. If you do this, you will probably fight even better because you would have an understanding of the mechanics of the world in which you are going to operate.

But if you are going to assert black power, or whatever it is you want to call it, and declare everybody else is a cheat, a liar and so on, I won't be able to believe it. And if I don't believe it, I am going to find it very difficult to give it my full allegiance.

This is why I do not paint white characters that are complete blackguards, because I don't think that is necessary for them to do the harm that they did. They were decent people with families, and that is the worst kind of danger:

when it comes from a decent man. It does not really excite me that a monster causes trouble. When an ordinary man causes havoc, that is more ominous.

Emenyonu: Do you see African literature now merging into one with black literature as a whole?

Achebe: There are sufficient similarities, for the two to be looked at in the same kind of way, but the details won't be the same, and these details are important. When you get down to the realities of the situation—the situation in Nigeria, the situation in Zambia, the situation in Ivory Coast and so on—there are tiny details that cannot be ignored. And these details will be ignored if you say that everything in Africa is the same as in America or in Latin America. This won't work.

There is some similarity. After all, what we are striving for is human equality and that kind of thing, and wherever you find people struggling for these ends, their struggle must have certain things in common. But even in fighting revolutions, the particular place where you are fighting your particular revolution is going to a large extent to determine tactics.

Emenyonu: Would you regard these details as the distinguishing factors between black literature and any other literature?

Achebe: Any other revolutionary literature? Yes.

Emenyonu: And would you go so far as to say that any black writer who is not incorporating these details is not writing a meaningful black literature?

Achebe: Well, I would suspect so, but I never really want to be dogmatic. I am sufficiently broad-minded to leave room for somebody to say that his own instinct tells him differently, and if he thinks this honestly and there is no falseness and no putting on airs about it, well, let him do his thing.

Emenyonu: In view of all this, what is your opinion about the present state of African writing? Do you think it is really sufficiently relevant to the issues of the day? And what do you say of its prospects for future development.

Achebe: Some African writing is meaningful and some less so. I think what is meaningful is what takes into account the past and the present. There are people who say forget the past. Well, you can't because the present comes out of it. At the same time, you do not want to be mesmerized or immobilized by your contemplation of the past to the exclusion of what is happening today. The most meaningful work that African writers can do today will take into account our whole history: how we got here, and what it is today; and this will help us to map out our plans for the future.

Emenyonu: Turning to your own recent work, I have read your short story in *The Insider* and another short story in *Okike* and, of course, your poetry, *Beware, Soul Brother.* Let me take the poetry first. Is this a new direction you are consciously branching off into?

Achebe: Consciously? Well, yes, if you like—in the sense that I know what I am doing. But in the sense of choice, it is not really that. The thing is that during the war I just wasn't able to write a novel or think of writing a novel. On the other hand, I was able to write some poetry, some short and intense pieces. Some of the poetry that has just been published was written during the war and the rest since the war ended. I also found that the short story seems more possible than the novel, so I have done quite a few short stories since the war ended.

Emenyonu: Are you writing or thinking of writing a novel at the moment?

Achebe: I can't quite make up my mind. I have the beginning of an idea for a novel—could be a novel, could be a play.

Emenyonu: A reviewer of the first issue of *Okike* implied that your tone, as evinced from your writings in that issue, now tends to be more violent and tense. Can you talk about how the war has affected your consciousness as a writer?

Achebe: That is very difficult and, in any case, it is not something I am very keen to talk about. Maybe it is still somewhat raw.

I have come to the view that you can't separate the creativity from the revolution that is inevitable in Africa. Not just the war, but the post-independence period in Africa is bound to create in the writer a new approach. This, maybe, was sharpened by the war, but in my case it was already there. The disenchantment with the fruits of independence was already there in the early '60s. *A Man of the People*, which came out in January 1966 and which I wrote in 1964 and 1965, shows quite clearly this new preoccupation with the reality of post-independent Africa. The war only emphasized our anxieties about how things are working out.

Emenyonu: Is post-independent Africa really as hopeless as the pessimistic ending of *A Man of the People* suggests?

Achebe: If you were convinced that it was absolutely hopeless, then you would just drink and wait for your death. But the fact that you are talking about it implies some optimism that somebody may listen, that there is still a possibility for change, so it is not entirely pessimistic.

But the situation is bad enough. One should not pretend that there is no problem when the place is full of problems. So one has to bring these problems out as forcefully as possible to draw attention to them. It has always been the method of teachers at all times to exaggerate in order to draw attention.

Emenyonu: Generally speaking, critics—western critics in particular— have been almost invariably favorable in their appraisal of your work, but this has not been the case with many other African writers. What is your judgment of the criticism of African literature by western critics—or black critics, for that matter?

Achebe: There again, I am not going to come down heavily on one side or the other. Until you have serious criticism by Africans of Africans, there are certain dimensions that are bound to be missed in the criticism of African writing. By serious criticism, I mean that the critic actually reads and understands the work he is criticizing. The problem at the moment is that we don't have many such people. We have far more western (European and American) critics, and in the absence of any serious contenders from Africa they are the ones in the field. Some of them have made an effort to understand, and sometimes they do and sometimes they don't.

The next stage should be for serious African scholarship to develop, and it must really be something solid, based on hard work and imagination. There is just a handful of African critics worth the name. I am sorry to say that, but it is the fact.

Emenyonu: Where does the indigenous African publisher come in?

Achebe: More or less in the same way as the African critic, because publishing involves a certain amount of critical judgment by the publisher. I am very keen on indigenous publishing. Before the war I was actively involved in setting up one such house. Unfortunately my partner [Christopher Okigbo] got killed in the war and I haven't been able to get round to doing it again. But there are one or two other people who are working in this area. All we can do now is to give them all our support.

Emenyonu: You are referring to the new Nwamife Publishing House at Enugu? Some of the things they have issued come from young, previously unpublished writers, particularly the authors in *The Insider*. Some of them are preoccupied with the bitterness of their experiences during the war. Do you see this trend as continuing in the writings that might come out of the East Central State?

Achebe: I don't know. But I do know that the experience of the last four or five years has been so enormous that there is no way you can talk about creative work from this part of Nigeria without taking it into account one way or the other. As more and more people feel that it is safe for them to say what they have on their minds, then we are likely to get more and more unorthodox opinions and positions. People have been through a huge experience and this thing is taking time to work out in all kinds of ways. It is not just cynicism, bitterness or pessimism. Irony and all kinds of things are mixed up with it. As time goes on, probably more mature positions and attitudes will begin to emerge.

Emenyonu: I have read some of your short stories before and after *Things Fall Apart* and I notice that some of the themes in your stories come up again in your novels. Are some of your major novels the outgrowth of your earlier short stories?

Achebe: They are, and it shows that the ideas in the novels are not new ideas. Some of them have been with me for years before I came to the novel. I am sure that if I had written poetry about the same time, you would probably find the same preoccupations. Certainly the preoccupations I have in my poetry today are the same that I have in the short stories I am now writing, and if I wrote a novel it would be the same. It is not the same story, but it is the same idea, the same theme, the same kind of attitude.

I didn't realize it for some time, but I had, in fact, used the phrase "a man of the people" before the novel, in a short story called *The Voter*. It was used in a different context, but it all goes to show that this kind of thing goes round and round in one's mind for some time before one actually starts working on a novel.

Emenyonu: There is a short story about intertribal marriage where the parents are strongly in opposition but are reconciled to the idea and the marriage takes place. In your novel *No Longer at Ease*, where you handle almost the same theme, you create highly inflexible parents and the marriage fails to materialize. Were you trying to reverse roles here and let the Old triumph over the New?

Achebe: No, I didn't think of it as such. I never will take the stand that the Old must win or that the New must win. If I wrote two stories in which the Old won in one, the New in the other, I would be quite happy. To me, that is the way life is.

In Obi's story the marriage didn't come through because the woman is tabooed, and cult consideration, not tribe, is the primary issue. The fact that they failed does not mean that I believe that all young men caught in such conflicts must go the way of Obi.

I never believe in taking firm positions and if I do two novels, I try to make sure that the same thing does not happen twice. Take, for instance, the stories of Okonkwo in *Things Fall Apart* and Ezeulu in *Arrow of God*. They are, to my mind, two completely different types of people. One is very dogmatic, in the sense of going by the past, and does not believe in change. Rather than have change he would kill himself. The other one is a more intellectual character. He surveys the whole situation before him and knows that change is inevitable in the world. He is not going to change his nature or his position, but he is ready to accommodate as much of this new thing as is possible for him without losing his important position in society. These two are quite different people, and yet both come to the same sticky end.

The point is that no single truth satisfied me—and this is well founded in the Ibo world view. No single man can be correct all the time, no single idea can be totally correct. If you pick any proverb that seems to put forward a particular point of view, you can always find another one that seeks to contradict it.

Emenyonu: But the sad thing in *Arrow of God* is that the very flexible nature of Ezeulu, which shows that he understands change in an intellectual way, is the thing that destroys him in the end. In *Things Fall Apart* Okonkwo remains stubborn, obstructing change, and is equally destroyed in the end.

Achebe: So there is no escape, up to a point. We are in it together. Those who are going to make it—if anybody is going to make it—are not going to make it because of the position they take, the strength of their character or the weakness of their character and the rest of society or at times the entire universe.

I don't think that man is strong enough on his own to counter these forces that he might come up against. He stands a better chance if he is operating from within his society. This is the value of a society like our traditional society where you were part of a bigger unit.

If you look at it really, Ezeulu was already going beyond the best interests of his society. He was carrying his logic as a priest to an extent where it begins to work against the people for whom the religion is designed. It is the good of these people that is the only good, as far as I am concerned, not the good of the logic or the good of the one man who happens to be king or priest or what have you. In the case of Okonkwo, of course, society was going to be more tactful, and he was going to leave them behind and come on his own. And these are the people who suffer.

Emenyonu: How about Obi in *No Longer at Ease*? Why does he suffer his type of fate?

Achebe: I think it is because he has come out of his society without joining a new one. If he belonged to the old society, the corrupt one, he would have known the rules and been well protected. He would not have gone to jail because he would have sent his steward to go and get the money. He had bits of his past and bits of the new morality he picked up in his studies, and he was completely at sea in the Lagos society. In other words, it is isolation that brings his fall.

I am not saying that one should never be isolated. Most of the great teachers and great revolutionaries have had to step out of their societies. But if you are going to do that you should know well in advance what you are in for and be prepared to suffer like Okonkwo or Ezeulu.

Emenyonu: Are there any aspects of your published novels that, given the chance, you would revise in any way?

Achebe: I would probably alter a few things in *Things Fall Apart*. But they wouldn't be basic things. I would not, for instance, change its society to the society of *Arrow of God*. The two books are complementary. There are little weaknesses that I might like to edit out in *Things Fall Apart*, some conversations that I would develop a little more, but no more.

Emenyonu: And in *A Man of the People*, would you say anything different about the masses whom you described as "the real culprits"?

Achebe: No, I would not change that at all. The masses have not changed. If I were writing the book today, the setting would be different. The charming thing about Africa is that yesterday is so different from today already, and this creates a problem for writers because some of the problems you discuss are no longer problems. Things have moved so quickly.

For example, *A Man of the People* with today's setting would feature the army instead of politicians. But the masses would still be as cynical, which is not to say that they should therefore be abandoned to their lot. The whole point of being a leader is that, in spite of the cynicism or the despair of the masses, it is your job to do something for them. They don't have to deserve it because they are law-abiding, sensible and obedient. After all, whether they are or not, they are still brothers, sisters, fathers and mothers.

If you create a situation in which they see certain values distorted, they tend to copy it and lose their own direction. But that does not absolve the leaders. The moment you declare yourself the leader of your people, you've taken on their vessel. You are "carrying" their god, and you have become their priest.

Emenyonu: Would it be right to say that you are disillusioned with the élite even before an élitist leadership comes into being anywhere in Africa?

Achebe: Yes. No country has so far handed its government to university professors yet, but some of them have had a hand in fashioning things and they have not shown that they were that different. Furthermore, there is an area where they are in charge—the universities. If we could expect any golden age from the élite we should begin to see it from the government of the universities. But what we see is, in fact, the same thing that happens in the society at large, and sometimes worse.

It seems to me that the basic problem that I hinted at in *A Man of the People* is that this generation, which is not used to good things, is not ever likely to produce the kind of leadership that you and I want.

It is my hope that when the next generation comes up and they are not so fascinated by wearing lace or by wearing gold that reaches the floor, maybe then we are going to find something different.

Chinua Achebe on *Arrow of God*

Michel Fabre / 1973

From *Echos du Commonwealth* (Pau, France), 5 (1979–80), 7–17. Reprinted by permission of *Commonwealth: Essays and Studies* and Michel Fabre.

In June 1973, I had the privilege of participating in a two-week seminar organized at the University of Missouri (Kansas City) by Professor Robert Farnsworth and devoted to Third World authors writing in English. The works of Chinua Achebe, from Nigeria, and of Wilson Harris, from Guiana, were studied in detail, with the novelists participating in the discussions as well as giving a few formal lectures. Other writers and critics—such as George Lamming, Derek Walcott, Kofi Awoonor, Paule Marshall, Jan Carew, Ivan Van Sertima and Peter Nazareth—were also in attendance at the seminar for varying lengths of time.

All formal lectures and panel discussions were recorded and videotaped, but I believe I was one of a handful of participants who privately taped the exchanges that took place every day after the study of specific works. From a half-dozen cassettes featuring Chinua Achebe, I have been able to put together the following "interview." It is largely an edited transcript, although great care has been taken not to alter what Achebe said in response to questions or reactions from our group. His utterances have sometimes been condensed, reorganized and put in a sequence which covers the various aspects of *Arrow of God* he commented upon at the time. This montage by no means intends to duplicate such useful interviews as Robert Serumaga's (*Cultural Events in Africa,* No. 28) or Bernth Lindfors's (*Studies in Black Literature,* Vol. 2, No. 1), which briefly deal with the novel. My aim has been to provide the student of *Arrow of God* with some hitherto unknown or little-known statements made by Achebe himself with a view of further illuminating the novelist's conception of his own work.

Out of what experience did Arrow of God *grow?*

Although maybe to a lesser degree than *Things Fall Apart,* the novel was inspired in part by my desire to revaluate my culture. Like many others, it had been branded as inferior and bad by British oppressors, when they did not say it was non-existent. It appeared to be a vital cultural necessity to fight and rebel against that view.

How is it that the title sounds so much like Conrad's Arrow of Gold?

The sounds are very much alike. I have said elsewhere what Conrad meant to me and I have talked about my relationship to his writings. The title, *Arrow of God,* is explained in the book itself: how Ezeulu stands for the instrument, the weapon of the god he serves.

What was your audience and what audience did you have in mind?

My audience is the whole world as a possible community, but one must also take into account one's actual audience. It is quite possible to love mankind and hate men. When I write, I always think of my hometown, my district, my province, my race. One must take into account those who speak a language which is exclusively yours and whose problems you share. Problems like oppression, like living in a given society. I began from the inside, in my own thinking, and worked out; and I hope that others will understand and get something out of what I am saying.

One finds in this novel a reflection of a kind of philosophy that expresses your faith, or lack of faith, in the culture and tradition of your people. How does this fit together with the sense of failure one distinctly gets from the stories of Okwonkwo, Ezeulu or Odili?

I do not know whether I am obsessed by failure, but that makes a better story than success. Really, I mean. I mean that failure is much more interesting; it is deeper and more moving, especially if one fails with dignity. This is important, and I tend to be drawn to it. Of course, one could write a comedy about failure, but one has to respond to one's leanings. Mine may be macabre, yet there is much interest when people die. To take a man like Ezeulu, for example, the important thing is not whether he really succeeded but his failure itself, the way it happens. That is much more important than any success.

Ezeulu was struggling with the white man, and his return, we could hope, would compensate for his struggle. But his people turned against him, and so the white man had it all his way. I was not saying, of course, that the white man is therefore right. What I was saying is that, in such kind of extreme situation, the important thing was that Ezeulu was able to fight and to cope, as best as he could, with the circumstances. Even when he failed, he failed as a man, you see. That is very important in our culture. The recent experience we had, in Nigeria, of the civil war, had this exemplified. There were leaders who showed up complete cowards and others, a few, of whom people could say, "This is a man."

When you talk about somebody and say, "He is a man," that means much in my culture. It means, here is a good person, a person who has been leading a right life. He is reliable and honest and you can stand by his word. He can take care of his responsibilities—familial, economic, as well as social and political. This is a measure of success, both material and spiritual. The important thing to ask of a man is: "How does he cope? How does he perform in an extreme situation?" That, in itself, is a story: not just how do you deal with it, but—if this is the case—how do you fail. In part, it is the story of Ezeulu. The way you fail is terribly important.

Can one say that Ezeulu's fall is caused by his own hubris?

Of course, at times, the high priest tends to confuse his own thinking with that of Ulu. He does not make the difference between the man and the god. But is this not natural on the part of a priest? Priests of all kinds, or political leaders, fall into such dangers.

Was Ezeulu really after power? After becoming a sort of king?

Ezeulu already has power—more power than anyone else, or nearly. And he certainly has enough strength and arrogance to attempt to assume a lot of power. But he does not want to become a king. One must be quite careful about this notion of becoming a king. In the book, Nwaka speaks of Ezeulu trying to be a king, but you must not take that word at face value, or, rather, in the European sense. The word is only used to speak of one who wants to become too powerful. Here, king would apply both to material and political power. And maybe I should tell you a story about the taking of titles in Ibo culture and how the title of king is said to have gone out of practice.

In Ibo traditional society there were built-in means of discouraging people from becoming too powerful or too rich, or rather of encouraging them to trade that power and wealth against honors and titles. If a man said he wanted to be the equivalent of a millionaire, although there is no such equivalent, the elders would say to him: "You want to prove to the village that you are wealthy, that you are a good and important man, then you must take titles." There were several titles, up to five of them. And taking titles would see to it that, in the process, the person would spend all of his money and this money would revert to the community. They would say: "To take this title, you will feed the village for a number of days and you will give each man who already has the same title a number of goats, or cows, or whatever." By the time the man had earned the title, his wealth was exhausted and he was no richer than his neighbors except in prestige.

And the amount of wealth to be given the village and the owners of the several titles would increase until one arrived at the title of king. The story about that title, the fifth title, also explains how this title went out of use long ago: the reason was that one was required to pay the debts of all the people in the community before one could become their king. Once you had done all the other things and acquired all the other titles, and fed the village for weeks, all the members of the community would come to you one after the other and tell you the amount they owed. Only when you had paid it off could you become their king. And this was enough to discourage all pretenders.

In the case of Nwaka, he uses the term "king" to talk about an individual who sets himself apart and against society by wanting to set himself above it. Such behavior would run against the social cohesion and group integration so dear to traditional Ibo communities.

Is there any clear relationship between religion and politics in Ibo society?

Religion, in present-day Ibo society, is a mixture of many religions—Christianity, the old religion, etc.—not to speak of the people who do not profess any religion seriously, although it is difficult to say that really irreligious persons exist. In the novel, for different reasons, I had to get some idea of sacredness both into religion and politics. This is, in my mind, the kind of link between Ezeulu and, not only the elders, but the British commissioners.

Does Ezeulu really try to use Christianity for political purposes?

Yes, he does. He is an intelligent man and can see what is about to happen. He sees that change is inevitable, and he tries to master the new forces, to use the new forces in order to retain his own position and to manage the inevitable changes in his society. This is the attitude of a clever intellectual and must not be seen in terms of religious beliefs—I mean, of adhesion, or not, to Christianity.

Ezeulu is no naïve man. He does not equate power and right. He is a shrewd political leader, too, when he recognizes the necessity for temporary alliances, with some whites, not as an aim but as a tactic. He pretends to welcome some changes in order for his society to absorb them instead of being ruled by them, so that his order, his religion, his tradition will survive these changes and ultimately regain power.

Earlier on, someone suggested that there is a sense of failure in my novels. Why do my heroes always fail, as Ezeulu does? Now, I sometimes use the word "fail" myself, and cannot blame anybody for using it. But I use it in a special way, because there is a very deep sense in which one can talk about Okonkwo or Ezeulu failing. It is a sense in which you see those two people standing for something. They stand for a way of life, a people, a vision of the world. Now, if a man knows what he stands for, it is difficult to say that he fails. Both men succeed in much the same way Christ can have been said to succeed. When you come to *No Longer at Ease* and find a young man who does not know what to stand for because he is confused, because things have been messed up, it is different. Odili has contradictory notions, some African, some European, and he lacks focus. This does not make his pain any lighter nor his tragedy less tragic, but it creates a different kind of tragedy—one that drags on forever. A sickness that drags on is a more serious matter: when you want to curse somebody, you curse him to die over ninety years. When you get to the time of *A Man of the People,* the situation is somewhat worse than in *Arrow of God;* although it is also somewhat better because, by that time, a certain polarization has begun to take place that begins to give coherence again. Only Odili does not see it until the end, and that is the point at which I decide to leave him for the moment, when he begins to have a sense of what needs to be done. Hopefully, when we go back to him, he may be clearer in his mind as to where he should stand. So, briefly, I do not think that the word "failure" explains the situation of these characters fully.

That kind of failure, if you keep it long enough in view, might take on another complexion. At the same time, I am not sure that Okonkwo's, or Ezeulu's, set of values really die. The simple fact that we are telling their stories and that some people may think, "Here is a man after my heart," means something, some kind of return or regeneration in the lives of their descendants. It is certainly hasty to apply words like "failure," you know.

Is suicide the ultimate failure, then?

Suicide is certainly the worst kind of end for Okonkwo. The reason he did it is suggested in his character. He was the kind of man who would go ahead and do the worst possible kind of damage to himself and to everybody. Just to show people. My father once told me: "Don't tell anybody, 'You don't dare do this,' because there is a kind of character who will go and do it. Nothing will stop him." Sometimes, as a kind of joke, a man will try to kill himself for the others to restrain him. He needs that kind of drama and attention. There was this extreme attitude in the young man. He would not leave anything unfinished after he had started; that is why he could not stop beating his wife.

How come women are generally secondary characters in the novel?

Well, women never saw themselves as secondary or inferior in traditional Ibo society. They were different, that is all. This did not mean a kind of masculine domination. I remember an uncle of mine who said, "There is nothing greater than a mother." My first cousins were my "brothers" in my language. We were cousins on our mother's side, which was more important than being cousins on our father's side. This is very central in what was going on—is going on—in my society. In fact, when a man died, he was taken to his mother's people to be buried. That showed the importance of mothers and women. Also, on the economic level, the market has always been there for the women to make money, and they have grown in importance. In traditional Ibo society the wife was economically independent.

What is the meaning of "son," when you write, at the very end of Arrow of God, *"Thereafter any yam that was harvested in the man's fields was harvested in the name of the son"?*

First of all, I'd like to say that, in general terms, the end of a story is only an end in one sense. It is a beginning in another sense because it is an open-ended kind of end. At the end of a page, another page is projected, like an echo or the pebbles you throw in a pond, and it goes on and on. This specific ending has all sorts of meaning for me. There is a suggestion of Christian ethics in "the name of the son," nearly in a caricatural sense. There is a bit of parody there, but it is not really parody because Christianity is not a joke, and suddenly what will happen to the Ibo culture is not going to be a joke. But there is an even deeper possibility in which the harvest in the name of the son becomes a reversal of the natural order. In the society we have been looking at in this story, you do not do things in the name of the son but in the name of the father. The legitimacy is with the elders, the ancestors, with tradition and age. We now have a new dispensation in which youth and inexperience earn a new legitimacy. This is something new and different. Wisdom belongs to the elders, but the new wisdom is going to belong to the young people. They are going to go to school, to go to church, and will tell their fathers what it is. This almost amounts to turning the world upside down. I think that Ezeulu himself sensed it coming; he had some kind of psychic vision. This is why he sent his son to the British. Something told him that it might be necessary. He found some other explanations for doing it, but in fact he sensed what he was doing. This was confirmed the first time he was interviewed by the English administrator Clarke, and Ezeulu looked up and the image in his mind was that of a puppy, something unfinished, half-baked, too young; and yet there was authority. Now, this reversal itself is tied up with the colonial situation. There is no other situation in the world where power resides with inexperience and young people. A young man would not approach the seat of power in England, but in a colonial situation he is given power and can order a chief around. In a very deep sense this reversal is the quintessence of colonialism. It is a loss of independence. These are some of the ideas that are implied at the end of the novel.

Was this the vision you tried to present in the novel?

I do not try to exhaust any vision in any novel of mine. I do not try to put in everything. I do not pretend to have worked out a neat view of the world. I am fully aware of things I would have liked to deal with and have not dealt with. Also, I do not operate in categories as some of my friends do. When a story comes to me, it comes complete; this means the kind of person who will tell the story is part of it, the kind of language used is part of it. It would have been very difficult for me to have put it to Obi to carry the story of *Arrow of God.* I don't know what the explanation is—you can work and find that out—but it seems to me that this is all part of the story. Now, if people talk about imperfect developments, they are free to do so. Even for me, these are not perfect models; they could have been improved. If you do not see certain things in my books, then I have not done things as well as I should have done; but I think you can easily see my idea of time, of the past, the present and the future as one. I stress the continuity of life from the child, the adolescent, to the old man and the ancestors. This is tradition. I am not using any kind of metaphor or genetic symbolism. The priest was a priest and he is the shrine of the goddess earth. His son sees things in a different way. Although I did not state this in a scientific, rational way, I say it in a very real sense. I attempted to describe in physical terms what was psychic—this belief that we are close to our ancestors.

You have written somewhere that you used English as a conscious artist, whereas Amos Tutuola, for instance, was a natural one. What do you mean by that?

Well, Tutuola has a fine instinct that helps him tell superb stories in a medium which is limited even by his knowledge of it. *Feather Woman of the Jungle* is proof of his talent. I say I am a conscious artist because I often make conscious attempts at recreating the turns and phrases of the vernacular while using English. Contrary to other writers of the English-speaking world, like V.S. Naipaul for instance, I do not feel much kinship, basically, with the English tradition although I use the English language. I have no thorough respect or worship for it. It is a very fine instrument, but not an object of ritual. I respect ritual, but it tends to make objects irrelevant to present-day situations when it extends to areas outside religion.

Interview with Chinua Achebe

Onuora Ossie Enekwe / 1976

From *Okike,* 30 (1990), 129–33. Reprinted by permission of *Okike.*

Enekwe: Why are you returning to Nigeria at this time, and what do you plan to do there?

Achebe: I'm returning to resume my life, if you like, in Nigeria. I came to the States on a short visit, to begin with. When I left Nigeria in 1972, I thought I would be here for one year, or at the most, two years. But it's dragged on beyond that to four years. So it's an overdue return, and I'm looking forward very much to my work at Nsukka.

Enekwe: What would you like to do, specifically, at the University of Nigeria?

Achebe: Well, I have so many things, I really don't know where to begin. I have so many ideas; there are so many things that need to be done, so many possibilities, you *know;* one is terribly excited, but at the same time, you're almost confused, because you don't know where to begin. But one can start from a personal angle. I'd like to complete the novel I'm working on. I had hoped to have at least the first draft ready here before going back. It didn't work out that way. I hope to complete it in Nigeria. So that's the first thing. Secondly, I want to see the work of the magazine, *Okike,* developed in its natural soil, with people who share the same kind of vision as I have. Thirdly, I'd like to pursue my own understanding and study of Igbo culture, which excites me more and more everyday. You can't do that from America—you need to get back to the soil. So, I'd like to get back, but I'm not sure just what specific areas.

This is one of the major cultures in Africa, and it's received scant attention. And somebody ought to get down to work on it, you know, just to uncover the mainspring of Igbo thinking. This is a major undertaking. And I'm not certain just what aspect I shall begin with, but that doesn't matter—this is the major area that needs to be attended to. So, that's the next thing that I'm excited about—getting back to Igboland, getting back to the study of Igbo people and Igbo culture.

Enekwe: Now, about your novel, does the delay have to do with what you wrote in *Morning Yet on Creation Day*—that we should not forget the past?

Is it related to the problem of delving into the causes of the Nigerian crisis?
Or is it simply part of your slow and meticulous writing habit?

Achebe: Well, I've had this question in a different way before, and I'm
sure I'm going to contradict myself here. I would say that the reason I didn't
come up with another novel was the civil war, and the crisis in Nigeria and
the problem of finding the kind of emotional and artistic stability—peace of
mind, if you like—that is needed. This is part of the answer, of course. I
think the crisis had something to do with it because I did abandon a project
of writing that I was already embarked upon. But I think that, as I look back
on that, there is a second element, which I have not until now talked about.
And that's the fact that I don't really feel that there is any obligation on my
part to produce a novel every other year. It's not my style, and perhaps I was
really making this point—it may have been unconscious—that one can get
into the habit of being pressured by one's publisher, one's readers, one's
fans—you know, everybody saying: "We read the last novel. Now when is
the next one?" And I think that is something that, for me, is not very desir-
able. I think I have to fight to work at my own pace. I think probably why I
began to think of this was that I saw a TV interview that somebody did with
Bernard Shaw on one of his visits to the United States. You know, Bernard
Shaw never liked Americans, and he was always off-hand. So this interview
was interesting because Shaw was almost anticipating his interviewer, and
saying, "Don't ask me 'what should we do' because when I was last here I
told you what you should do and you haven't done it." So I think that I have
a kind of feeling of: "Well, I've written these novels, which are important in
my view, and they have not been fully, adequately, dealt with. So why should
I write a fifth, and a sixth?" Now, that's one point of view. You may think
that this is just an excuse, but in a way I think that there's something quite
fundamental there. I think that the job of my readers is to get the maximum
out of what I have done.

I too have to sit back—especially after the number four—and assess what
I have been doing, ask myself questions and see if there is need for new
departure. Because it's so easy to get into the same routine. A novel every
two years; perhaps, improving technique. But I'm not interested in that. I'm
interested in doing something fundamentally important—and therefore, it
needs time. And what I've been doing, really, is avoiding this pressure to get
into the habit of one novel a year. This is what is expected of novelists. And
I have never been really too much concerned with doing what is expected of
novelists, or writers, or artists. I want to do what I believe is important. And

so I've been thinking; I've been working out things in my mind, and part of it is the Nigerian crisis. I have to ask myself: "What happened to Nigeria? What happened to my relationship to Nigeria? What happened to the Igbo people in relation to Nigeria? And how are we going to deal with this in future? Should this kind of thing ever happen again, how would we deal with it? How does Nigeria move on into this stage of evolution? And these are very important questions. And I don't think you can answer them if you're busy churning out one novel after another.

So the kind of thing I want to do in the interim is a book of essays, which could pull together some of my thoughts in the past, but also include some of the more recent things that I have been thinking about. And this seems to me necessary. You can clarify your own thinking much more directly in an essay than you can do in a novel. A novel is like life. I mean, there is no way a novelist can be held to account for what happens in a novel. I mean, even a character you like can be totally odious to other people. So a novel is not a way to clarify your mind. An essay *is*—it's logical. And so I think probably I needed to take time off to attend to the logic of a situation.

Enekwe: Thank you very much. You talked about dealing with some aspects of Igbo culture. You would like to get back to study the Igbo culture. Some time ago I heard that you were planning to write an Igbo dictionary. Is this true? If so, what are your plans?

Achebe: No, it's not true. I'm not planning to do an Igbo dictionary. I think that's something that people in linguistics should be dealing with.

Enekwe: In 1974, during a conference in Columbia University, you disclosed that you were developing an inclination—or rather, that you have a talent for the theatre. Earlier, in an interview at the University of Washington in Seattle, you had expressed an intention to write plays in the Igbo language. What is your concept of theatre?

Achebe: Well, I don't know that I can answer the question of concept, because I really would prefer to produce a play and then from that play, discuss my concept of theatre. In other words, there is a certain artistic inevitability in creation which I do not want to anticipate, to pre-empt. I have certain ideas, certain theories about theatre and language in our situation, which I'd like to try out before I begin to pontificate.

I think, for instance, that one of the problems with modern Nigerian theatre is the language—the English language. You are likely to produce theatre for the West rather than theatre for Nigeria, if you didn't stop to think about the language problem. Now you might say: "Well, isn't that the same with the novel; isn't it the same with poetry?" No, I don't think it is. Art is a convention. There are various forms, various conventions, which are applied. But once you choose the convention I think you are *bound* by the rules of that convention. Now, the theatre, being a very direct, almost participatory form, does require a different convention from the novel. You go to watch a play, you see actual people moving, and talking on the stage. If you are reading a novel, you don't see anybody. You are using your imagination. So what I'm saying is that it's a different convention.

In a novel, once you accept that the whole thing is make-believe; once you accept that you are reading printed words on a page, and you come across characters, and so on, this is all a kind of pre-arranged convention, and you accept it. And so if you read about Okonkwo, a traditional Igbo character in the English language, you know that this is a convention anyway; there is a kind of filter—somebody's telling you what happened. Even if you are reading the words of Okonkwo, you know that it was written by somebody else—by the author, or narrator, whatever you call him—there is an agent between you and Okonkwo, telling you the story. And however you work this out for yourself, if the novel is successful, you *do* accept the convention, and you stop asking questions. Now, I think, if I were to put Okonkwo on the stage, and if I were to put English words into his mouth, it would be a different problem altogether. The convention would no longer hold. Because each time Okonkwo talks, he would be violating something quite fundamental. He would be talking about experiences and life and history in a language which has nothing to do with that life or experience or history. And each time he opens his mouth, the audience is reminded that there is a convention—a translator, a medium—between him and the audience. And I think this is almost an insuperable problem, and this is why I began to think that if you are going to work in the theatre, at least part of the action, part of the dialogue, of this theatre must be in the language of the characters. Because you see a character is there on the stage, alive, and even though he's only an actor, pretending to be Okonkwo, he's *there*. He's visible to you; he's flesh and blood. And if he were to speak in a language that Okonkwo did not understand, there's a major problem there: a problem of artistic credibility. So when I work, I'd like to experiment with the Igbo language as well as English, where it is appropriate.

There are vast areas. If one is writing a modern Nigerian play in which

modern people like you and me are at work, it would be better for me to do
it in English, because we talk in English; it's not the only language we speak,
but we use it quite extensively. But going back to Okonkwo, to Ezeulu, it
seems to be inappropriate.

The Critical Generation
Rosemary Colmer / 1980

From *Ash Magazine* (Adelaide, Australia), 5 (Winter 1980), 5–7. Reprinted by permission of Rosemary Colmer.

Chinua Achebe was born in Eastern Nigeria in 1930. He is best known for his novels, *Things Fall Apart, No Longer at Ease, Arrow of God* and *A Man of the People,* the last of which ends with a coup d'état which seemed prophetic of the political upheavals which broke out in Nigeria within weeks of its publication and which led to the Biafran war. Since the war, Achebe has published a book of short stories, a volume of verse and a collection of critical and autobiographical essays. He is the author of four books for children. He is currently the head of the literature department of the University of Nigeria at Nsukka.

He visited Adelaide as a guest at Writers' Week in March 1980, where he was invited to deliver an address on the theme of myth, symbol and fable in African literature.

Colmer: How important are myth, symbol and fable in African writing?

Achebe: Well, it's important, but in all the years in which I have been writing and talking and lecturing I've never talked about myth and symbol and fable. I think we take them for granted and maybe that's the way it should be really. In African tradition we do not separate things quite as much as the Western world does, and myth is the raw material, it's the substance of stories, it's the substance of the creation stories, which are basic. For me this is the first time really I'm giving any thought in that sense to it, and even attempting to read up what there is in the way of literature—and it's really amazing some of the extraordinary things that have been written and said about this.

Colmer: You find in your own language, the Ibo language, many proverbs which are almost an embedded fable. They refer to a story which is well known, or they suggest a story: "If a man carries ant-ridden faggots into a house he must expect the visit of lizards". Things like that. They suggest a little mini-story. Do you think that's a feature you would acknowledge?

Achebe: Yes, that is the same way of thinking, if you like. It's the same way of perceiving the world, of perceiving reality. If you like, you can start from metaphor. Now the metaphor is a form of symbol. From there you go to a proverb, which is a little longer, more extended, and a finished statement; then to a fable, which is longer still; and then perhaps to a myth, which could be a very long story indeed. But behind all this is the idea of comparison, of metaphor, of relating one thing to another.

Colmer: And you feel that this is important in your own writing?

Achebe: It is very important. Oh, yes, it is very important.

Colmer: Two of your novels are historical novels, *Things Fall Apart* and *Arrow of God.* Why did you choose to explore the history of Eastern Nigeria?

Achebe: Well, because we all have a history. Just as we have a front and a back, we have a history which is our back, and our front which is maybe our future, and our present is somehow in between these two, and you cannot deal with a total experience without taking this into account. In our situation it is especially important because our history has been interfered with seriously, grievously. In fact it has been said that three or four hundred years ago we were taken out of our history and dumped into somebody else's history. We lost the initiative—the historical initiative—and therefore for us it is a matter of life and death that we recapture that initiative, and we situate ourselves again in the mainstream of our own thought and feeling and experience and perception. This is why it is very important that we understand who we are. When people talk about their identity, it's a word which is so often used today that it has almost become a cliché, but it is nevertheless a very important concept. You must know who you are before you can deal with any problem.

Colmer: I believe that in a sense your own generation is the most cut off. In your book of essays, *Morning Yet on Creation Day,* you suggested that as the child of a Christian family you looked down on your fellows who carried beautiful African pottery when they went to fetch water. That must in a sense have cut you off from quite a lot of the life of traditional Africa.

Achebe: Yes, when I was young we were the most cut off, but if we are thinking of today, we are the best situated, because our children have absolutely nothing to cling to in terms of our history, unless we do something about it. We were cut off compared with my father's generation and my grandfather's generation, but the situation has been getting worse and worse, and in a way I think my generation is a critical generation because we do have an awareness of that past. My father had an awareness of it because he lived it, so he could tell me about it, like the people of his generation who are still around. Now the generation after me, unless we deliberately, consciously set about to teach them, will be much worse than I was, and that will be the end of the story.

Colmer: I believe you have just come from visiting the East African writer, Ngugi wa Thiong'o. I understand that he's working on a novel in Kikuyu and translating it into English. What do you think of that kind of idea within the West African context.

Achebe: I saw him very briefly and he confirmed that he had written a novel in Kikuyu, and we talked about writing in African languages in general. This is something which exercises the mind of most serious African writers because there is a definite problem there. I have talked about this. Even as you write in English you are aware that there is a problem which you are not touching, and so there is the awareness of the problem. The question now is, what do you do? Some people say: okay, stop writing in English, go back and learn your language if you don't know it, and write in it. Some people would say: okay, let us all learn a new language—because the first suggestion (you write in your language) raises problems of mutual intelligibility. Even within one nation, like Nigeria, you could create a situation in which 250 writers would be writing in 250 languages. That's the extreme, of course. I mean that may never happen, but you could easily have 20 to 30 languages going in Nigeria. Now what does that say to the concept of the Nigerian nation, which is a shaky thing at the best of times? So this is one problem which you have to deal with. And so some people come up and say: why don't we all write in Swahili; which seems to me very fanciful, because there's no way in which existing writers in Africa could all switch over to Swahili, and I don't see it becoming reality in the near future. So I don't see much future for it. The problem is not resolved. Ultimately I think each writer will have to make a choice. I told Ngugi when we first met that I have a plan to write a play, not a novel, in Ibo, because it seems to me that drama is the first place, the most crucial place in which to deal with the language problem.

Colmer: Because drama is more immediate?

Achebe: More immediate, yes, and the paradox of writing an Ibo story in English comes out in all its starkness on the stage. I mean, it's difficult to swallow. The convention of the novel manages to circumvent it somehow, but if you are putting a play on the stage, it's a different thing. And in addition it's also very satisfying. I have watched Ibo plays on television and they

are much—infinitely—better than plays performed in English, in terms of the
actors, in terms of the dialogue and so on. So I had had this project for a long
time. And Ngugi said yes, he had the same idea. If he hadn't been in jail, he
would not have written a novel in Kikuyu. So I don't know. It would be
interesting to see what happens to that novel now. It would be interesting;
one would want to see how it developed. But it is a problem that we have not
solved and we are concerned about.

Colmer: You mentioned that Ngugi has recently been in jail. How far do
you think that the writer ought to involve his writing in political issues?

Achebe: Oh, as much as possible. I don't think a writer can avoid political
issues, although writers are different, they are different human beings, and
the way they perceive their involvement will differ from writer to writer and
also will differ from country to country. It depends on what is going on in
the country. Quite often it will determine for the writer what form his
involvement should take. But politics as a subject, I think that's an absolute
necessity for the writer.

Now if you are in a country which is reactionary and capitalist like Kenya,
very capitalist and reactionary, then I think the chances of getting into difficulties with the regime are immense. I think Nigeria is going the same way.
The difficulties would be immense. But for some reason Nigeria has not,
fortunately, had the same kind of monolithic power, governmental power,
that Kenya has had, and this is really what saves us from the fate of Ngugi.
It's not because Kenya is more capitalistic than Nigeria; it is simply that there
is a diffusion of power, there is inbuilt opposition in the Nigerian situation.
The fact that you have 19 states, for instance, each under a governor who
may have his own personal political ideology, saves the situation a bit.

But the writer can't avoid involvement, because politics is a fundamental
theme of our lives. It's the way that people are governed and I think this is
very important.

Colmer: At a rather different extreme from political writing, you're also
interested in writing for children. How did you become interested in writing
for children?

Achebe: It's a long story. Many years ago I noticed that my daughter, who
was then quite little, just beginning to go to nursery school (we lived in Lagos
then), was developing very strange notions about race and colour. She
couldn't have picked up any of that from home, so my wife and I tracked it
down to the racially mixed school that she attended, and I immediately wrote

in protest to the headmistress, a white lady. Most of the teachers were white. And we also found that it wasn't just that, but the entire educational system, including the books they read. So even if the teachers did nothing at all, the books would have done it. Some of the books were frankly racist, and I paid for this with my money, you know? And I just didn't see that, why this should be so.

At the same time a very good friend of mine, the poet Christopher Okigbo who died in the Biafran war, was then representing Cambridge University Press in Nigeria. I'm not sure now how it happened, but he urged me to write a children's book for Cambridge University Press, and so I did. It was not something which had occurred to me until then, but these two factors, my daughter not having anything safe to read and the urging of Christopher Okigbo, made me write the first children's book, and I found it was fun. It was not very easy but it was fun. In fact I had to do the first one twice. After that I realised it was really very important to do, and I have since written four children's books.

Colmer: In fact your latest writing is for children?
Achebe: Yes.

Colmer: Do you feel that you need to live in Nigeria to write?
Achebe: I think so. I think I need the Nigerian environment for what I think is important. I could write anywhere but I think it's not really a question of putting something down. I want to be doing something which is important in my own view. It doesn't have to be important in the view of publishers or critics or anybody. For instance, what I write for children does not come out in my C.V., but it seems to me to be very important. The essays hardly do, but again these are important. So it is where the problem is, as far as I am concerned, that the writing should be. There is really no way you can be dealing with the problem of Nigerian children in the United States, for instance. So it is that kind of thing that makes your residence important. But it is not difficult for me for instance to sit in Australia and write a novel or perhaps two novels, but I think after a time what I brought with me would be finished, and I would need to renew my contact with my sources and with the people for whom I write primarily.

Colmer: You are involved in editing a magazine which publishes quite a lot of writing by young African writers. How do you see the function of your magazine, *Okike?*

Achebe: Well, it is what you have said: it is a forum for writers. Books of course are the major forum—this is what a writer is aiming at ultimately—but before that great novel, before the great poem, you want a place where people can experiment, where they display their shorter work, where they try things out, and *Okike* is one. You want a place where critics can review what is produced and talk about it. This is the place of the magazine, and it is essential for the health of any literary tradition, especially a new one like ours where we are still arguing about criteria, about which language, all kinds of things. You want a place where these things can be talked about and so this is the reason why nearly ten years ago I began this journal which has been going, a little shakily to begin with, but I think now we are quite firmly established.

Colmer: You're very busy at the moment with your teaching and so on, but presumably you will find time to write, and certainly there have been the children's books recently. When can we expect the next novel?

Achebe: Well, that is a question that every critic and every publisher asks. I don't know. Actually I have been working on something intermittently for quite some time now, and all I can say is that I have not felt the urgency to write a novel. If I had, I think I would have written one because it is not really very difficult to put one together in terms of technique which one has acquired over time. But somehow the urgency has not made itself felt to me so I have just been going at it at a very, very slow pace, and I think some time it will come. This year, this last year, has been particularly difficult in terms of time. I've never really complained about time until now, because I've always had enough time for anything I wanted to do; but this year I am doing something that I never thought I would do, which is administrate a department. I thought all that was behind me. I did my administration in radio nearly 20 years ago, and I thought I'd done my bit. But this year something exceptional happened, so I've not had as much time as I wanted. Maybe at the end of this year I should be able to give more time and get the novel out of the way. I think it's time, too, I think it's probably time that I wrote another novel.

Colmer: When you do, can you tell me what themes you'll be following up? What is your main interest in the novel at the moment?

Achebe: Well, it's very difficult for me to talk about something I have not written, because the way I work, I'm really very secretive you see, and also very superstitious in this way, because there are things you don't talk about too much or they go away, and I find the same thing if I'm building up an idea. I think it's best not to talk about it; otherwise the talking takes the excitement. But I think I can say it will be an attempt to bring together the various strands of experience that I have been experimenting with in my other writings.

I hope it will be different therefore from the others because it is this bringing together. But beyond that, I think I will leave it until it happens.

An Interview with Chinua Achebe

Kalu Ogbaa / 1980

From *Research in African Literatures,* 12 (1981), 1–13. Reprinted by permission of Indiana University Press and Kalu Ogbaa.

This interview took place on 11 April 1980 at the University of Florida at Gainesville, where Achebe was participating in the fifth annual conference of the African Literature Association.

Many foreign readers are greatly attracted by the cultural information they get from your novels about traditional Igbo society. Do you consider these novels a competent source of that kind of information?

Yes. What I'm doing is presenting a total world and a total life as it is lived in that world, and you cannot do that in a vacuum; I cannot do it in a vacuum. I am writing about my people in the past and in the present, and I have to create for them the world in which they live and move and have their being. If somebody else thinks, as some do, that this is sociology or anthropology, that's their own lookout. It is the life of the people I am writing about. Therefore, if someone is in search of information, or knowledge, or enlightenment about the total life of these people—the Igbo people—I think my novels would be a good source.

How would you advise foreign readers, who are alien to the culture about which you are writing, to approach your novels?

I don't advise them at all beyond the novels. I think just in the same way as I got myself sufficiently informed to understand the culture in which Dickens set his characters or the environment in which James Joyce situated his stories, in the same way as anybody who is genuinely after whatever virtues literature gives and wants to get them from my books, indeed from African books, he must be prepared to get himself immersed in the life of the Africans. How he does it is not for me to say, but I think he would fail unless he displayed an openness of mind and a readiness to accept another way of looking at reality. This turns out to be difficult for many people in the West, but that's not my fault; it's their fault. And it's up to them to do something to correct that defect—the defect of self-centeredness.

I say that it's not a universal fault because, as you yourself know, the Igbo culture lays a great deal of emphasis on differences, on dualities, on otherness. This is why we do not find it difficult to accept that other people somewhere else might be doing one thing differently from ourselves. Look at our proverbs; they are full of statements like "Ọdi be ndi adirọ be ibe fa" ("What there is among one people is not among another"). It's as if Igbo culture is constantly anxious to remind you of the complexity of the world. And so you are ready for it. Now, if you're brought up in a culture which is fanatically singleminded in its own self-centeredness, then you've got a job to do to correct it—it is a liability and no one but yourself can correct it.

As a creative writer, you have done much in the way of correcting misinformation about Igbo culture. How do you regard the work of Igbo literary critics? Do you think that they have done enough to interpret the messages borne in your novels?

I think some of them have. I mean, there have been outstanding examples. It would not be proper, in fact, to get into names, but I think I should mention that there are people like Emmanuel Obiechina and Donatus Nwoga who have done very serious work on my novels or more generally on Igbo culture as seen through our literature. But there have been others who have been somewhat casual or even negative in their attitude. I'm thinking, for instance, of a certain fellow who was claiming that *Arrow of God* was written by his uncle, which led to the rather curious situation in which the fellow was dismissed as irresponsible by a white critic! It really should have been expected that some Igbo critics would have shown as much concern as the white critic about matters of critical responsibility in our literature.

I do think that what you need is a fair number of indigenous critics who are on the ball because they see literature as a serious matter (our people do not take it seriously enough; I think we are still too complacent). And the next thing you know we will be complaining about Americans, about the British, running around telling us about our writers. And yet there is not enough dedication and diligence among our own critics. I'm looking forward to a change in this for it is absolutely important. If literature is important, then criticism of literature is also important, and we should get more and more people who are ready to read the books. Read the books first. It's not enough to say, "I am a Nigerian, therefore I understand Achebe." No, you've got to read what I have written. If not, an American who has read it would be a better critic than yourself.

Do you think the white man's culture succeeded in destroying Igbo culture completely, or did it just injure it a little bit?

Culture is not as fragile as we sometimes think, but it is not granite, either. A culture can be damaged, can be turned from its course not only by foreigners. Let's get this absolutely clear: a culture can be mutilated, can be destroyed by its own people, under certain situations. Maybe we could return to this later on because I think the Igbo people are in many ways today doing as much as, or more than, the British ever did to destroy their own culture. Take the question of these comical chiefs that you have now—400 in Anambra State and 400 in Imo State. This goes against all the history and tradition and philosophy of Igbo people. But that's by-the-way—no, I mean that's a digression.

The Igbo culture was not destroyed by Europe. It was disturbed. It was disturbed very seriously, but this is nothing new in the world. Cultures are constantly influenced, challenged, pushed about by other cultures that may have some kind of advantage at a particular time—either the advantage of force, persuasion, wealth, or whatever. But as I said initially, a culture which is healthy will often survive. It will not survive exactly in the form in which it was met by the invading culture, but it will modify itself and move on. And this is the great thing about culture, if it is alive. The people who own it will ensure that they make adjustments: they drop what can no longer be carried in transition; they drop whatever seems like excess baggage so that they can continue their journey. We're all engaged, we're all embarked on a journey through history. So I think what has happened is that we still have the fundamental principles of the Igbo culture. Its emphasis is on the worth of every man and woman. Every man has his *chi* and every woman has her *chi*. Nobody is useless; that's one thing we have not jettisoned. I am as good as the next man.

From this flows the idea that in the deliberations of the people everybody should participate. It's a democratic principle which is very deeply embedded in our culture. We don't send representatives—you go yourself. But that was all right in the microstate of the village. Today our situation is different; we can no longer all appear in person. So our culture has to make some adjustments to find a way of dealing with this new threat to its egalitarian philosophy. This is what I mean: How do you send a representative? And you can see that our people don't know. From recent experience in politics, you can see that our people simply have no idea how to choose their representatives. And it's not surprising because we didn't have representatives in the past. So this is something our culture has to learn. Like the adaptable bird in our proverb, we must learn to fly without perching or perish from man's new-learnt marksmanship. So there is the need for a culture to be alive and active and ready to adjust, ready to take challenges. A culture that fails to take challenges will die. But if we are ready to take challenges, to make concessions that are necessary without accepting anything that undermines our fundamental belief in the dignity of man, I think we would be doing what is expected of us.

So, in other words, when people describe your novels as protest novels, you accept the term protest *to mean that you are protesting against the European disturbance of African culture as well as the disturbance that comes from within?*

Yes, yes. I think that protest is not a very good word, but we use it quite often, and whenever I use it, I use it in a very general sense, the sense in which we all admit that there is a lot to protest against in every life, in every community, in every civilization. If things were perfect, there would be no need for writers to write their novels. But it is because they see a vision of the world which is better than what exists; it is because they see the possibilities of man rising higher than he has risen at the moment that they write. So, whatever they write, if they are true practitioners of their art, would be in essence a protest against what exists, against what is.

All your novels contain incantations, proverbs, and aphorisms used by the priests, chiefs, and elders. Were you very conscious of their poetic qualities or were you more interested in the traditional philosophy they convey as you wrote these novels?

There is no need to separate the two. You see, this is a western attitude to things. Our people have always taken a more holistic approach. So when people ask me, "Is it this or that?" It's both, it's both. A proverb is both a functional means of communication and also a very elegant and artistic performance itself. I think that proverbs are both utilitarian and little vignettes of art. So when I use these forms in my novels, they both serve a utilitarian purpose, which is to reenact the life of the people that I am describing, and also delight through elegance and aptness of imagery. This is what proverbs are supposed to do.

What of the dramatic values of the costumes and postures of the Egwugwu?

I do not attempt too much description in my writing of the actual physical appearance, the face or faces. I do a certain amount, but it's not a preoccupation with me. I go over this rather fast because I am concerned about other things. But when it's absolutely essential to draw attention to the physical appearance of the person or spirit or how he is dressed, then I would do so. But basically, I think that costume belongs to drama. You can only give an impression, some kind of impression, that something looks like this. I do not know whether I'm making myself clear. It's not basically my function as a novelist to concentrate on the appearance except where it is absolutely essential for the story.

But we must not attempt to be too prescriptive or dogmatic. Rigid distinctions tend to put us into difficulties because *drama* is an abstraction from something which is total. Take, for instance, the appearance of Ezeulu to reenact the coming of his God and the consecration of the first Chief-priest. He has to explain who he is and he goes back to history and myth. That whole episode is drama. But if you ask an Igbo man what is going on, he won't say that this is drama or that is religion. It is all: religion, drama, and mythology. Everything is rolled into one in the service of art and society.

Do you consider the Igbo rituals and ceremonies in your novels a photographic reenactment of traditional Igbo rituals and ceremonies? If so, does your writing them down vitiate or promote their oral performance? Put differently, some people are talking about oral literature, others call it oral performance, and still others believe we are simply dealing with literature.

I don't mind what anybody calls anything as long as we are up and doing. I think the people in oral literature have a lot of work to do in collecting, analyzing, and presenting what we have. They cannot stop a novelist from using what he wants to use from this tradition. Such borrowing doesn't prevent scholars from doing their own job. The fact that I have a pumpkin ceremony in *Arrow of God* does not prevent an oral literature scholar from going to Umuchu where—and only where, according to Nnolim—the thing exists and recording it; or going to Ngwa where, according to Amankulor, a pumpkin festival happens one month before the New Yam Festival and is dominated by women. So the novel does not prevent a documentation or presentation of what we have in other art forms. I think that, on the contrary, it should encourage such documentation.

You are saying literature encompasses all these variations?
Yes, yes, yes!

Many African scholars, especially those who receive their higher educa-
tion in Europe and America, come back to African countries disillusioned
with the white man's religion. Do you think there will be a time in the future
that they will consider going back to practice traditional African religion
such as the society of Okonkwo had before "things fell apart" for them/us?

I don't think people go back, if you see what I mean. It's not really a
question of going back. I think if one goes back, there's something wrong
somewhere, or else a misunderstanding. In other words, you assume already
that he is ahead and returning. When we talk of going back, I suppose we
mean metaphorically. I guess we mean searching around for alternatives.
There are alternatives which say something about religion, about morality, in
a way other than the Christian-western-European, which are indigenous to
our culture and which some of our best people, even the Christians, never
abandoned. There is really no question, in my mind, of going back. If one
religion fulfills a certain need for some people, I'm not about to prescribe
how they will make use of it. Other people may not need it at all. As we
know now, some people feel they can do without any kind of formal religion.
So you can't say, "Oh, let us all go back" because our attitude towards
religion and what religion does for each and every one of us is different.

But that's not what we're talking about. We are not talking about the forms
or manifestations of religion—like whether somebody has a sacrament with
God through Christian communion or somebody else has another sacrament
in which he breaks kola in the presence of his guests and his God and ancestors. I don't think these two things conflict. We must realize that our ancestors
were wiser than is often made out. They were around in our environment for
thousands and thousands of years. They learned a lot about that environment.
And if we think that we are wiser than they because of thirty years or so of
mixing with Europe, I think we are sadly mistaken. And the day will come
when we will rediscover some of their values and attitudes—for instance,
their attitude to family. We see the western people that we are copying are in
trouble with their families. So why go and copy people who are in trouble?
It may be, in fact, that what they need is help from us. If you meet someone
who is in distress and has collapsed, do you collapse beside him? No, what
you should really do is give first aid or send for a doctor.

What kind of trouble do you have in mind? Is it the problem of one man
having one wife? Or do you mean the kind of moral support that somebody
receives as a result of the extended family system?

All that, all that! I think that the respect that fathers and mothers had and still have in Africa (and this extends to all old people, not just one's parents) is very valuable. The respect you give to age is very valuable to you because an old person has been around a long time and has encountered a whole lot of things you haven't seen. You may think, "This is an old man; what does he know?" But you are wrong. Respect is not only valuable to you, it's also valuable to the old people for they are senior members of the society. If they feel they are needed and that their advice is useful, they will remain alert. They will not simply go to pieces. I've known old people in my village, some of whom were said to be 100, who were still very alert in their minds because they knew that if there was any land quarrel, they would be called. They had a job; they were not useless. If you render somebody useless—that is, every-body above fifty—then they become useless. They grow senile, they lose their mind, and they decay. They have an irrational fear of growing old, they make pathetic concessions to youth, and society suffers by being frozen in adolescence.

As a writer, you have played the roles of a teacher, a social transformer, and even a revolutionary in Biafra. How did your insight as an imaginative writer help or inhibit you in carrying out these roles?

Well, I don't think that's a very easy question. I think I can sense what you are driving at. In a revolutionary situation, in a situation of great danger, in an institution and regime of violence, for instance, what does a creative artist do? This is a question which I will not presume to answer for everybody because a writer is a human being. He is not just a writer; he is also a person. He is a member of society. Therefore, he must decide what role, besides that of writing, he can play. He must decide that himself. I decided that I could not stand aside from the problems and struggles of my people at that point in history. And if it happened again, I would not behave differently.

But there are limitations, you know. For instance, in that kind of situation there is bound to be pressure to think alike. There is bound to be pressure, maybe, to surrender some of your cherished ideals. There may even be the danger (and this is not just talking about Biafra) of forgetting that art is not "brother" to violence. The writer has to keep reminding himself all the time that even where you think violence is inevitable, you still should realize what it is; you do not pretend that violence is good. It may be inevitable but it's not good. So when I see people talk about revolutionary violence, I think the artist has to be very careful. There is revolutionary violence, okay; but the artist would be endangering himself the moment he begins to write a poem which talks about the flowering of bullets. Bullets do not flower! It's tricky to get into that situation. I cannot say more than I have said, but I'll simply say again that an artist has to have his wits around him because he is stepping into a very dangerous domain. Fundamentally, art is on the side of life.

However much you may wish to deny it, people know and believe that you have a peculiar insight as a writer and that you occupy a very privileged position in society. That's the reason why they rely on you to help in a revolution, not only to preach against violence, but also to probe the future and advise them.

Oh yes, I think that within your power you should do all that. I'm simply giving a kind of signal which I have noticed (not just out of the Biafran experience) about a total allegiance to a regime, for instance. Revolution will be prosecuted by people. And the artist who gives his total allegiance to a group of people is likely to be disappointed, is likely to find sooner or later (and more likely sooner) that the people are not all that he thought. So he should hold himself in some kind of reserve. This is all I'm saying. There may be an occasion for him to back out. And he should not destroy this possibility, this chance.

Kolawole Ogungbesan uses quotations from your public addresses, lectures and interviews to point out how you have encouraged the African writer to play a meaningful role in his society: the writer as a teacher, a social transformer, a revolutionary, and an actor rather than a reactor—roles which he alleges you and Christopher Okigbo played in your native Biafra. He adds that while such crusading roles may not be wrong in themselves, they inhibit the production of long-lasting creative writing. Would you like to comment on this observation?

No, no, I think that's nonsense. Ogungbesan, unfortunately, is dead. He died last year. It's unfortunate, I think, that I should be dealing with that kind of thing in his absence. But it doesn't matter. The trouble is, he had a problem with Biafra, like many Nigerians who were on the federal side, and their problem was compounded by the fact that they won the war. So they feel justified in whatever they thought and felt during that crisis, because it's very easy to imagine that right and victory are on the same side. So it's the problem Nigerians have with Biafra which is coming through in Ogungbesan's comment. He didn't think, for instance, that the poetry I wrote during the war is poetry. Perhaps he was right. Except that other people—those in Biafra with me, but especially those in neither Biafra nor Nigeria—think otherwise. (Two examples are Donatus Nwoga and Eldred Jones.) I received a letter from an Irish poet, a very good Irish poet, in which he said, after reading my poems, that he was full of envy. In his own situation he wished that he or *any* of his countrymen in Ireland could write even a few lines as grave and moving about their problems. And he added, "This is not only your best work but also the best war poetry that has come out from anywhere in a long time." This is from someone I didn't even know. He may be overenthusiastic—this Irishman, and many others like him—I don't know. But put that beside Ogungbesan's view (and it's not just Ogungbesan; it's a whole group of people who were bitterly opposed to Biafra.): "This is not poetry; this is nonsense; this is sentimental." So you realize then that you are perhaps not dealing with literary criticism; you may be dealing with political prejudice, ethnic prejudice, and that kind of thing.

In an interview at the University of Texas in Austin in 1969, you said, "I believe it's impossible to write anything in Africa without some kind of commitment, some kind of message, some kind of protest." Given the kind of political and literary strides that Africans have made, do you still believe African writing today should continue to be protest writing? If so, protest against whom and what?

Well, I think that I've already touched on that. The problem is the use of the word *protest.* It is too vague a word—too vague in one sense and too exact in another sense. Protest means from someone against another. But the way I prefer to see protest is that assumed mission, that natural condition of the artist to be protesting against what he is given. As an African, I have been given a certain role in the world, a certain place in the world, a certain history in the world; and I say, "No, I don't accept these roles, these histories— distorted, garbled accounts. I'm going to recreate myself." I'm protesting against the world. But if we are talking about a novel like *A Man of the People,* the protest is clearly more localized. I'm talking about the politics of the country after independence. I'm protesting against the way we are ordering our lives. So I think protest will never end. The need for protesting will never end. I don't think it's a question of protest against Europe or simply protest against local conditions. It is protest against the way we are handling human society in view of the possibilities for greatness and the better alternatives which the artist sees.

Foreign commentators like David Carroll and Lloyd Brown appear to have got the message in your novels and this is why they have been able to write

very brilliant essays juxtaposing your balanced view of Africa and the preju-
diced view of Conrad's Africa, "the heart of darkness." If you were to write
a novel today, what would its message be?

Well, that's a secret. I don't talk about something which hasn't been written because it inhibits the creative process.

But to take up what you were saying in the introductory part of the question—I mean, the people you mentioned—I feel at this point that the high
standard of criticism from people like David Carroll and many others has
raised the tone of our criticism immensely in the last several years and that
we no longer see the kind of critical dilettantism we saw initially from people
who were not really qualified either by temperament or training to get into it.
They were doing it maybe because nobody else was. And now we have some
very acute, some very sharp people. It's a challenge to the African to be up
and doing instead of just sitting around and complaining about "all these
people running around and writing about our authors." Many of these foreign
critics are doing a lot of good work. Not so long ago an Indian magazine
called *Literary Half-Yearly* devoted its pages to my work. Contributors were
from all over the world and most of them from the Commonwealth. Now,
one of the things that struck me particularly was a piece by an Australian
woman on *No Longer at Ease.* You know, that is a book that has not, in my
view, received as good and perceptive attention as it deserves. And this Australian had somehow got into the relationship of blood between Obi and his
mother (which is an important key to an understanding of the story) in such
a way that I was absolutely astounded. This comes from taking literature
seriously. Whoever she is, wherever she is, she took this book seriously and
was able to uncover an important layer of its meaning. Maybe this is not the
question that you're asking, but I thought I should mention this first as a
tribute to what, at the level of criticism, some foreign critics and scholars are
now giving to African literature and also as a challenge to our own people to
get cracking. There are still areas where our people have an advantage, but
that advantage will come to nothing if they do not read the books, if they
don't take literature seriously, if they are consumed by prejudice, envy, whatever. Some of them, strangely enough, do not seem to believe that literature
is important even when they make a living teaching it! Or are they? These
things will have to change.

Many people regard you as a creative mentor. What advice do you offer to
them that would help them start their creative writing careers?

Well, the advice that I always give is that they should start and they should strive to be themselves, to achieve honesty of tone, to achieve authenticity of tone, and not to pretend to be something that they are not; not to pretend to feel something that you know you don't feel just because you heard it is the right way to feel about something. Posturing is a disease which artists are very prone to. "What does an artist dress like? What does he wear? What kind of life does he live?" Things like that. "Then I will do that and become an artist." No. I think you should get to work with seriousness and not copy. No artist should copy another. We all probably start off imitating, but ultimately a good artist will soon find his own voice and will use it.

Your answer may have rendered my next question irrelevant, yet I think I should ask it. That is, you seem to have influenced directly or indirectly almost all the Nigerian novelists. Do you foresee a time when that influence will produce artistic monotony in the Nigerian novel?

No, it shouldn't. I think influence is not a bad thing. You can influence people in positive ways. I have dealt with certain things so the next person doesn't have to go over the same ground, but that is not to say that the story of our past is finished, which is the way many people seem to take it. That is absolute nonsense. We haven't even started. We don't know who we are yet. So I think there are thousands of stories that can be written out of our past and our present and our future. The kind of influence which I would like to think that I have had is a positive one. We may say, "He has done this, okay. It is possible to do something even better." It is possible now that we know we can write. "He has used language in a particular way." It doesn't have to be Queen's English. It doesn't have to be pidgin. It is possible to do something else in the process of that recreation of ourselves that I was talking about. It is possible even to recreate the language that we are using. It's possible to go from there to push the English language to a limit or reject it. I mean we can say, "No, we've come to the end of that; I want to write in Igbo" or something like that. All these things would be, in fact, a reaction to me as one of the first writers, and all this would be positive. But we should not sit down and say, "Achebe wrote about Ogidi; now I must write about Umuoji" and then repeat the same thing. No, that's not what I am saying.

Some of us aspire to make a career out of teaching your works. Do you have any advice for us?

No, I think you are doing a fine job and you should continue. I think the teaching of literature should go on and even increase because I think it is very important. When we talk about the confusion in our culture, about no morals and so on, where do we get these things in the modern world if not from literature? I mean, we don't have the social institutions that we had in the past in which the values of the community were transmitted. How do we transmit a national culture to Nigerians if not through works of imagination? This is something that our people have not paid attention to. We are talking about modernization, industrialization, and so on, but we do not realize that we cannot even industrialize unless we have tackled the mind, the imagination, and thus the attitude of people to themselves, to their society, to work, and so on. How do you do these things if you cannot get to their minds, to their imaginatiion? So literature is not a luxury for us. It is a life and death affair because we are fashioning a new man. The Nigerian is a new man. How do we get to his mind? Is it by preaching to him once in a while—by the leaders? No, I think it is something solid and permanent that we must put into his consciousness. That is what he reads, what he believes, and what he loves. We must dramatize his predicament so that he can see the choices and choose right.

Chinua Achebe: At the Crossroads

Jonathan Cott / 1980

From *Parabola: The Magazine of Myth and Tradition* 6.2 (Spring 1981), 30–39. Reprinted by permission of *Parabola*.

Born in 1930 in Ogidi, Eastern Nigeria, of devout Christian parents who baptized him Albert Chinualumogu, Chinua Achebe "dropped the tribute to Victorian England," as he puts it, when he went to university, and took his first name from his last. "On one arm of the cross," he remembers in his autobiographical essay "Named for Victoria," "we sang hymns and read the Bible night and day. On the other, my father's brother and his family, blinded by heathenism, offered food to idols. . . . If anyone likes to believe that I was torn by spiritual agonies or stretched on the rack of my ambivalence, he certainly may suit himself. I do not remember any undue distress. What I do remember was a fascination for the ritual and the life on the other arm of the crossroads. And I believe two things were in my favor—that curiosity and the little distance imposed between me and it by the accident of my birth. The distance becomes not a separation but a bringing together like the necessary backward step which a judicious viewer may take in order to see a canvas steadily and fully." It is this canvas that Achebe brilliantly creates and displays for us in his four novels—*Things Fall Apart, No Longer at Ease, Arrow of God,* and *A Man of the People.*

Achebe informs us that his mother and elder sister used to tell him tales when he was a child—folk stories that had "the immemorial quality of the sky and the forests and the rivers." And like other West African writers such as Amos Tutuola, Wole Soyinka, J.P. Clark, and Christopher Okigbo, Chinua Achebe has drawn literary sustenance from folk tales as well as from legends, jokes, riddles, and, especially, proverbs. "Proverbs are the palm oil with which words are eaten," he tells us in *Things Fall Apart.*

"Our ancestors," Achebe affirms, "created their myths and legends and told their stories for a human purpose (including, no doubt, the excitation of wonder and pure delight). . . . Their artists lived and moved and had their being in society and created their works for the good of that society. . . . In a recent anthology, a Hausa folk tale, having recounted the usual fabulous incidents, ends with these words: 'They all came and they lived happily together. He had several sons and daughters who grew up and helped in raising the standard of education of the country.' As I said elsewhere, if you consider this ending a naive anticlimax, then you cannot know very much about Africa."

Today, as Nigeria (the most populous and one of the most prosperous countries in Africa) becomes increasingly developed economically

and technologically, we are continually reminded in Achebe's writings
that as we inevitably move forward, we must at the same time remember where we began; and that if the adults forget, then the children and
the stories they like best will remind them.

Chinua Achebe is currently head of the Department of English at
the University of Nigeria, Nsukka. The recipient of many awards, including an honorary Doctor of Letters degree from Dartmouth College, he has traveled and lectured in countries all over the world. As
unafraid and unashamed of gentleness as of strength, he has a bearing
and voice that bespeak an unusual mixture of quietness, intensity,
humor, and commitment. Our conversation took place in London in
the summer of 1980.

Jonathan Cott: In your fable *How the Leopard Got His Claws,* you first
describe the animals of the world at peace with one another. "They sat," you
write, "on log benches in the village square. As they rested they told stories
and drank palm wine." But later, after selfishness and cowardice have upset
the animals' communal harmony, the leopard—now forced into the role of
violent avenger—says: "From today I shall rule the forest with terror. The
life of our village is ended."

This reminds me of the conclusion of *A Man of the People,* in which you
write: "The owner was the village, and the village had a mind; it could say
no to sacrilege. But in the affairs of the nation there was no owner, the laws
of the village became powerless." It seems to me that the idea of the "village"—connected as it is with the notions of the possibilities of community,
truthful language, and the attainment of real individuality—is central to all
your work.

Chinua Achebe: My world—the one that interests me more than any
other—is the world of the village. It is one, not the only, reality, but it's the
one that the Igbo people, who are my people, have preferred to all others. It
was as if they had a choice of creating empire or cities or large communities
and they looked at them and said, "No, we think that what is safest and best
is a system in which everybody knows everybody else." In other words, a
village. So you'll find that, politically, the Igbos preferred the small community; they had nothing to do—until recently—with kings and kingdoms.

Now I'm quite convinced that this was a conscious choice. Some people
look at the Igbos and assert that they didn't evolve to the stage of having
kings and kingdoms. But this isn't true—the Igbos have a name for "king,"
they have names for all the paraphernalia of kingship—it isn't as if they

didn't know about kings. I think it's simply that, looking at the way the world operates, they seemed to have said to themselves, "Of all the possible political systems, we shall insist on the one where there are only so many people." So that when a man got up to talk to his fellows they knew who he was, they knew exactly whether he was a thief, an honest man, or whatever. In a city of eight million people, you can't know your neighbor. And that means you have to set up a system of representation: you choose a delegate to speak for you. But the Igbos didn't want someone else to speak for them.

The Igbos are so ambitious that everyone wants to be a king, in fact—this is the strange thing about it. And I'm not being facetious, because what happened at the end of the Biafran war is that somebody in the Nigerian government thought of the idea of letting the Igbos have chiefs.

This is the same thing the British tried and failed to do. But this time it worked. In every village now there's a king—they call themselves *kings*— these are illiterate traders who made money at the Onitsha market! So the Igbos now have 600 chiefs or more throughout Igboland. And we are a people who are reputed, who are *famous* throughout the world, for not having kings. I'm saying it to make the suggestion that there must obviously have been a predilection in our character for ruling others, and it was that instinct, if you like, that the culture was fighting. I think a good culture fights against the instincts of destruction. And this held as long as we had the initiative to control our own history. In recent times this has changed, and the situation is different. Now, the kings we have today aren't going to do any harm, they have no real power, they're really clowns. But the fact is that in the Igbo language, "King" means enemy. The culture was right.

And this is quite central to my fiction and to my analysis of the problems of creating a new nation today. Obviously, we can't go back to the system in which every man is turning up at the village square—that's in the past. But we have to find a way of dealing with the problems created by the fact that somebody says he's speaking on your behalf, but you don't know who he is. This is one of the problems of the modern world.

J.C. In *Arrow of God* you write: "The festival brought gods and men together in one crowd. It was the only assembly in Umuaro in which a man might look to his right and find his neighbor and look to his left and see a god standing there." So your idea of the village seems to include the possibility not only of political participation but of a spiritual one as well.

C.A. Definitely, you're absolutely right. It's a world of men and women and children and spirits and deities and animals and nature . . . and men and women both living and dead—this is very important—a community of the living and the dead and the unborn. So it is both material and spiritual, and whatever you did in the village took this into account. Our life was never compartmentalized in the way that it has become today. We talk about politics, economics, religion. But in the traditional society all these things were linked together—there was no such thing as an irreligious man. In fact, we don't even have a word for religion in Igbo. It's simply *life*.

J.C. As a person who grew up with the values of village and who now lives in a country that is rapidly being modernized, you seem to be in the position of someone who has found himself standing at the crossroads.

C.A. Those who live at the crossroads are very lucky, and it seems to me that there will never be this kind of opportunity again. My generation belongs to a group whose fathers—my father, for instance, although a converted Christian, was really a member of the traditional society—he was already full-grown in the traditions of Igbo life when he decided to become a Christian; so he knew all about our culture. My children, however, belong to the world culture to which American children belong. They went to school in America for several years and liked the same kind of music that children in America and England enjoy. But I'm in between these two. And we can talk about "transitions"—it's a cliché, since every day's a transition—but I think that I'm much more a part of a transitional generation than any other. And this is very exciting. Of course it carries its penalties, since you're in no-man's land, you're like the bat in the folk tale—neither bird nor mammal—and one can get lost, not being one or the other. This is what we are, we can't do anything about it. But it does help if you have the kind of temperament I have, which tries to recover something from our past. So you have one foot in the past—my father's tradition—and also one in the present—where you try to interpret the past for the present.

J.C. The sociologist Philip Slater has written about the difference he sees between the "community" and the "network." By the former he means the people whom we live with, and by the latter he is referring to the people we communicate with professionally throughout our own particular country or even throughout the world—just as you have a readership and attend conferences in many different countries.

C.A. I think there's a certain strength in being able to have one foot in the network and another foot in the community. But if one forgets one's foot in the community—and that is quite possible—one can get carried away into the network system. And this is a real problem for us—for the African intellectual, the African writer. I've sometimes complained about African writers who blindly follow Western fashions with regard to what an author should be writing, saying, or even looking like . . . what ideas he should be expressing, what attitudes he should be having towards his community, and so on—all taken from the West—while we forget about the other part of our nature which has its roots in the community. So I think we have the responsibility to be both in the community and in the network. This is a challenge—it's very exciting and also very perilous.

J.C. You yourself are at the crossroads on many levels—spiritual, political, intellectual—and you have chosen to write for both adults and children. It's as if you've decided to balance and integrate all of these levels and activities.

C.A. Yes, I do that consciously. I think this is the most important and fascinating thing about our life—the crossroad. This is where the spirits meet the humans, the water meets the land, the child meets the adult—these are the zones of power, and I think this is really where stories are created. The middle of the day is a very potent hour in our folklore—noon. This is the time when morning merges into afternoon, and that is the moment when spirits are abroad. When the adults go to the farm and leave the children at home, then the spirits can come into the village.

I've talked about the "crossroad hour" in one of my poems—this hour when the spirits appear—and it is this transitional period that manifests, I think, the great creative potential. It's an area of tension and conflict. So I deliberately go out of my way to cultivate the crossroad mythology, if you like, because I think it's full of power and possibility.

J.C. In *Things Fall Apart,* Okonkwo tells his son Nwoye "masculine" stories of violence and bloodshed, but the boy prefers the tales his mother tells him about Tortoise the trickster, about the bird who challenged the whole world to a wrestling contest and was finally thrown by a cat, and about the quarrel between Earth and Sky—stories for "foolish women and children," as Okonkwo thinks of them. But in *No Longer at Ease,* Nwoye—now the father of the protagonist Obi—forbids the telling of folk tales to his son because he has become a Christian and doesn't want to disseminate what he now thinks of as "heathen" stories. All of this reminds me of the constant attacks against fairy stories in Europe by Enlightenment spokesmen and by any number of rigid moralists and educators during the past two centuries.

C.A. I think that stories are the very center, the very heart of our civilization and culture. And to me it's interesting that the man who thinks he's strong wants to forbid stories, whether it's Okonkwo forbidding the stories of gentleness, or whether, later on, it's a Christian who, so self-satisfied in the rightness and superiority of his faith, would forbid the pagan stories. It is there in those despised areas that the strength of the civilization resides—not in the masculine strength of Okonkwo, nor in the self-righteous strength of the Christian faith. The stone which the builders reject becomes a cornerstone of the house. So I think a writer instinctively gravitates towards that "weakness," if you like; he will leave the "masculine" military strength and go for love, for gentleness. Because unless we cultivate gentleness, we will be destroyed. And this is why you have poets and storytellers, this is their function.

J.C. The psychologist James Hillman has talked of the importance of "restorying the adult."

C.A. This is what I've been trying to say when I talk about weakness and strength. You see, "restorying the adult" is a very interesting phrase because what, in fact, is the adult as distinct from the child? The adult is someone who has seen it all, nothing is new to him. Such a man is to be pitied. The child, on the other hand, is new in the world, and everything is possible to him. The imagination hasn't been dulled by use and experience. Therefore, when you restory the adult, what you do is you give him back some of that energy and optimism of the child, that ability to be open and to expect anything. The adult has become dull and routine, mechanical, he can't be lifted. It's as if he's weighted down by his experience and his possessions, all the junk he's assembled and accumulated. And the child can still fly, you see. Therefore the story belongs to the child because the story's about flying.

J.C. In your autobiographical essay "Named for Victoria," you've mentioned that, like Nwoye, you were told stories by your mother and older sister. So you were lucky enough to be "storied" at an early age.

C.A. I was very lucky, but I would say that that was traditional. Any child growing up at that time, unless he was particularly unlucky, would as part of his education be told stories. It doesn't happen anymore. The stories are now read in books, and very rarely is there a situation in which the mother will sit down night after night with her family and tell stories, with the young children falling asleep on them. The pace of life has altered. Again, this is what I meant by saying that our generation is unique. And I was lucky to have been part of the very tail-end of that older tradition. Perhaps we may not be able to revive it, but at least we can make sure that the kind of stories that our children read carry something of the aura of the tales our mothers and sisters told us.

J.C. In traditional oral societies, the storyteller would employ intonation, gestures, eye contact, pantomime, acrobatics, and occasionally costumes, masks, and props in his or her dramatic presentation.

C.A. Yes, that's right and the loss is enormous. And all I'm saying is that, rather than lose everything, we should value the written story, which is certainly better than no story at all. It's impossible in the modern world to have the traditional storytelling. But I think that perhaps in the home we should not give up so quickly. I find, for instance, that when I write a new children's story the best thing I can do is to tell it to my children, and I get remarkable feedback that way. My youngest child, incidentally, writes stories of her own! . . . But the storyteller today has to find a new medium rather than regret the passing of the past. Television is there, we can't do anything about it, so some of us should use this medium, we should do stories for television.

J.C. You've often stated that stories impart important messages to use and that they are repositories of human experience and wisdom. Your children's stories are, of course, excellent examples of this notion.

C.A. I realize that this is an area where there is some kind of uneasiness between us and the Western reader concerning just how much of a "message" is suitable for a story. I'm not talking about "preaching," which isn't the same thing as telling a story. But to say that a good story is weakened because it conveys a moral point of view is absurd because in my view all the great stories do convey such a point of view. A tale may be fascinating, amusing—creating laughter and delight and so forth—but at its base is a sustaining morality, and I think this is very important.

Going back to the Igbo culture, the relationship between art and morality is very close, and there's no embarrassment at all in linking the two, as there would be in Western culture. The earth goddess Ala—the most powerful deity of the Igbo pantheon—is also the goddess of the arts and of morality. I would say that Ala is even more powerful than the supreme god because of her closeness to us: the earth is where our crops lie, where we live, and where we die. And any very serious offense is called an abomination—the literal translation of "abomination" in Igbo is *nso ani* (*nso* = taboo, *ani* = earth)—*that which the earth forbids.* That's what you say for the worst kinds of crimes like murder and rape. But Ala is also, as I said, the goddess of art.

My concern is that stories are not only retrieved and kept alive but also added to, just as they always were, and I think this is really what a living traditional storyteller would do. I loved the stories my mother and elder sister told me, but there were always little changes here and there. And this was part of the entertainment—you hear a tale a hundred times, but each day there was one additional little twist, which was expected.

There's that combination of stability and change. You mustn't change it so much that you don't recognize it—that would be unacceptable. The child wouldn't accept tinkering with the folk tale to the extent that it becomes something else. But little twists now and then . . . yes.

J.C. It's strange but obvious that it is children—the seemingly least significant members of society—who are given stories about the most important matters—selfishness, pride, greed, the meaning of life and death.

C.A. That's right, and this is wonderful for children. I think the adult sometimes loses sight of the nature of stories. But these great fundamental issues have never changed and never will. I mean, children always ask the same questions: Who made the world? How come some people are suffering? Who made death? And to think that we have somehow moved on to more "adult" subject matters is simply self-deception. What we do, of course, is quite often get trapped in trivia. . . . we get carried away. But the basic questions are still the same, and this is what children's stories particularly deal with.

I think that mankind's greatest blessing is language. And this is why the storyteller is a high priest and why he is so concerned about language and about using it with respect. Language is under great stress in the modern world, it's under siege. All kinds of people—advertisers, politicians, priests, technocrats—these are the strong people today, while the storyteller represents the weakness we were talking about. But of course every poet is aware of this problem. . . . And this is where children come into it, too, because you can't fool around with children—you have to be honest with language: cleverness won't do.

We lost belief at our cost. Lines from an Eskimo poem called "Magic Words": "That was the time when words were like magic./The human mind had mysterious powers./A word spoken by chance/might have strange consequences./It would suddenly come alive/and what people wanted to happen could happen—/all you had to do was say it," take you right back to the beginning of things. "And God said: 'Let there be light' "—he didn't do anything, he just said it. And you can also look at the Aborigines in Australia who are somehow closer to the beginning than ourselves: you have the same feeling there that the word has power.

J.C. I wanted to ask you about your first children's book, *Chike and the River.* The name Chike has *chi* in it, and so does your first name, Chinua.

About *chi,* you've written: "There are two clearly distinct meanings of the word *chi* in Igbo. The first is often translated as god, guardian angel, personal spirit, soul, spirit double, etc. The second meaning is day, or daylight, but is most commonly used for those transitional periods between day and night or night and day. . . . In a general way we may visualize a person's *chi* as his other identity in spiritland—his *spirit being* complementing his terrestrial *human being;* for nothing can stand alone, there must always be another thing standing beside it."

C.A. When we talk about *chi,* we're talking about the individual spirit, and so you find the word in all kinds of combinations. Chinwe, which is my wife's name, means "*Chi* owns me"; mine is Chinua, which is a shortened form of an expression that means "May a *chi* fight for me." Chike is a shortened form of Chinweike, which means "She has the strength or the power." And that's what that little character has—he has the power.

J.C. In *The Flute* and *The Drum,* you also suggest that one shouldn't tamper or fool around with the spirit world.

C.A. The question of frontiers is very important—you must not overstep them—and those frontiers are set up in every space and time: there's even a frontier to ambition. One of the most typical Igbo tales is about a proud wrestler who has thrown every challenger in the world, and so he decides to go and wrestle in the land of the spirits. A very good wrestler would have a man playing the flute for him—singing his praises on the flute—so his praise-singer begs him not to go to the spirit world. But he says, No, I'm bored, there's nobody in the world who can challenge me, I must go there. So they go. And when they arrive there, the spirits come out to wrestle with him—one after the other—and he beats them all. And then he begins to boast. He says, "What sort of spirit world is this, the famous spirit world, can't you find somebody who can give me a proper fight, is there nobody else?" The spirits have a consultation and tell him, "Well, there is somebody, but we think you shouldn't fight him." He responds, "No, if there is anybody at all here now, I must wrestle with him." And this person is his *chi*—his personal spirit—and when he comes out he's very unimpressive, as you would expect, very weak and hungry-looking, thin as a rope. "Who is this?" the wrestler asks. They tell him that this is the man who will challenge him, and he laughs. But his *chi* moves towards him and with one finger picks him up and smashes him on the ground. And that's the end of our great wrestler.

We create these tales and fables, like God creating man in his image. These folk tales aren't just decorative things, they tell us so much about the people who make them. And when told to children, they're intended for their safety, for their survival in the world.

J.C. Chike goes from his village to Onitsha, a famous market town which you've written about elsewhere, stating that "it sits at the crossroads of the world. . . . Because it sees everything, Onitsha has come to distrust single-mindedness. It can be opposite things at once. It was both a cradle of Christianity in Igboland and a veritable fortress of 'pagan' revanchism." It was always the "marketplace of the world," a place where "riverain folk and the dwellers of the hinterland forests met in guarded, somewhat uneasy, commerce; old-time farmers met new, urban retail traders of known and outlandish wares." And it always attracted "the exceptional, the colorful, and the bizarre."

C.A. It's almost a mythical city, with all those extraordinary people, not the least of them Dr. James Stuart-Young—a scholar, mystic, and trader—a crazy Englishman who arrived, it seemed, from nowhere and who claimed to be a Ph.D. And he was an egalitarian! In those days he fought on the side of the people against the big British and French commercial concerns—multinationals, as we now call them. He was a one-man band who lived and died in Onitsha. I saw him once when I was a child—a tall, bald-headed Englishman. I loved Onitsha then and I love it still. It's different now, of course, since it was bombed, and it's been rebuilt, but it's still very vital. And I think that this vitality is the main quality of the "crossroads."

Chike was my first children's book. I enjoy writing for children, it's very important for me. It's a challenge which I like to take on now and again because it requires a different kind of mind from me when I'm doing it—I have to get into the mind of a child totally, and I find that very rewarding. I think everybody should do that, not necessarily through writing a story, but we should return to childhood again and again. And when you write for children it's not just a matter of putting yourself in the shoes of a child—I think you have to be a child for the duration.

J.C. It seems that, in the African tradition, the infant is generally thought of not as a kind of *tabula rasa* but rather as a little messenger whose presence is a gift from the other world.

C.A. I think that the idea of the child as messenger is certainly prevalent. My wife has been doing some work on the notion that children are supposed to be born, to die, to come back, and to repeat cycles of birth and death—this is a very common and popular belief among the Igbos. It was meant to explain the high rate of infant mortality, of course, in the past. And in doing this research she's encountered stories about how children come from the world of over there into the world of men. It's very interesting to discover the attributes they're supposed to come with. The fact is that there's a bargain made, there's a discussion concerning what you'd like to be and what you'd like to do that takes place before the child comes over here. So the child is not a *tabula rasa,* he or she is someone who has already negotiated *over there* its entire destiny. And the child comes to the borderline, and there is somebody there—perhaps a group of people—who tries to talk him or her out of what he or she has agreed to be—they want to discourage the child from aspiring too greatly. So what I am saying is that the child comes with a whole realm of experience. Of course, these are really metaphors for explaining reality. But a child isn't a clean slate, it's got all its genes from its ancestors—what he or she is going to be is more or less fixed in the genes, among other things.

I believe that in bringing up children it's the adult who learns. As a parent I know that, and so this leads to a humility. I think this is very real. Now, that's not permissiveness, that's not to say you must never correct a child, because we're talking about the years of experience the child cannot possibly have. But if you accept that the child comes from somewhere else, you can renew your acquaintanceship with that world through the child. I think this is a very good way of putting it because these are metaphors for our experience. We really don't know. We're simply trying to use words as images to convey vague but insistent notions that visit us.

In the past, our people, when a child was born, would go to a diviner, to find out which of the ancestors it was who had come again. They went back and said, "Well, who's this newcomer, this man's father or this man's grandfather?" So this child was not new. And once they established who the child was, they gave him all that respect. I don't know how it operates, I don't know whether it means that this is exactly the same person or just somebody who has aspects of the character. This is a mystery to me and it must remain a mystery to us. But I'm saying that, as a metaphor, people do come around in that way—children are supposed to be reincarnations of their grandfathers, not of their fathers. And quite often there *is* a very close relationship between grandparents and their grandchildren.

I have a poem called "The Generation Gap," which talks about that specifically, in terms of the pattern of the coming and going of the moon. There's usually some friction between father and son and that would explain why there should be complicity between the child and the grandfather—they have one common enemy [laughing].

J.C. The Ijo of the Niger Delta have a proverb that goes: "He's of goblin ancestry who knows not whence he came." And this might imply that there is and should be a connection not only between grandfather and grandchild but also between the adult and his sense of his own childhood, since both connect one to one's past.

C.A. Yes, that's right, because if there is a constant coming and going between us and the world of the ancestors, which is what my people believe, then it's in fact the child who can tell you about that world since it's coming from there—it's not the old man who's *going* there but the child who's *coming* from there.

J.C. In all your work, the grandfather casts his shadow on the grandchild, the village on the city, and the pagan tradition on the Christian one.

C.A. The duality. Things come in twos. "Wherever something stands, something else will stand beside it"—this is another very powerful Igbo statement. It's absolutely true, and it's when someone refuses to see the "other" that you have problems.

Achebe Interviewed

D. V. K. Raghavacharyulu, K. I. Madhusudana Rao, and B. V. Harajagannadh / 1981

From an appendix to B. V. Harajagannadh's unpublished Ph.D. dissertation, "The Novels of Chinua Achebe: A Study," Nagarjuna University, India, 1985. Published by permission of B. V. Harajagannadh.

Following is an account of the interview given by Chinua Achebe on 11 March 1981, at Madras, during his lecturing assignment in India. The interviewers were D. V. K. Raghavacharyulu (DVK), K. I. Madhusudana Rao (KIM) and B. V. Harajagannadh (BVH)

DVK: Professor Achebe, we in India have taken a lively interest in your fictional work, and your Ibo Quartet comprising *Things Fall Apart, No Longer at Ease, Arrow of God* and *A Man of the People,* has had a great impact on the Indian readers. Your novels depict a sociological situation, in which individuals brought up on the values of the past are made to confront the realities of the present, experiencing in the process several kinds of conflict and tension. Social change and culture-shock are aspects of Indian life in our times, and the Nigerian situation seems to correspond to our own, and we wonder whether this similarity is not, at least in part, responsible for our response to your work.

Achebe: I am glad that my novels do attract such attention from the reading public in your country, and not only from the university academicians. In the final analysis, a writer of fiction must proceed from his own specific local reality towards the universals of human experience and, should I say, of human aspiration. At the same time, the particulars of one's own culture must be the defining framework for a novelist. My situations and characters are drawn from the Ibo society, whose tribal structures of value, attitude and norm, have been subjected to heavy pressure from the western impact. I am not interested in making value judgements, but as an artist the major premise of my work is to show and tell how the individuals, caught in social and institutional change, respond in terms of their deep psychic urges—the irony, the tragedy and the glory of the human predicament, in short. As a matter of fact, the conventional Ibo society had certain shared values, a world-view, if

I may say so, and certain personality goals, a behavioural model, and a mythic-ritualistic strategy of communal action. The advent of the colonial and post-colonial institutions has tended to erode these conventional life-styles and patterns of human relationships. I am not concerned with which is better, the old or the new, the African or the European; both have possibili-ties, imponderables and ambiguities. But in their encounter and confrontation both have tended to shift away from their primary or radical assumptions throwing up unpredictable, contingent realities. Gain and loss are perhaps eventually balanced, but for the novelist there is here rich material to deal with, in terms of narrative and characterization. And, certainly, too, there is a possibility for the ironic development of various points of view.

BVH: Would you say that in *Things Fall Apart,* your protagonist, Okon-kwo, represents such a situation? For instance, doesn't Okonkwo represent the kind of individual who would be a misfit, even a tragic or heroic misfit, in any given society, in the tribal Ibo society, or the changed westernised Ibo society?

Achebe: This is true—to a point, of course. Okonkwo is unaccommodated in both worlds. His loyalty to his chi—or personal, indwelling God—works in an ambivalent manner. A chi affirms what a person does, and a person confirms what his chi prompts. But the point is, Okonkwo loses control, self-mastery, and drifts precipitously towards tragedy. But circumstances have also a heavy hand in it. As a chronicler of life, it has been my business to contemplate the whole process of cultural change and present Okonkwo in the total perspective of the two orders—not so much in conflict merely—but in subversive collaboration against an objective perception of a reality. Okon-kwo is cut off from reality, and becomes a victim of illusion, of a false perception of himself. Hence his self-governing chi cannot hold him together, he falls apart; so does his outer world, which suffers an ecological, historical and existential breakdown and displacement.

BVH: Doesn't *Arrow of God* present a slightly different situation? Isn't Ezeulu, the priest of the Ibo tribe, a much stronger, hence a more heroic figure? He inhabits a more complex, almost hieratic universe which demands self-sacrifice, valour and vision. The destiny of a whole society is in his hands. For instance, his paraclitean responsibility is much more a matter of his adherence to tribal ritual than that of Raju, the reluctant saint in Narayan's *The Guide?*

Achebe: I am not quite familiar with Narayan's work, but I presume your comparison implies an interesting insight from the point of your own reading. But I do agree with you when you say that the threatened loss of ritual content in *Arrow of God* is more serious than the disintegration of personality in *Things Fall Apart.* But I must also say that the duality that prevails in the Ibo world-view is not simply a dialectical opposition of two spatio-temporal concepts. Two things make one rather than divide further into four, and so on. Myth in the African context, as it is perhaps in many non-western cultures, is not the opposite, much less a negation, of the real. It reinforces, structures, rationalises reality. Ezeulu's calendar of events leading to the Yam Festival is not merely an announcement. It is an annunciation of the Invisible Present, or the Eternal, if you might say so, and hence even in his apparent personal failure, Ezeuelu becomes an arrow in the bow of God. All his actions and reflexes are ritualistic responses to a mythically ordained view of reality. *Arrow of God* is a novel of African Being and of African Becoming as well. There is no dichotomy in this, but rather a unitive principle of viewing two as one, many as one, instead of one as two, or one as many.

BVH: *No Longer at Ease* and *A Man of the People* are less dense with Ibo myth and ritual and seem to be narratives of the conflict between morals and manners in a changing society. You seem to be more preoccupied in these novels with the synchronic rather than the historical situation. You almost give the impression of being a happy humorist, a genial satirist, exposing the corruption, the duplicity, and the gullibility of leaders and people in the post-colonial world. This brings an inevitable comparison between these novels and Mr. Naipaul's *The Mystic Masseur, The Mimic Men, The Suffrage of Elvira* and other political satires in Commonwealth literature.

Achebe: I believe I should agree with you. The protagonists in *No Longer at Ease* and *A Man of the People* represent the present generation, with the historical situation very much behind them. They are ordinary, almost unheroic, but they are entirely representative—I believe that the novelist as teacher has some function, some role in society. And even satire must speak in undertones of humour rather than in overtones of indignation. It was great fun, and joy, writing these novels. But the reference to Mr. Naipaul is teasing, almost intriguing. I do admire Mr. Naipaul, but I am rather sorry for him. He is too distant from a viable moral centre; he withholds his humanity; he seems to place himself under a self-denying ordinance, as it were, suppressing his genuine compassion for humanity. His style is all too perfect, steel-bright, metallic, and so forth. But I am a different kind of writer, at least.

KIM: Naipaul is of course obsessed with form and style—almost to the point of being puritanical. But I wonder—if Mr. Naipaul is all that self-centered and self-righteous. Doesn't he, for instance, in *In a Free State, Guerrillas* and *A Bend in the River,* offer a new perspective on modern man—rootless, placeless and homeless, but certainly deserving sympathy, understanding and compassion?

Achebe: What I mean is, there are many omitted possibilities in the works of writers like Naipaul, and my interests are different, and lie elsewhere. Perhaps the Caribbean situation lends credibility to the kind of work undertaken by Mr. Naipaul. But I am aware that there are writers over there, like George Lamming and Wilson Harris (and Tutuola, Soyinka and Ngugi in Africa too), whose novels are more kindred in spirit and I am more at ease with their work. To some extent these writers share my own concern with man in crisis in terms of African sensibility—call it Négritude if you will, not in its purely political sense—and in terms also of the felt life of individuals shaped, of course, by the dynamics of the meeting of two cultures, which is inevitable. I have been interested in how the ensuing struggle for self-reference shapes and changes the texture of the human personality. What happens to the individuals—Okonkwo, Ezeulu or others—is known, but the diffused tumult arisen out of the tragic encounter is more important for my fictional treatment than the political outcome or result in purely historical terms. You may say that character interests me more than the circumstances in which my people and the society are placed.

DVK: Having done us the honour of visiting our country, have you had an opportunity of getting acquainted with our writers, particularly those using English as a medium of creative expression?

Achebe: I wish I had. But my visit, though not the first, and I hope not the last, has only been for three weeks—and here there has been a cultural miscalculation—three Ibo weeks are twelve Indian days—and I must get back. I am of course aware of the work of Anand, Raja Rao and Narayan, though my familiarity with their works is not as deep as it may be expected. But at Mysore I was excited by my encounters with such brilliant, if abrasive, creative writers as Anantha Murthy and others. I have in fact made my visit to India a modest pilgrimage to the land which had invented the zero in the past and, in our times, the Commonwealth concept. It is a convenient fiction and has held out many possibilities for creative discovery and self-dramatisation.

KIM: Is there any aspect of your work to which you feel greater attention should have been paid by critics and scholars?

Achebe: Yes, indeed. My fictional work has received the courtesy of wide critical response, although what I do as a novelist is independent of what others say about it. But sometimes I do feel that my work in children's literature and in the field of literary criticism has not been given the attention it deserves. I personally have derived great satisfaction from writing for the children. Writing for the children is a greater challenge and opportunity than writing for the adults. The mythic and the real merge in natural symbiosis in the radical, undifferentiated innocence of children. And a creative writer must in a sense become a child to capture the flavour and essence of life.

BVH: Are you currently at work on a new novel?

Achebe: Yes. I must confess that I can share a secret with you before it becomes a public scandal. I have a work in progress—a novel which I hope will win favour with my readers. But it will not be prudent on my part to speak more about an unborn child.

DVK: You have referred to your interest in literary criticism. In fact your academic background, which includes higher studies in the United Kingdom and prestigious teaching positions in Nigeria and abroad, finely blends with your concerns as a creative writer. You have also been intimately associated with various literary and educational journals in Africa and have been doing excellent work as editorial advisor for the Heinemann African Writers Series in projecting the contemporary cultural image of Africa. Your *Okike,* which corresponds to *Srijana* in our language, has indeed been the organ of African Renaissance. In your own criticism, especially in that directed to the study of fictional works, you seem to imply that a novel has not only an ontological but also an epistemological centre. In other words, would you suggest that fiction may very well be a vehicle for knowledge, the kind of knowledge which could not be had as convincingly from any another conceptual tool?

Achebe: Now, that is a most interesting question, but difficult to answer over a cup of tea, or is it a cup of coffee? I understand that in India the South is the coffee zone, and tea is a punishing kind of status symbol. Well, let me see. Yes. I think I would basically go along with what you have said. Fiction is certainly one of the most effective ways of getting at truth—or certain kinds of truth in any event. That is what myth is in most non-western cultures, as I have already said earlier. Myth is not a surrogate for, but an efficient agent of reality. For instance, scientific axioms and assumptions without which there can be no science; the equator, an imaginary or fictitious line on paper, still defines and formulates the globe of the earth. "Willing suspension of disbelief," as Coleridge says, or the will to myth, is at the root of aesthetic response. Or take Commonwealth literature itself—a useful fiction, but still a fiction of the non-existent Commonwealth—for which your own leader Nehru was responsible, which has in many ways defined the reality of English literature for our time. Extending the argument, in a serious sense, the novelist makes use of fiction to adumbrate, demonstrate and enact truth—the truths of life, of man, of the world, of the future. The African writer finds the fictional mode quite natural and integral to his culture, thanks to the syncretism of oral and tribal art traditions in Africa. Take Tutuola, for instance, where the very modern questions of freedom and responsibility, of complicity and escape, are compellingly drawn in the narrative idiom of folk-fiction. Of course, there can only be one Tutuola, but that is another matter.

DVK: As there can only be one Chinua Achebe. You have yourself turned Ibo traditional materials to wonderful fictional use. So, may it be inferred from what you say, that the novel as a literary form need not be written off. This, particularly at a time when epitaphs are being prepared to celebrate the death of the novel or certificates to announce the birth of the anti-novel, the anti-anti-novel, and so on.

Achebe: The novel is, I think, still alive, and has great potential, particularly in the African cultures. It is a good job waiting to be done. It is still a bright book of life.

BVH, KIM, DVK: Thank you Prof. Achebe, for a most interesting interview. We wish we could spend more time with you, but we see you are already looking at your watch to keep time for another important engagement. Thank you.

Achebe: I must thank you, indeed. It has been for me an educative experience, I should say. Thank you.

Giving Writers a Voice

Lindsay Barrett / 1981

From *West Africa,* 22 June 1981, 1405–07. Reprinted by permission of *West Africa.*

Chinua Achebe's position as one of Africa's most respected novelists has been consolidated over the years by the fact that he has also been one of the most consistent organisers of activities that could lead to wider acceptance of the writer's role in modern society by the community at large. His involvement with the Mbari Club before the civil war, and his founding of the *Okike* literary journal after it, are two of the instances of this concern and dedication that spring easily to mind. Achebe's own work and the attitude that he encourages among new writers are indices of his commitment to the growth of literate expression as a creative force with a political and social responsibility. It is not surprising to find him now spearheading the call for an association of writers in Nigeria, that will enable them to have a more effective voice in commenting upon and helping to direct the affairs of that nation. On June 26–28 at the University of Nigeria, Nsukka, the first convention of Nigerian writers will be convened under the concerned gaze of Chinua Achebe.

Achebe teaches at the University, but he is spearheading this move in conjunction with other writers from other parts of the country as a pragmatic and non-academic exercise. Last week he was in Britain conducting a series of readings and lectures in various places and Lindsay Barrett was able to pin him down for a few moments to discuss the implications and the motivation of this convention with him, and also to talk about the nature of the journal *Okike* which he has edited continuously since its inauguration 10 years ago. Below are some highlights of the conversation between them.

L.B. Chinua, who are the guiding lights behind this convention or conference?

C.A. There are no guiding lights as such, especially at this point. It was my idea to invite my colleagues, fellow Nigerian writers, to come together and decide whether or not they should have an association of writers. I personally think we should have such an association. The last effort that I remember as being along these lines was before the civil war, in 1966. We had the small beginnings of an association. It was called SONA, the Society of Nigerian Authors, and I think it ran for about two years. I was the President when the civil war broke out, so I feel that I have a responsibility now to revive it, or revive something like it, something bigger really, because what I am attempting now is to bring in writers in all languages, English and Nigerian languages, to set up an association, which will be useful for the writers, a kind of trade union for them. But I also think it will be very valuable to the country, to have a forum where one can feel the pulse of the writers.

L.B.: What would be the main things that such an association could achieve for the writers and the country?

C.A.: I would leave this to the association once it has been set up to decide. I think that one of the benefits for the writers would be to provide a kind of cover for them. I think there is strength in numbers but you have to organise the numbers well. There are questions of copyright and all kinds of things like that, which, at the moment, are handled haphazardly, and I think if we had an association now, we would begin to look more closely at the things that are of common interest to us.

L.B.: Do you plan to model this association on the lines of any existing organisation in other parts of the world?

C.A.: No, I am taking no definite steps in any direction, I simply want to call people together and say to them: "Look, this is my idea. I think we should be organised, how do we go about it? Do you agree?" And if they say yes, then we can begin to elect officers, set up committees, work out modalities. One other thing that I should mention is that I am inviting two writers from abroad, Ngugi wa Thiong'o from Kenya, and Kofi Awoonor from Ghana, because I think that while the emphasis should be on a national association, we must not lose sight of the international implications. I would like this association to have an eye on the African scene at the same time.

L.B.: Under what auspices are you organising this convention? Is it in your capacity as Head of Department?

C.A.: Hold on. I am no Head of Department at all. I am simply using my position as I explained to you, as the former President of the defunct Society of Nigerian Authors, to call for this conclave. As you also know, as the editor of *Okike,* I have a forum around which to rally people, and I was going to organise this meeting to coincide with the tenth anniversary celebrations for the journal. As it turned out, that idea was not well received in some quarters, and I thought that it was perhaps necessary for one to be tactful in this situation, so I separated the two happenings. I was able to get a small grant from the Nigerian Council of the Arts, the Secretary of which, Frank Aig-Imouk-huede, is also a well-known writer. I shall also be appealing to publishers to help out. The University of Nigeria is also being very helpful; in fact the Vice-Chancellor has expressed great happiness at the idea and is prepared to support the convention. So you see, I am just gathering aid from all quarters.

L.B.: Will it be a very long conference?

C.A.: No, it will be very brief in the first instance. We shall assemble on Friday, undertake the main business on Saturday, and disperse on Sunday.

L.B.: How many writers are you expecting?

C.A.: It is difficult to say. We have sent out several scores of letters and we shall also put out an advertisement in the press. But really everybody is welcome, everybody who regards himself as a writer in Nigeria is welcome to come and participate.

L.B.: Now this is *Okike*'s tenth year of existence. How continuous has its publication been?

C.A.: It has been quite continuous or rather consistent in its publication over the ten years, and this is something that I am quite proud about. It has not been as regular in terms of the period of publication that we visualised when we started, but it has been consistent. We had intended to appear regularly three times a year; that has not been the case always, but we have managed to continue to appear at least once each year. We have number 18 in press at this time, and by the time we hold our little celebrations in October we should have number 19 ready.

L.B.: When you originally decided to start *Okike* did you intend it to be purely a literary magazine or was it supposed to take the place of *Black Orpheus* which was a much more general magazine with a broad interest in all the arts? [Note: This question was necessary because Achebe was one of the main African supporters of the journal *Black Orpheus* which largely shaped and expressed intellectual creative achievements in Africa of the '50s and '60s. When *Okike* was started, it was just about the time when it was clear that in spite of efforts to avoid it, the demise of *Black Orpheus* was real.]

C.A.: I did not intend it to repeat what *Black Orpheus* had already done. Each magazine must have a personality of its own. I did not intend *Okike* to be quite as broad in its interests as *Black Orpheus,* but at the same time I did not intend it to be purely "literary" in the sense of being academic or anything like that. It has been somewhere in between.

L.B.: What has been *Okike*'s main thrust and impact on the African literary scene over the last ten years?

C.A.: I think it has helped to provide a forum for discussing what our literature is and should be about. A magazine should not dictate, but should provide a forum for discussion and we have been quite active in that area. It has also provided a forum for new writers. There are some people, I am glad to say, who were first published—first saw the light of day, so to speak—in the magazine. For example, Odia Ofeimun, who is a very well-known poet in Nigeria and abroad, when he sent his first poems to me, he was totally unknown in wider circles, and there are a few others. I think in these two areas, the provision of a place where short works of fiction and poetry by both new and established writers could be published and a forum in which to discuss the ideas behind literature, the journal has been very useful.

L.B.: You have been the editor and founding father of *Okike* all along, so what is your impression concerning the direction in which *Okike* has helped to point the writers of Africa?

C.A.: I don't like to see my role as one of setting directions. This is something which I try to avoid. I work towards creating a forum in which people can find their direction, in which there will be a free and open discussion of possibilities. There is no one direction for the creative arts: there is no one direction for literature. I think airing of views, clearing of obscurities, are useful functions. I think every genuine writer will ultimately find what his direction should be, and a good journal gives him the opportunity to find this out for himself.

L.B.: But I still believe that there are some areas of what you call "obscurity" which *Okike* has been devoted to clearing up and thus have become identified with the journal and with you. For example, it seems that the writers who have been associated with you and *Okike* over the last decade are people who have come to the conclusion that literature should be committed to the social realities of their communities, and that one can see in literature of both English expression and the vernacular mother tongues of Africa, a unity of equal importance. Don't you believe that in its determined promotion of these principles *Okike* has been quite different from the journals that have gone before?

C.A.: What you say there is true. I happen to accept those two principles, but for me these are basic. I don't see how anyone can conceive of literature without commitment or how anyone could hope to ignore literature in African languages, and the very name *Okike,* which is an African word meaning creation, is significant. I thought what you meant by direction was stylistic or doctrinal: we don't want to give that kind of direction. In that respect I believe that *Okike* is different from what has gone before, and I also hope that it will be different from what follows it. A new journal will arise some day which could carry these principles forward in other ways.

L.B.: Do you see the convention then as being in any way an extension of your work with *Okike?*

C.A.: Yes. Well, everything that has been done in the area of creative writing could be brought into a convention like this, and especially in the area that you have mentioned about the dynamics between writing in English and the Nigerian languages. It will be interesting to see what comes out of the convention on this subject.

Those Magical Years

Robert M. Wren / 1983

From Robert M. Wren's *Those Magical Years: The Making of Nigerian Literature at Ibadan: 1948–1966* (Washington, DC: Three Continents Press, 1991), 53–66. Reprinted by permission of Lynne Rienner Publishers, Inc.

Achebe's new house in his ancestral town, Ogidi, its style clean white-concrete contemporary, was on an unpaved road that narrowly angled off the old highway. It's in an area of large old houses, most of which poorly survived the civil war. Building materials, scattered about, made the house look unfinished.

Achebe showed the rest of the house, almost finished and already furnished. Upstairs were conventional large bedrooms and baths, with stairs from the main kitchen to a locked door—locked not so much against servants as against armed robbers—and, to the front, an open staircase to the reception hall. The lounge and dining room were under a single high ceiling, but the dining area was elevated about two feet, with a chrome steel railing. The living space below, where we talked, was grand enough for the large furniture.

Achebe remembered Adrian P.L. Slater—"Apple" Slater—very well. Slater had taught at Government College, Umuahia, when Achebe was a raw youth from the Nigerian "bush." Achebe knew very well [Slater's] teaching was important. "[He taught us] a little elementary logic," he said, "but the instruction was, to Class One boys, very useful. It's elementary, but you need proper instruction to understand it. This is particularly important for us. If you were to divide the world into the scientific and non-scientific people, we would be in the non-scientific. We are a magical people, if you like; the logical thinking of the sort Slater taught us does not come automatically. Take, for example, a taxi-driver; if he has an accident he does not see himself as responsible, because he thinks in terms of magic. The man who died must have done something: that is why he came to his sad end."

Achebe went on to say that his education was a singularity, an unreproducible event. "The teachers took chances with us, because they could. The selection process for getting into a place like Umuahia meant we were not an average group. The whole school was just two hundred; my class was thirty-two. It's impossible to recreate that kind of thing today. No one is going to allow you to have a school and admit only thirty-two students. I'm not myself unduly worried about elitism. It's become a dirty word, but any system has to have an efficient corps. In an army every other word, is 'special.' You have an elite corps. When things get tough, you send them; they break it up and move out. Then the other soldiers will go in. I don't think it has anything to do with democracy. The real problem is that when you set up an elite, you give them privileges, and then you recruit the wrong people into it. If you look for an elite corps of soldiers [now], you recruit the children of generals, who are not necessarily the best soldiers.

If we had an elitist school today, I would never have got into it. My father would not have had the money, nor the car to drive me there. In those days, we were children of poor men. There was no rich boy in Umuahia; there was only this strict competition. I went to Umuahia on my own. My mother, my father would not have known how to get there. They wouldn't have known what the whole thing was about. I came in answer to a letter from the principal inviting me." He told this like a stand-up comedian, astonished at his own ignorance. "It said 'Please acknowledge receipt.' But to me that was simply a fancy way of ending a letter. When I got there, there was this big white man who said, 'Oh, yes, Achebe. Why did you not reply?' I said I was confused. And I stammered something, that I did not know I was to reply. And he brought out a copy of the letter and said 'please acknowledge receipt—what does this mean?' I had *no idea* what it meant! And those thirty-two boys came from bush schools, from all over. Even from as far as Cameroons. So it was not a corrupt kind of elitism, which is what you would have today if you set up separate schools . . ."

"We did a lot of reading," Achebe went on. "That was one of the things they insisted upon. Slater had you read something like thirteen novels every term, on your own. You just went to the library and read all those books." Achebe's face lit up, remembering. "The principal was a mathematics man— one of his favorite phrases was 'Excessive devotion to work is a real danger!' He said it like a proverb, all the time. We needed to be told that. In our environment, you studied. You didn't drink [from the sacred spring] for pleasure! What the school tried to break was the habit of swotting. So there were rules, rigid rules about when you could read your mathematics, or physics, or whatever. At other times you had to read a novel, or write letters—or you could play ping pong . . . Things were so informal! I think what was really effective was this business of going to the library and reading anything you liked, whatever you could lay your hands on." Achebe was enjoying this, and he had us laughing with him, at lines that aren't funny at all in cold prose, like his imitation of a teacher, Charles Low—pronounced with an Australian "o." "After Slater, we had an Australian, a very eccentric man. He taught English, but he was very different from Slater. Low was totally unstructured. He would come into the class without any ideas as to what you were going to do that day. He would start something, and then he would wander off and talk for about forty minutes. And he would say, 'That's an important digression!' Now most of what he *did* was digression, but it was fantastic. He read Latin in Melbourne and Oxford, Latin and Greek, and he had a prodigious memory. He practically knew *Paradise Lost* by heart. That was *one* passion; the *other* passion was cricket." We'd been laughing a good deal, so Achebe put in a warning, "we had people like that; he was effective . . . I'm not making fun of him . . ."

"The library was excellent for those days, and even for today. I still remember walking into this long room with incredibly neat bookshelves. I'd never seen so many books in my life. When I finished at the University, I came back here and I taught for a little while at a school at Oba—just a few miles below Onitsha—the Merchant of Light School. They had no idea of a library. This was a revelation to me, to see that at Umuahia we were so privileged. Not just Umuahia. A few others—Government College, Ibadan, King's College in Lagos, and the one in the north—those students, whether they were soldiers or doctors, they'd write well. Let me give you an example. One of the first books to come out of the war was by Alexander Madiebo, who was the general commanding the Biafran army. It was beautifully written. The general was one of the boys who was coming into class when I was leaving. At Umuahia we also had a military corps. One of the masters had been a captain during the war, and he started a little military training program for those who were interested. And of the first batch of Nigerian officers who went into the army, quite a number came from Umuahia." (He put one such officer into *Anthills of the Savannah*—as a military dictator.)

[Achebe talked] about several Nigerian masters: "W.E. Alagoa's still alive. He's a Rivers man—from the same family as your friend Professor Alagoa. He taught chemistry. He came from King's College, and he taught there. I.D. Erekosima—he's still alive, too. He was a genius, really a great mathematician. They didn't have opportunities—well, there was no university around then, so he went to Yaba Higher College after Umuahia. I think he was one of the foundation students, one of [the Reverend Dr. Robert] Fisher's boys, the first headmaster. Erekosima was really named John Bull. Many of the Rivers people had the names given them by the traders. He came back to Umuahia to teach—physics, mostly—but he could teach anything. G.J. Efon died last year. He was a very popular science teacher, physics."

Achebe had originally qualified to study science at Ibadan. "At the time I was starting at the University, I thought I could do anything. I had maybe a slight bent to literature. But I enjoyed chemistry; I enjoyed biology. Physics wasn't—I enjoyed it too, but I didn't enjoy mathematics the way I enjoyed other things. Now, as a result of the entrance examination, I was a 'Major Scholar.' There were just two Major Scholars in any year, and about seven or eight Minor Scholars; the rest were fee payers. So I was a Major Scholar for science. It was a rather aristocratic kind of thing; Major Scholars each had a room to himself. At the old site, the others shared rooms." Was the old site terrible? No, because, by Nigerian standards, what the British "suffered" was luxury. "There was no lack of comfort at the old site. It had been an army camp during the war. We had stewards in the dining rooms, as in the British system." He laughed. "We certainly had no lack of water or bread! But," he went on, "I realized that the kind of interest you needed to pursue education was not the kind required in secondary school. It was clear to me early in the first year that I didn't want to do the grinding work in physics, or ultimately, in medicine. I didn't do well. I lost interest entirely. When I went to the dean and said I wanted to change, he said, 'How do you know you can do the English? and history? I mean, you came here on a scholarship because of your . . . ' He brought out the scores. He said, 'Go and talk to the Dean of Arts, and if they will take you, we'll see.' So I did, but I lost my scholarship.

That year, my brothers pitched in. My immediate older brother was a junior civil servant. He'd gone through secondary school, had not gone to university, and was working. He was in Ibadan, and was about to come home on leave. You were given money for transport and so on, by the government. He decided he would cancel his leave and give me the money to help me with my fees. And my older brother, with whom I lived my last year in elementary school—he's now a priest—he had absolutely no doubt that I should go back, and then to apply for a government bursary, which I got in the second year. Getting through the one year was quite traumatic. A large number of students were destroyed in that first year. I changed my course, but some people were thrown out of the university on the basis of the first year exams. It was a big thing, in the newspapers; there was an outcry from the *Pilot*." The *West*

African Pilot, founded and edited by the great nationalist Azikiwe, was the gadfly. "They had a cartoon of the principal, Dr. Mellanby, with a basketful of young undergraduates; he's throwing them out of the window from a tall building." We all laughed at poor Mellanby, but Achebe cared about the failures. "Many of them went abroad and came back with excellent credentials, but there were a few who were crushed. I know one young man who never recovered from that year, who went off his mind."

He remembered—"Joyce Garnier—no—oh, yes, Green"—with an ironic smile. "She was a Victorian; she taught Tennyson. She was the one who promised to explain to me what the short story was, but she never did. There was a kind of departmental prize that was to be given, and we were supposed to write a short story. I had never written a short story before, so I wrote one. No prize was given, although they said there was some 'interesting effort.' I was mentioned as one of the 'interesting' ones. Miss Green said something about—that the problem with mine was that it lacked the form of a short story. I said, 'What is the form of a short story?' She said, 'We'll talk about it'; she'd find some time and explain. I reminded her in the course of the term and she—well, at the end of the term I reminded her again, and she said, 'I read your short story again, and I don't think there's anything wrong with the form.' "

Prize or no prize, students had their own journals. "The *Herald* was the establishment journal. It was 'serious' and 'literary.' Serious in quotes because I think *The Bug* had its moments of seriousness too. But the *Herald* was where you had the essays, the new poets, and so on. I was recruited into the editorial committee and was elected editor in my third year. *The Bug* came down as a kind of rough thing, to lampoon people, and that was useful. But another thing was that it tended to concentrate on the girls.

There were not many girls in those days. Some of the attacks were quite ungentle, to say the least. On one occasion, one of the girls nearly committed suicide, an overdose of sleeping drugs. You know who, actually, but I won't mention her name. Those two journals kept the campus vibrant. Later on another paper came out, which came into conflict with the *Herald*. The *Herald* was rather anomalous, funded by the University, but controlled by the students. The election of the editor had nothing to do with the students. It was by a small committee, self-perpetuating, if you like. In my time as editor, pressure by some elements of the Student Union to take over the *Herald* made things become uneasy. I don't think it would have been right for the editor of this journal to be elected on the floor of the Student Union, like the president or secretary. The University sided with us, and the Student Union leadership broke away and set off another journal. In the end I think both journals suffered, and died . . .

I was confused, as a student. I started up with medicine, then went into English and geography and history. And then comparative religion came. It was a latecomer to the campus, and there was this Dr. Parrinder who had spent about twelve years as a Methodist missionary in French-speaking West Africa, in Dahomey, and had written a book called *West African Religion*. I heard from other students the kinds of things they were doing. It wasn't theology at all; they were comparing religions—all the way from Akan [in Ghana] to the Cameroons. I dropped geography and picked up this new thing, to see what it was, this religion. There was a bit of Christian religion, yes, but not much. Parrinder was a very enthusiastic and knowledgeable teacher. I don't know if Parrinder turned me toward the study of religion, but he certainly enlightened me. I already had the interest, even if I didn't know it. I certainly had an interest in our gods and religious systems. In those days, the teacher mattered a lot. News about who was an excellent teacher spread through the university, no matter what department you were in. You would find people going into the lectures by Keith Buchanan in geography because he was a fantastic lecturer. Physics people would come. It was the same when Parrinder began, and later on when the Professor—he was James Welch—came. Welch was a distinguished person who had worked as a missionary in the so-called 'country.' He'd gone back to England, been chaplain to the king, and he was the head of the BBC religious service. Mellanby brought him out as a Professor of Religion. He handled the Christian side, and Parrinder the West African. Between them, it was a very exciting course . . .

So when I got to Ibadan I began to see religion differently. I think that must have helped a lot. I began to see that all the things I took as the gospel's truth were being interpreted academically. I began to say, well, it doesn't really matter. You can be a Christian and yet be able to worship your ancestors. I think that was the difference. That was a revelation, yes."

Another influential lecturer, Achebe said, was Alex Rodger. "He came to us at the end of my career there." Rodger thought that one of the novels he assigned might have been Hardy's *The Mayor of Casterbridge*. Achebe said, "Not in my year. We read *Far from the Madding Crowd*. But I took to Hardy immediately. What appealed to me was his sense of reality, which is tragic; it's very close to mine. I think for the same reason I took to A.E. Housman. There are a lot of funny things, a lot of comic things that happen in the world, and they're important. But I think that the things that really make the world, the human world, are the serious, the tragic. And this is, roughly, what Hardy says to me; this is what Housman says to me. It is, you know, the man who fails who has a more interesting story than the successful person. If you ask me why, I don't know . . ."

Achebe felt that simplicity was part of their seriousness. "Because the tragic situation is very simple; it's not 'convoluted' at all. I mean, the man who strives—there's no reason he should not be happy, why he should not reap some reward, achieve some success. That's not a complex thing at all. And Hardy knew that, and Housman knew it."

He finished study at UCI, as did many others, without plans. "I had no idea of what work I wanted to do. These days, students get so edgy, and I don't blame them. In my time, getting a job was no problem; people were looking for you. I just didn't think of work or how I was going to go on. Things looked a bit nebulous to me; I thought there was still so much I wanted to know, but just where to find it I wasn't so sure. Professor Welch came in at this point. He was very fond of me, thought highly of me, and he said, 'I'm going to write my college—Trinity College—to give you an exhibition.' And he did. Now, whatever happened, nothing came of it." He didn't want to elaborate; it was an old sensitive point. "Then I came back here to Ogidi. A friend of mine who did mathematics said, 'What are you doing? Come to Merchant of Light. They're looking for a teacher of English. They'll pay you anything you want to earn.' So we went down to Oba, and I got a job teaching English and history there. One day I received a letter from the broadcasting people, saying, 'We have been advised by Professor Welch, and we are looking for—' well, I don't know what they said they were looking for—" but he got the job. He remained in broadcasting until the civil war.

On the political interests of the students, he said: "We were very political, yes. The period was full of constitutional conferences—in '50, in '53, and so on . . ."

I said to Achebe that Ken Post thought that the intellectuals were disillusioned about the politicians. Part of the deal had been preservation of the country's three regions, a British requirement that the politicians should not have agreed to. Achebe hesitated because he'd given the subject a great deal of thought. "This, the predominance of the north, by its size, in Nigerian politics was old, as old as the Nigerian nation. Before 1914, seasoned colonial administrators urged Lord Lugard to break up the North." Sir Frederick Lugard "unified" Nigeria's two parts, leaving a divided, minority south as a danger for time to deal with—which it did, at a terrible price. "If you are going to have a proper balance between the north and the south, you can't have this mammoth, this huge thing that is bigger than the two southern parts together. But Lugard didn't care for the south, you see." I did indeed see; Lugard's letters showed that he detested the hot, damp, and ungovernable south, and loved the north for its despotic rulers and docile people. "He just had no interest in the south—and he said so. He wanted the north to dominate, he said, deliberately. We didn't need the conference in '50 to see this.

What I do remember in the '50's as a source of great disillusionment was the introduction of ethnic politics, with the arrival of the Action Group on the scene." The AG was a nationalist political party founded by Obafemi Awolowo to secure Yoruba interests, which he thought were not adequately served by the National Conference for Nigeria and the Cameroons (NCNC). The NCNC had been founded by the long-time nationalist Azikiwe, he of the *West African Pilot,* and of Igbo origin. The two-party conflict became intense during the 1951–52 elections. "That," Achebe said, "is the disillusionment I remember. As for the structure, we had no illusion. It's still clear to me today that the British had no interest in the South. Robertson, the last Governor General, was saying exactly the same thing. He was talking about the dignified northerners, the polite—and so on—and on the other hand the vociferous and bad-mannered Igbos. This was an old thing, and the north in time simply began to capitalize on it with the Sardauna [of Sokoto] eventually speaking for them." The Sardauna, Sir Ahmadu Bello, became the most powerful man in newly independent Nigeria, and he was among the first people assassinated in January 1966. "Religion doesn't come into this. The British are fascinated by Islam, whether it is Lawrence of Arabia or something else. And, yes, by aristocracy," Achebe said, laughing, "and by horses to ride!"

Were Achebe's English lecturers inclined to socialization with students? "The system was not informal at all. There were *attempts* to create bridges. But students—there was no doubt at all, in that generation of teachers, that students were students! Mellanby was a good man. He joined things like—for example, we had a dancing club. I was very fond of dancing in those days, and we did all kinds of dances, you know, whirls, fox trot, rumba, tango, and then someone introduced us to the Scottish reel, and we learned even that. Mellanby was very fond of it. And he brought the Governor of Nigeria, Sir John McPherson, who was visiting the campus, to come and join us in the Scottish reel. And that was a big thing, because there were two rival groups, the Dancing Club and the Social Circle. And we were the ones, you know, we were the ones patronized by the Governors of Nigeria! I remember going to Mellanby's house, maybe twice, for lunch when there were visiting dignitaries from abroad. But my real connection with him is that his wife was a lecturer in history. She was a very good teacher, one of my favorites, and I was one of her favorite students. So I was invited. I don't think there was too much communication between staff and students. It wasn't that kind of society. They tried to institute the Cambridge/Oxford thing about having a tutor, a 'moral tutor,' I think he was called. The moral tutor had about five students assigned to him. My moral tutor was John Potter, who was a very eccentric person. He was an Anglican priest who lost his faith and became an agnostic—and a very good teacher of history. He invited us to lunch a couple of times . . .

Faith is not a matter of desire or intention. I have no faith in any religion, so there's no point in pretending that I have more faith in the efficacy of traditional religion, in the sense in which my grandfather had it, than I would have in Christianity the way my father had it. Things have changed. The world order in which the gods operated, the way that those people saw it, I cannot accept. But that doesn't mean—" He laughed, interrupting himself. "No! I can go to church without their dragging me! I was prevailed upon by the Bishop of the Niger to propose a toast to the Archbishop of Canterbury when he came. I don't object to that kind of thing, because I have a lot of ties with the Anglican church, as you know, but I don't have my father's faith, or my brother's. He was the one that my father took to the church. I didn't know this until he told the story on the day of his ordination. My father took him to St. Philip's Church and offered him to God, you see. So that's fine, but I cannot pretend that my life is organized around traditional religion. For the same reason, I would not fill my house with masks, which are not supposed to be in the house anyway. If I found one that was absolutely beautiful, and I could deal with it, I would. There's a lot of posing about all this, and I think all religions do the same thing. If your view of the world is scientific—and my view of the world is scientific—then you don't accept the role of the gods in the same way that my father would." Had Achebe reached that point of view before he went to Ibadan? He had.

After graduation, was there an Ibadan community? "I still maintained an interest, because I had friends—[Momah] was a librarian in Ibadan. He was my best friend; he was the best man at my wedding. I often went to Ibadan. Later on, my wife was a student at Ibadan. Our wedding took place in the Chapel of the Resurrection. That was in '61. Okigbo was living in Ibadan, though not in the University." That would be when he was Cambridge University Press representative, and writing poetry. "And in those days, Ibadan was on the way to the east, from Lagos, and I was in Lagos from '54 to '58, and then back in Lagos from '60 to '66. So I was in the east for only a short while. Ibadan was very much on the route. I went to Molly Mahood's Inaugural Lecture; I went up from Lagos. I knew Chris Okigbo well, very well. He was in Umuahia in my time; he came there two, two or three years after me. And he came to Ibadan after me. I wouldn't know about Ben Obumselu's friendship with Chris. Ben didn't go to Umuahia; he went to DMGS [Dennis Memorial Grammar School, at Onitsha].

I knew J.P. Clark only through the student publications, until later, after he graduated and came down to Lagos to work in one of the newspapers. That's when we became close. As a matter of fact, when the crisis started in '66 he was the first person I saw—well, he came to me the day of the coup. We had our Friday meeting of the Society of Nigerian Authors at the Exhibition Centre on Marina. J.P. had just read *A Man of the People,* the only copy in Nigeria that day. It was to come out the following Monday. I read my advance copy and passed it on to him. You know how he says things." He imitated Clark's severe enthusiasm. " 'Chinua, I *know* you are a prophet. Everything in this book has happened except a military coup!' This was on Friday, January 15, in the afternoon. The next morning, which was Saturday, I went to work in Broadcasting House and found the place surrounded by soldiers. I had no idea what was going on. They looked at my pass and saw that I worked there. They said, 'There's been a coup. Nobody knows where the Prime Minister is!' J.P., who was by this time teaching in Lagos University, dashed over to come tell me that there had been a coup. When he got to the gate, he was nearly shot by these soldiers, because he had no business there. You know how he is."

Amos Tutuola had been published in London, and Cyprian Ekwensi in Nigeria, both with some success. Had their publication motivated him in any way? "Yes, those matter in the sense that one didn't think of publishing a book as something impossible. Now nobody ever doubts his ability to publish a book in Nigeria—so that's a major gain. Though that is not enough to determine the kind of book you write."

We were, I thought, finished, and we were getting up from our great chairs, when for some reason Achebe was reminded of remarks made by Professor Welch, remarks that caught perhaps the meaning of the education Welch and his fellows had been attempting years before at Ibadan. Achebe quoted

Welch: " 'I'm an Englishman, you see. You are Africans; you are Nigerian, you know. Very soon you will be running your own business—independence. We can't teach you how to run Nigeria. We are not experts in African religion or anything. We can only teach you what we know. After that you can do what you like with it.' " Achebe went on, "I think this is the thing. It doesn't matter really what you teach; it is the spirit. I think that the best teachers in Ibadan, in Umuahia, seemed to be formed by that spirit. They weren't teaching us African literature. If we had relied on them to teach us how to become Africans we would never have got started. They taught us English literature; they taught us what they knew. But they had a passion, if you like, for whatever it was, and they conveyed it. And a good student could take off from there."

Literature and Conscientization:
Interview with Chinua Achebe
Biodun Jeyifo / 1983

From *Contemporary Nigerian Literature: A Retrospective and Prospective Exploration,* edited by Biodun Jeyifo. (Lagos: Nigeria Magazine, 1985), 3–19. Reprinted by permission of *Nigeria Magazine* and Biodun Jeyifo.

Jeyifo: Well, as I told you, this interview is essentially meant to reminisce on the past and examine the present and perhaps look forward to the future. So I suppose we should start by going back to the beginnings. If one may state what is now a commonplace, when you started writing, there were not too many other Nigerian literary artists on the scene. Of course there *were* literary artists in the oral tradition. But there were no *writers,* so to speak. What started you on this vocation? One has read in fact that you went to Ibadan initially to read medicine.

Achebe: Yes. Well, you know, what you went into a university to read in those days was not really very much related to what your real interests were. Well, sometimes, if you were lucky, the two might coincide, but I do know that the university existed mainly to raise you from one class to another. It had little relationship to such things as what your *real* interests might be— literary, philosophical, whatever. You were simply looking for the shortest, the quickest avenue into the "senior service." Well, I'm putting it a bit crudely and of course there is no way of knowing whether if I'd gone into medicine and become a doctor I would still have written my novels. I mean it's not the first time that such a thing has happened. But I gave up my study of medicine because I discovered that I hadn't really thought about it. And being an average student in both the arts and the sciences at that time—in fact I think I did a little better in the sciences than in the arts—it was a question of following that advantage and I thought I would get a degree in medicine. But after one year in Ibadan, I matured a bit, and knew that although I could have gone on and become a doctor, I wouldn't have enjoyed that vocation. So I moved into the liberal arts. Of course at that point I wasn't thinking of writing at all.

Jeyifo: Although you had written at Umuahia.

Achebe: Yes, I was the editor of my house magazine and the school magazine, and I'd written a few odd things here and there. But as I said, those were not such "literary" things. I enjoyed stories and read novels a lot. The decision to become a writer—it's difficult for me to say when it happened because, as you said, there were no writers. Well, there were a few names. Cyprian was beginning to write. And then while I was in the university, Tutuola came out.

Jeyifo: Had you actually heard of Tutuola by the time you were writing *Things Fall Apart?*

Achebe: Oh yes, of course, I was in my penultimate year at Ibadan when *The Palm-Wine Drinkard* was published, and I was also a student of Parrinder who played a role in connecting Tutuola with Faber and wrote an introduction or something for Tutuola's second book, *My Life in the Bush of Ghosts.* So I did hear of him, although I didn't meet him until years later. These were however marginal. So it wasn't like now, and it's difficult to imagine how different it was. I mean now, every child I meet tells me he or she is going to write!

Jeyifo: So, later on, when you decided to be a writer—you've since then formulated some very clear ideas, some very clear purposes which impel you to write. For instance, to write a truer and more meaningful and relevant story about the way our people lived in the past as a corrective to some of the things which had been written by others before you started to write. So were these ideas conscious at that point?

Achebe: They were not very conscious at the beginning. You know, the way a writer works—a lot of his motivations are instinctive and subconscious. It's easier to perceive after the event, which is not to say the ideas were absent. It's only that I didn't sit back and say I'm going to write ABCD, you see. It's more like an urge to express yourself—self-expression, which is a human thing. I think this is something which is basic to our nature, whether you do it in painting or music, or whether you just talk. I mean people who dramatise themselves. I'll tell you something. When I was in the BBC staff school, I'd just finished *Things Fall Apart* and my friend then who was in the same course with me, Bisi Onabanjo . . .

Jeyifo: The present Governor of Ogun State?

Achebe: Yes, he was urging me to show this thing to our teacher at the BBC staff school, a novelist. But I was very shy—I envy some of the children today who are so sure they want to be writers!—I was hesitant, but Bisi kept urging me until one day I walked up timidly to the man and said I'd written a novel. This man was a well-known novelist himself in Britain . . .

Jeyifo: Who was he, by the way?

Achebe: Gilbert Phelps. And like every other writer, you know, you don't want an invasion of your privacy by anybody, so he said rather evasively that he would look at it, and I then showed it to him and, well, he liked it. And from that moment, I was launched because it was published by Heinemann, and he showed it to them. So the story got around—and this is really what I'm talking about—and one of the instructors said, "I hear you are writing a novel; is it going to be like Cyprian Ekwensi's?" And I said, without meaning to be rude, "I hope not!" And then, you know the British, he said, "I hope not too!" Well, you know, everybody has his own idea—I mean Cyprian had developed one style and kind of writing and I had no intention to imitate or repeat what he had done. Tutuola was a total world of his own, too. And I must say, I was completely impressed by Tutuola from the word go. I mean, this thing about Nigerians not liking him at the *beginning;* that did not apply to me. It just did not apply to me—although I didn't go about shouting anything about him. But that was one different style and approach and everything, and Cyprian was another, and I wanted something of my own.

Jeyifo: So in that case, still on this subject of *writing* as a vocation, is it possible to date *when* you actually began to see writing—I hesitate to use the word "mission"—you know, as a vocation?

Achebe: Yes. Well, I will say yes and no. Because you see, the moment I became conscious of the possibilities of representing somebody from a certain standpoint, from that moment I realised that there must be misrepresentation, there must be misjudgment, there must be even straightforward discrimination and distortion, and this was clear from European literature which I read as a student. In secondary school, one didn't feel that way. For some reason, maybe one simply had not grown up sufficiently. Reading Alan Paton and other writers, you know, you tended even to identify with Europeans. Because this is the thing really: a writer controls . . .

Jeyifo: Can seduce . . .

Achebe: Yes, controls your response by the way he stacks the evidence for or against, you see. We should have immediately identified with the Africans but this was impossible because the dice were loaded against them, the way the story was told, the way the author took sides. And being children, you could not perceive this, you simply didn't want the adventurers to be harmed by the savages!

Jeyifo: That still happens by the way, as unfortunate as it may sound. Tarzan films and Kung Fu films . . .

Achebe: Yes, and on many different levels. I mean, I've heard a student, a third-year student, saying that if the whites (this is talking from the Christian angle), that if the missionaries had not come here, we would all be slaves still. I mean, you're right; it's not as if we've emancipated ourselves. Individuals can, of course, if they have the kind of exposure and intelligence that one should have in our situation. I think one can emancipate oneself and see that the story you are reading is written by somebody with a point of view, with a position. I think once you discover that, you are on your way.

So that's the kind of beginning I had. It's quite difficult to say, but I'm quite sure that by the time we were reading our set-books at Ibadan we were not as innocent as we had been in secondary school—just enjoying adventure stories. We were able to say: I don't think this is fair or right! I remember one of the brightest students in my class, Olumide, saying something to the effect that the only moment he enjoyed Joyce Cary's *Mister Johnson* was the moment when Johnson was shot! This horrified our English teacher. But you can see that we were beginning to struggle out of the position into which we had been placed. And if one exaggerated, that should be understood.

So I think it was at Ibadan that my feeling about literature, the vocation, began to form.

Jeyifo: There's also an element that—although one can say that your development, your beginnings, also marked a point of beginning for contemporary Nigerian literature, not in an absolute sense but in a relative sense—it also seems that, in your writings, one perceives there to be other beginnings too, in the sense that one sees that you show a certain sensibility, an awareness of oral resources, which you exploit and use a lot. How did this emerge? For instance, were you quite conscious of the story-telling art in the oral context?

Achebe: Oh yes, I was always fascinated by our traditional stories as a child. I was always fascinated by the stories of my people, always intrigued and fascinated by our festivals. You know, when there was a new dance, a new masquerade coming out, I would want to see it. Now we were not supposed to be eager to see all this, you know, as Christians. My father was a very staunch evangelist, he had taken the church and education, missionary education, to, oh, practically everywhere in our part of the country and on both sides of the Niger.

So we were very proper Christians; we were not supposed to be interested or excited by the things of the "heathens"! But I should say here that my father, who should have shown the example, showed sometimes he was ambivalent; he would be offended if a masquerade came out improperly set up. Now, you wouldn't think that he had any interest in whether a masquerade was properly done up or not. But it was later, after he had died, in fact only in the last couple of years, that I realised that before he became a Christian, he had been a sensational masquerader himself, and that the masquerade which he carried was so famous, for its agility and its dance . . .

Jeyifo: How was it that you only stumbled on this fact after he had died?

Achebe: Because he never told us! He never mentioned anything about that. But you see, it shows that, although he had turned his back on those things for whatever reason, he instinctively responded to good form, to the artistic element in our tradition. So it was that element, particularly the artistic element in our culture that attracted me; a good story, a good dance, a good piece of music, anything that was done well, won my respect.

And that was just an alternative to what the Christians were saying. I mean, I did not doubt the Christians' theology or anything like that; it seemed very obscure, but I didn't have any reason, at that stage anyway, to query it. But it seemed one reality, and another reality was that in the village.

Jeyifo: As all of this developed—well, you've done other things all along apart from writing—you were in the external service of the old NBC. Did you at any time consider writing as a full-time activity, as an option?

Achebe: Well, again, you see, I couldn't have because there were no precedents, really. Okay, Cyprian had written books, but he was a pharmacist, and then he came into broadcasting. And Tutuola was in the Labour Department and somebody, in fact, the Director-General of NBC, brought him in to give him a break, and he put him in the stores of NBC. Hence, writing was something you did in your spare time; it was not supposed to be a profession in that sense. It never occurred to me that you could earn a living from it. Indeed, it never occurred to me that you could make any money at all out of it. I was not very well informed about the American situation at that time where a few writers perhaps could become quite wealthy. That sort of thing didn't cross my mind. And even if it did, I wouldn't have had the confidence to launch myself into it. I enjoyed the other things I was doing as well. Broadcasting at that point was a very exciting thing to do. And I learnt a lot by handling scripts; I was involved with the spoken word programmes. I was never an announcer, I was a producer. So I learnt a lot. We did short stories, short talks, fifteen-minute talks, debates, current affairs, and so on. But the short story was really my special talent, and I encountered a lot of ideas just handling that, converting what is written on paper to what you can speak.

In a way that's pretty close to having to deal with dialogue in the novel. And even "tongue twisters"—there are things you don't think about until you put somebody on the air. I remember one day, (I think it was the man in charge of the Nigerian Ports Authority who wrote a very fine script) and when we started recording him, he got to a point where he just stopped! He just couldn't go on and the whole thing was ruined!

Jeyifo: Because it was a live broadcast?

Achebe: Yes. And, you see, what was down on the script was something like "six storied shed," you know, a lot of "s" piled up, and this was a thing which when you read with the eye you can't see it, but in reading aloud you are tied in knots, you can't say the word! So, the profession of a producer in radio was very useful to me, very useful.

Jeyifo: Also, at that point in time, although you didn't go on to become a full-time writer—I'm talking now of the early sixties to the mid-sixties— there began to emerge something of a community of writers and critics, all being part of the general intellectual class, the intelligentsia, but occupying a rather special place within this emergent national intelligentsia. And of course, with hindsight, one can see that writers have played a very crucial role in contemporary Nigerian history. Can you reminisce about this—your colleagues, the Mbari, *Black Orpheus,* a lot of activity . . .

Achebe: I think what was happening then was an indication that there was a certain ferment in the society. It was not just one person or two people, but something general, something in the air, something that had to do with the fact that we were about to become independent—I'm now talking of around 1958 when *Things Fall Apart* was published.

I actually wrote it while I was in Lagos. I started broadcasting in Lagos, then I was promoted Controller, Eastern Region, at the very young age of 28, because the whites were leaving in a hurry. So I went as Controller to Enugu and I was there when *Things Fall Apart* was published, and within two years, you know, we were independent and we wanted to set up our own international broadcasting, external broadcasting and all of the three Controllers, Badejo in Ibadan, Ladan, he's dead now . . .

Jeyifo: Umaru Ladan?

Achebe: Yes, that was his name; he was in the North, he was the most junior. Badejo was already moving to become Director-General, so I was made Director of External Broadcasting. I therefore went back to Lagos which was closer to the centre of activities in those days, the real "production centre" being Ibadan, the university, and Lagos being a sort of periphery. But there was a general atmosphere of optimism which was created by this independence which came in 1960.

Jeyifo: Almost a sense of a renaissance—apart from the *political* independence, also a *cultural* renaissance.

Achebe: Oh yes. We were rediscovering ourselves, we were about to take our lives into our own hands again. You see, we were going to take the initiative again in our history, because this is what colonialism and all that meant: a loss of initiative and you just have no say in who you were, your own self-development and all that. And there was this feeling that at long last all this was coming to an end and one was intoxicated and it produced this feeling of euphoria. We had a story to tell, we were a different people, we must tell this story, and we insist on being listened to.

Jeyifo: If I may generalise a little on your works, especially the earlier ones from this period, something strikes me immediately from what you say now, which would seem to be that there's a displacement somewhat in the sense that your works from that period—I'm thinking of *Things Fall Apart, No Longer at Ease, Arrow of God*—were not so optimistic! Maybe the sense of a new beginning shows in the energy of the writing—that is, in the sense of form—but in the themes you were exploring, you were not so optimistic.

Achebe: Well, this is a very interesting angle. I don't think I've ever had to answer it in this form! Okay, if you were so enthusiastic, why didn't you write enthusiastic novels? Well, I suspect that has to do with my own nature and character; but also I think it has to do with what I consider the proper role of art, you see. I think that art is an alternative in the imagination to the reality all around us. And I think all artists, whatever may be their particular strengths and weaknesses, are doing that. They are giving us something that is not already given, something which is not flying around the life of the community, the life of the individual, as they see it in reality, and something else which we see through the imagination, which mixes, interpenetrates the two realities. I think this is our role. I think this is what happens when there is *optimism*.

I think the writer must retreat instinctively into this kind of reserve. Because he knows, through his imagination, through his intelligence, that it can't all be that sweet. The writer instinctively says that this is very good, that we should be happy and gay and optimistic, but from this reserve which comes from all kinds of sources—your intelligence, your experience, other people's experience that you have absorbed—that something must be lurking, some danger must be lying in wait. I think this is one of our roles—we just don't get lost in the celebration, like everybody else, you see. The prophets come up when things are going very well and they start proclaiming doom! I think this is partly the answer to your question. This is our role, and I think it is proper too, to always call attention to it because humanity is not new; we've been around for ages, we've made the same mistakes over and over again. History is full of periods when we are carried away by optimism, and in reverse there are periods when we suffer great hardships and we are crushed morally, mentally and psychologically, and the writer comes up, an artist, somebody, and he holds up some hope of a greater tomorrow, whatever it is. And I think these things are essential for keeping a kind of even keel so that society doesn't lose its head in enjoyment or is not crushed in despair.

Jeyifo: Within that general pattern, critics on the left have pointed out something which may be an *Achebe dimension,* a personal dimension: that there is a pervasive sense of irony. You seem to be particularly sensitive and responsive to the unintended consequences in human affairs and history, a detachment from history. What do you say to this?

Achebe: I think this is part of my awareness of the complexity of reality. There is a dimension to things which I don't know exactly how to explain. And that's what you might call the unintended. I've used the phrase *"powers of event"* in the *Arrow of God,* when the *"powers of event"* achieve their own logic. For instance, you've already worked out things in considerable detail and you expect this to happen and that to happen, and then suddenly these things don't happen as you planned them. Something else, the unforeseen, chance, whatever it is, intervenes.

I don't think we should ignore this force or phenomenon, whatever it is, maybe providence. If you are religious, you will call it God. But there is that dimension over which you have no control. So I make allowance for that, because my view of reality is that it is at once simple and extremely complex.

Again, talking of this ambivalence of the writer, to simplify it by showing that this relates to that, this has happened before, this is like this, by even the use of metaphor one then begins to see that this complexity is actually not so terrifying.

If this has happened before, and our ancestors have coped with it, then there's no reason why we of this generation could not deal with it. So that's a kind of simplification. We are not then crushed; because if we are dealing with something you've never seen before, never heard of before—nobody has ever seen it—how do you begin to handle it? So, you simplify by metaphor and analogy. That's one rule.

Now, when something is too simple, on the other hand, it's the job of the writer to complicate it! Because it cannot be as simple as that. If it was, then there would be no problem in the world, but you see, a writer comes into the relationship and dredges up all kinds of frightening possibilities. And then what seems a simple thing is made not so simple. And it's the same artist even dealing with these realities. And I think this is the proper role of art.

Jeyifo: May I ask you a question which I've always wanted to ask you? I know it's always a little too bold to see a writer in terms of his fictional characters, but I personally have always wanted to ask if there is something of Achebe in Obierika in *Things Fall Apart?*

Achebe: Yes, that is very bold indeed! Well, the answer is yes, in the sense that at the crucial moment when things are happening, he represents this other alternative. This is a society in *Things Fall Apart* that believes in strength and manliness and the masculine ideals. Okonkwo accepts them, in a rather literal sense.

Jeyifo: And quite disastrously too.

Achebe: Yes, quite. Actually the culture "betrays" him. He is "betrayed" because he's doing exactly what the culture preaches. But, you see, the culture is devious and flexible, because if it wasn't, it wouldn't survive. The culture says you must be strong, you must be this and that, but when the moment comes for absolute strength, the culture says, "No, no, hold it!"

So, Okonkwo says, "Where is this coming from? I mean, you've said it's good to be strong, and so on!" The culture has to be ambivalent, so it immediately raises the virtues of the women, of love, of tenderness and so on, and holds up abominations. You cannot do this; even though the cultural norm says you must do it, you cannot. So you evade, you leave it for somebody else to do! Obierika is therefore more subtle and more in tune with the danger, the impending betrayal by the culture, and he's not likely to be crushed, because he holds something in reserve. You therefore find me more in him, than in Okonkwo. Although I think every character that a writer creates ultimately comes from himself, his experience, his own imagination, and therefore also represents some aspect of the writer, even if the writer says this part of me is something to avoid, to keep at a distance. Because we really have no facility for exploring what we don't know. It doesn't need to have happened to us physically but in the imagination.

Jeyifo: On the question of the imagination, you once gave a lecture in Ife,

a convocation lecture titled "The Truth of Fiction," in which you assigned to
literature something a little different from what you had said in other essays—for instance, in "The Novelist as Teacher." Here, you assigned to literature a conscientizing capability, a means to imaginatively project oneself
into a reality which is not immediately coincident with one's own situation.
Do you think this is adequate for the kind of society that Nigeria is now?

Achebe: Well, it has to be because I think our failure as a nation is a failure
of the imagination, if you think deeply about it. Whatever ills you care to
take up and explore, you would see that if our imagination was working
properly, our own self-interest would stop us from doing many of the things
we are perpetrating, such as injustice to other people. In the long run we are
digging our own graves. If we really could project into the skin of the beggar
under the bridge in Lagos, we would immediately start doing something to
bring about a just society. It is that lack of imagination which I think is at the
root of cruelty. One is cruel because one is not imaginative enough.

Now I see what you mean. How can we wait until every commissioner,
every politician, has become imaginative? No, I don't think we can wait, and
society doesn't have that kind of patience. If one still says what one wants to
say, or still does what one must do, it's not because we expect people to start
behaving like oneself or accept what one says. Even if they accept, they'll
say you are a man of the future, or something like that. But our imagination
is faulty. Now, we may never be allowed to correct our imagination before
we are overtaken by something else. This is the tragedy of it.

We may be so crass and cruel that the man on whose back we are sitting
will cut off our heads before we've had a chance to mend our ways. I'm not
holding for preventing that from happening at all. I'm merely saying that,
barring revolution—which I cannot say will come tomorrow or the day after,
I do not know—we still have an option to improve our situation, even if this
means that when the danger comes, it will not be so brutal, because they will
say we give you some credit for your goodwill. That's not impossible and
that's not to be underrated. I mean, it's rather like what was said by Malraux
in *Man's Fate*. There's one image which he uses there which I think is very
effective for me. There's a man who needs surgery; he is very ill, he's also
running a very high temperature. There is really no conflict between the nurse
who comes in and gives him aspirin to lower the temperature and the surgeon
who is getting ready for the surgery, you see. The surgery may be inevitable,
I don't know; but there's really no conflict, unless the nurse is saying aspirin
is all that is required.

Jeyifo: Yes, that is the crucial distinction, the crucial element which I wanted to indicate, because it does seem that if, as you say, a large part of the problem is a failure of the imagination, a large part of it is also due to *imaginative* exploitation of downright cynicism. There are a lot of very cynical people who control our lives and are very imaginative.

Achebe: Yes, yes. People's vile imagination.

Jeyifo: In fact, you do make a distinction in that essay, "The Truth of Fiction", between what you call malevolent fictions and beneficent fictions.

Achebe: Yes. You see, one is really talking in metaphors. You know, we are dealing now with areas we cannot really be absolutely sure about. We are now sinking into the subconscious and all that kind of thing. But it seems to me that a really imaginative person cannot be evil—a man in my view of the imagination, who can put himself in the shoes of his neighbour. I mean, this is what all the religions are teaching—that man is your brother; you are not of the same parents and all that, but you have to imagine, you have to bring your own imagination into play. As we say in our own languages, this is your mother's son, which is nearer than "brother." And once you've said that, you accept that it is very difficult to be the way you were before. So I think this is the area where art with its ameliorative, curative powers can operate.

Jeyifo: Moving to more specific areas of your total activities, you've also at various times, including now, been an editor. In fact, you are the editor of perhaps the most stable journal so far—*Okike,* and also you've been a publisher at different times. What I see in this, perhaps simplifying a lot and also generalising a lot, is an attempt to define yourself as an intellectual, an artist, in relation to an immediate audience. And this audience wasn't there when you started—an immediate audience, a community of letters. Do you have any reflections to offer on this, any opinions on this problem, which is really a vast one. You've also been the editorial adviser to Heinemann's African Writers Series.

Achebe: Yes, I think I can reflect, in the sense that a lot of what's happened here, a good part of it, has simply happened. Some of it I've then decided to promote. And I've been learning as I go along. Our society is a "new" one; writing of the kind we do is also new, as we were saying earlier on, and so one cannot come to it fully sure of all the answers.

Which is not to say that a writer's basic instincts are changing. No, I think a writer's basic instincts must be inviolate; there must be complete integrity there. So this is why when I hear writers say, "Before I used to do this; now I've seen that my ways are wrong," I feel that's too much like born-again

Christians! And I have great suspicion of people who have these instant conversions; I think there is something specious about it. I think the basic thing in the equipment of the writer, which is his integrity, is there from the beginning. He doesn't learn it half-way through his career. Your soul as an artist cannot be something which you are tinkering with along the way. You may say the emphasis has changed. It's really a matter of emphasis rather than of absolute distinctions.

Again we are talking of ambivalences. Things come in twos, nothing is absolute. It's the man of action, the politician, who is allowed to see things in their absoluteness. And he's usually quite wrong and dangerous. A writer must keep that reserve, recognizing that although this is true, but . . . That "but" is terribly important and while we are experiencing our contemporary history and so on, we are seeing mistakes—maybe not mistakes—wrong emphases or even emphases that become outdated, because things move very fast in our situation. I mean, the twenty-first century is almost sixteen years away and we are running like mad. So what was the right emphasis yesterday may not be quite right today, so we must be agile and flexible and imaginative. I'm not saying we should be different people from what we were yesterday. And one of the areas where this flexibility is called for, is in our relationships; how do we get to the people, to our audience, to our nation, to our country. If I was writing novels and I thought that, well, novels only reach a certain number of people after five years or something, it is quite permissible to say "well, what else is there to do which might get my voice across as quickly as possible?" It might be an essay, it might be a play on the stage, it might be radio or television or whatever; I think these are simply "dresses" you can change, "shoes" you can change. But your basic integrity demands that you don't lie about what you see; you shouldn't. You don't touch it up so that it looks acceptable because somebody else is saying so, because America is saying so, because Russia is saying so. You may be right or you may be wrong, but this is what you see. You may say what you see, but it's not for you to start monitoring and censoring what you see, maybe in keeping with what somebody else sees.

Jeyifo: One final question. You have been honoured as a writer, an artist, around the world. One particular honour, and this is a paradox, one that came late, relative to the others, was the Nigerian national honours, and even that was highly controversial. A few people thought that you should not have accepted the honour, since, in their view, the people who were giving the honour were not much different from Chief Nanga. How do you react to this? And if I may sum it all up: what is Nigeria to you? I sense that your acceptance of that honour had a lot to do with this question—what Nigeria is.

Achebe: That's a very important question and I am aware of the doubt expressed by people, especially by my colleagues in the writing profession. I should state that I did not feel that the moment somebody offers this and you say yes, there is a certain compromise. You don't accept with the right hand and slap the person with the left hand. But my view of this is really quite simple. I am a Nigerian. Nigeria, with all its faults, is the country where it pleased providence to put me. Now, I am not one of those who will say Nigeria is an absolute good, that even if Nigeria is cutting my throat, I should be singing the national anthem. That's not my kind of patriotism. But this is where I am. There was a time, as you know, when I was quite vocal in my condemnation, in fact my absolute rejection of Nigeria. That's one individual's action. Now, I do not then become a stateless United Nations citizen. Okay, I wanted to break out of Nigeria, not because I didn't like Nigeria, because I was always fond of this country. But the experience one went through at a particular period was so bad, that one really had to say no. That was not to be; so we reconciled ourselves with this experiment—it's still an experiment—called Nigeria. It is not a great country. In fact I've got a book which should be out in a short while, called *The Trouble with Nigeria.* I do not think Nigeria is a great country, contrary to what Shagari and others may be saying. It's not true, you see. I listed all kinds of things about Nigeria which in my view would make it one of the worst countries in the whole world, one of the least attractive places on earth. But it's my country and since, as I said, providence put me here, my role is to make this place more habitable than I met it. That's our role, that's the role of every generation, and that's what civilisation is about. I do not think that I have any right to move to America or Britain or France or the Soviet Union and then live there because those societies work better than mine. Because I know that those societies were created by human ingenuity, by human intelligence, by good leaders, by writers. So I have to deal with Nigeria.

Now one of the weaknesses of Nigeria is failure to accept merit and quality, in various areas—in the sciences, in the arts, in everything. Politics is all that matters here. If you seek the political kingdom, everything else will be added unto you.

Jeyifo: A failure to establish a criterion of achievement.

Achebe: Yes, we don't know it. So when, in a fit of absent-mindedness, or whatever, the Nigerian nation says we recognise your achievements as a writer and we give you a medal, I don't see that I should reject it. Not that I need that medal. In fact, it was Femi Osofisan who said I didn't need it. Of course, I didn't need it and this was all the more reason why I thought I could take it, because I really didn't need it. But for me, it meant that for the first time literature was being accorded a certain recognition. And while I was going to receive it, I was also writing a speech—this was before anybody else knew that this was going to happen—a speech in which I was going to say precisely this: that nobody is going to buy me with honours, and that I think that this will not be the end because we should have a situation in which national honours are given to writers, given to painters, given to sculptors, given to journalists.

What we have here—if you go round this campus, you'll find student hostels are named after politicians that you cannot remember one year after they leave office. Statues are raised to politicians the first year they are in office; universities are named after living politicians. Now, I think this kind of thing is wrong. And if we can change the emphasis ever so little by bringing in scientists and writers, we will be encouraging other scientists, other writers. Politics is not the only way. And I want a situation in which literature, as a matter of routine, becomes something which Nigerians talk about and recognise. Now if my accepting national honours will do anything in this connection I will be quite satisfied. There should be recognition of the arts in our political culture.

Achebe on Editing

G. D. Killam / 1984

From *World Literature Written in English,* 27, 1 (1987), 1–5. Reprinted by permission of *World Literature Written in English* and G. D. Killam.

Chinua Achebe held the Commonwealth Foundation Senior Visiting Practitioner Fellowship at the University of Guelph in 1984. This is a talk that he gave on the educational and literary uses of folk orature at a workshop sponsored by the Guelph-Yaoundé Project on Education for Self-Reliance.

I am glad we have this booklet to sink our teeth into because having something concrete before us is a great help; it saves us from excessive theorizing. Some of the points I had wanted to make earlier but didn't find an appropriate opening now seem easier with actual texts before us. The educational validity of material of this nature requires a lot of thought, and this is where I think what we were saying earlier about the role of the university is so very, very important because once we have the oral or written material before us, certain judgements must be made. The selection from a vast body of oral material is the first judgement and I want to say that from my experience it is not enough to be romantic about this. You know there are many romantics around and I have nothing against them. Like what we were saying in the morning, that some people would prefer a situation where there is no blackboard, nothing at all, in their school. Some people are simply excited by that kind of thing. But I am not because a blackboard is not only necessary but easy to come by. All you need do is rub part of the wall black and that becomes a blackboard. We shouldn't be trapped into the kind of thinking that says the more deprived we are or the more primitive a thing is, the better. My experience is that not all of oral literature is of acceptable quality. Now this would displease purists and some kinds of scholars. But we must decide in which of two ways we should approach oral material. We can come as anthropologists, take what there is and just freeze it. I don't deny that there could be a certain value even in that because sometimes you just want to know exactly what there is. But another way in which this material can be used is the way of the poet.

This is the dynamic way. It is not static. I'll give you another simple and silly example. Last year we were recording old traditional epic poetry from the Anambra flood basin of Igbo land. And one of the poets was describing how the hero cut down a mighty forest. This forest belonged to a god, which landed the hero in considerable difficulties we won't go into. But the size of this forest, the way it was described was startling. It stretched *from here to Lagos.* Now obviously that cannot be the tradition. The poet had changed whatever was there because he knew that putting it this way would make an impact of size on his particular, modern audience. In the past he would probably have said Idu, the name of the old kingdom of Benin. But now he could talk about Lagos which conveyed to his hearers the same notion of distance. I have myself attempted the same thing in some short stories, some children's stories, because it was always clear to me that in the oral tradition no two tellings of a story could be exactly the same. The important thing is not to deviate so radically that there will be problems of recognition. If you have ever told a child a story again and again, you will understand what I am driving at. A child will accept, even expect, variations and innovations every time. But if you try to change the nature of the story, he will not accept it, you see; he will say "That is not the story." But if you merely add a little twist, that is fine. I'm saying all this because I think that anybody working in oral tradition will encounter it, and the purists who will say, "This is the way the story is told, and why are you trying to change it?" And I think we should make up our minds what the answer should be.

Take the story about a king and his five wives which is in our booklet. Now this is not a good story and it's also in my opinion not good entertainment. It is not a good story because it is saying that four daughters are not as good as one son. There are many stories like that in our tradition, and I don't think that this kind of tale has a place in modern teaching, in the modern school situation anywhere. I feel very strongly about this. I feel we should be very careful about this because what you might be doing would be reinforcing elements of tradition which are no longer usable. And there are many, many such elements. We don't just say "Oh, this is in the tradition, so we must have it." I don't accept that. Some of our responsibility as teachers is to move civilization ahead, and I don't accept immutability as a necessary basis for our work. As it turns out, as I said, this story fails not only in content but also simply as a story.

I have used oral tradition in two kinds of stories. One is called "The Flute." Now this is the story of a child who forgets his flute in the farm. It is a fairly common story in Africa. When the child and his family reach home at dusk, he remembers his flute and wants to go back for it. But that is not permissible. You see, the world is divided. Spirits have their own time. We have our own time. You go to the farm in the daytime; in the night it is the turn of the spirits. So if you go there at night, you are breaking the law of jurisdictions and you can expect all kinds of problems. So when this boy wants to go to the distant farm at night, his parents beg him not to go. But still he goes. And so in one sense this is a story about disobedience. And true enough, the boy meets the spirits. All of this is in the tradition. What is not there is the king of the spirits saying to the boy: "Why did you disobey your parents?" Being a spirit, you see, he has seen far away right into the boy's home, before he came. So he says "What about your mother? Didn't she promise to buy you another flute on the next market? Why did you disobey your mother?" The boy looks down, he knows he is beaten, you see, he knows about disobedience. He rallies and says, "That flute, I made it myself; it is the only thing that I could call my own." Now I put that in, quite shamelessly, you see, because I think you require that kind of justification for disobedience. Children may not ask you, but it will be bothering them, you know, if you tell them, "You should obey your parents." Why is it that this boy didn't, and yet he is rewarded in the end? Now I insist the question should be asked. So the boy gives a good answer and the spirit says indulgently: "Well that is not good enough. But I like your spirits, I like your guts." So the point is made that obedience is still the rule, but courage is also important. And we make the point that the song which the boy makes about his flute lying out there all alone, in the cold, is another saving grace. And so, making things—a flute or a song—adds to build up the story, I think. And that way, the idea of making things, which I feel very strongly about, is injected into the story without destroying it. That is what Senghor was talking about, incidentally: that we have become a society of consumers. We don't make things. Making things is very important. Any chance one has to sneak it in, to smuggle in something about making, would be justified in terms of what our traditional culture intended art to do. Art was intended to be useful, to be entertaining, yes, but also to be doing something useful in the society.

The other story I did for children is called "The Drum." That again is from tradition, a traditional story about the doings of the tortoise during a time of great famine in the land of the animals. He goes in search of food; he's just wandering, miserably, and then he stumbles, by sheer accident, into the world of the spirits, and he is rewarded with a drum that produces food.

So the tortoise takes this home and beats it and feeds the animals. Now I decided to make a political story out of this, by making the tortoise want to use the power that he has over the other animals to attempt to become their king. And he is succeeding! One can see the kind of king tortoise would become from what is already happening, and the way he is carrying on. He sets up a committee for the coronation, and makes the biggest animal his drum major! The elephant beats the drum too heavily and breaks it. It is a very desperate situation. The tortoise tries to patch it up but it won't work. So he says to the animals: "Well, don't worry; after the coronation, I'll go back and get a new one." But the animals reply; "No drum, no coronation." So the tortoise is compelled to go on a second journey which is faked, and this is the whole point of the traditional story. Adventure, fine. Faked adventure, no. Because in faking it, all the things that happened by chance before are now contrived and false. I won't tell the whole story because I think you should read it. But to cut a short story shorter, the tortoise goes away from spirit-land lumbering a heavy drum which he discovers on his way does not dispense food but assorted punishments—masquerades that whip, bees and wasps that sting. The tortoise decides when he returns home that it is only fair that the animals should share his unhappy experience just as they had shared in his feasts. I don't think I have altered the meaning and flavour of the story. In my own estimation what I have done is to make it applicable to our situation today. And I believe that this is what the makers of these traditions intended to do—to tell stories that would be applicable to that day, and I believe these stories are evolving slowly through the millenia until our own time.

I am not talking here about the act of collecting the material in the field. I think the collection should not be tampered with at that stage. The people who collect should go ahead and collect. I am thinking of the work of the committee which produces the books—the final books. They are the ones who should worry about the kind of thing I have been talking about. Much of what they do may not raise this problem at all. But when it does, as in this thing about the king's five wives and the son being the only valuable child, I think that the committee must descend on it like a ton of bricks. But let me say once more, let's not inhibit the collection. I think that those who collect or bring in the material should go out and do it. Thereafter comes the editorial stage where the final decision on the literary quality, on the content, on the ideological—yes, even the ideological content of the story—is discussed. Incidentally we must be ready to plough through masses of collected material to discover a few nuggets of real quality. Well, out of this lot before us, apart from this play, the tortoise play, I don't really see any other which gets into the final stages of the book—not yet. That is masses and masses of material out of which a little at a time will be selected. And it is this gigantic process of distillation that is the role of the committee.

[Question from the floor.] I have difficulty with one aspect. You made a comment about adjusting to modern situations, and I realize that the role of the female of course has improved greatly over the past few years. However, what I have difficulty with is that you would deny a child this tale as it was, not recognizing that the tale, I would hope, would be used in conjunction and with guidance from someone else. Therefore it would be with an understanding that this is the way things *were* as opposed to denying it and denying the fact that woman was looked on as being inferior at one time.

[Answer.] Yes, that is a decision to take. But when you are dealing with this kind of situation (and you are not dealing with a *dearth* of stories, you are dealing with an abundance) I don't myself see the point of choosing a bad story simply because it is there. Unless there is some other compelling reason. If this story were so well told that we must use it but let us be aware of objections a, b, c, d, that would be a different matter. The point I'm making really is that if I were handling this, I would not use this particular story, because I'm not denying the children anything, and this is the way I bring up my own children: that I do not accept that a boy is superior to a girl. Therefore, telling them stories in their formative years in which this kind of tale is fostered seems to me to be wrong. I mean I don't give them poison, and then promptly administer an antidote.

Since I've been here I've seen two references to Africa on television. One of these was a large crowd of disgustingly dirty African children. Just masses and masses of them. The program is about birth control, you know? Now dirty children exist in Africa; that picture was taken somewhere. But it is also a fact that wherever Africa is mentioned in the West it is in connection with bad news. This is the image. Nothing good is happening there. So it is a question of selection. I think one should realize that you have a responsibility, in this kind of situation, that what you select can have an importance beyond the mere fact that it is true or false.

[Question.] I think what you're saying is that we have to select, we have to make conscious selections according to the aid of the needy one. Because I can see that for instance that story you were talking about, the girls and the boys and so on, that would be probably all right for someone who is more

mature and can see that difference between the past and the present, whereas for the children, in the modern context you want to portray an image that you would like to foster.

[Answer.] What society wishes to foster. This is what education is about. It entails an enormous responsibility. If your judgement is wrong, then that's too bad. But then, why are you sitting here around a table, deciding on stories? I mean isn't it because you are arrogant enough to think that you can safely take certain decisions for the benefit of children?

[Question.] I remember seeing in a book of stories where the government of Mozambique did a story just like the one we were just talking about, where the people had to play all kinds of tricks in order to survive. In that situation, like characters in a folktale, the people had to play around in order to survive the massive oppressional people, the colonialists, the Portuguese. In the end they give the moral of the story that . . .

[Answer.] Well let me warn you that these things behave like a two-edged knife. I am not here propounding that a government should issue short stories. What I am saying, as I address a group of poets and writers and educationists who should have no difficulty understanding how subtle this process has to be, is that you cannot lay down the law, which is what governments are good at. I think that this is something of the instinct. If you have a group sensitive enough to good writing, to good stories, to the needs of Cameroonian education, they will know what to do. We don't need to turn it over to a committee of inflexible idealogues to tell us what stories to use.

An Interview with Chinua Achebe

J. O. J. Nwachukwu-Agbada / 1985

From *Massachusetts Review,* 28 (1987), 273–85. Reprinted by permission of *Massachusetts Review.*

This interview took place in October 1985 in Chinua Achebe's office at the University of Nigeria in Nsukka, where he has been emeritus professor of African literature since 1983.

J.O.J.N.: Professor Achebe, do you have any grouse with the new evolving criticism in Nigerian literary circles which insists that art must be in the service of the Social Revolution, must be ideologically committed, that is. Considering that you had once condemned "art for art's sake" for the African creative writer, is this recent critical temper an extension of what you had always meant or a distortion of it?

   Achebe: It is a distortion! I think that what we have now is one form of extremism meant to counter an earlier extremism. I think it was an extremism to talk of "art for art's sake," which is simply to say that even if the world was falling into ruin, the artist should be carving his little piece of ivory, as Jane Austen would say. Certainly this kind of position is false because it is extreme. An artist in my view is always afraid of extremists; he is always afraid of those who claim to have found the ultimate solution to any question. Often an artist will find himself dancing to a different beat. A Black American writer once wrote a very good novel called *A Different Drummer,* showing that the artist is always drumming differently. Now if you criticize or condemn the extremism of the bourgeois society, which is satisfied to free art from social responsibility, and then move right across the spectrum to the other end, or with the pendulum to the other extreme, and say that no art is possible unless it is committed to something you define, this is also a fallacy. This is the situation I think you are referring to. In other words, one makes a certain valid point and carries it to the extreme. At this point it becomes not just false, it also becomes dangerous. I think artists invariably rebel against that. That is precisely why an artist will never get into any rigid association. Even if he is in such an association, you will find him saying things that are quite strange for that association. Let us leave politics and look at religion, says the Catholic Church, which is a fairly rigid ideological, intellectual system. If you take a writer like Graham Greene, who is a converted Roman Catholic, you will observe that he is all the time writing about bad priests. That is what an artist does. If he were to behave in the way these ideologues are suggesting, he would only be writing about the perfect priest because he believes in the church, and therefore must uphold the dignity and authority of the church. But the real, genuine artist will not do it. In the same way, if he gets into a political association he will observe that real life is not as simple as the scheme of life drawn up in political manifestos. Almost always he will find himself reflecting this. Anybody who is surprised by this does not know what an artist is or what his true function should be.

J.O.J.N.: I had to raise the question because anyone attending our literary conferences will observe an evolving coterie of critics who will insist with vehemence that every work be ideologically committed. Works that fall short of their criteria are immediately hammered and battered, sometimes with a somewhat caustic language . . .

Achebe: I know what you're talking about and where the people you're talking about are. Some of them are quite vocal and quite active. They don't worry me because I don't think they have anything of importance for me. But I am worried in another sense because there are people who may be misled. I think it is a fad, a fashion which will pass. It enjoys some stronghold in certain universities in this country and it sounds glamorous and full of fire but in the end it is sterile. What worries me is that some writers may be misled. I will give you one example. There was one short story written by Kole Omotoso which I once published in *Okike*. That was not a good story. I published it because it was an example of a story written to satisfy this new dogma. And Kole Omotoso, being within easy range of the pronouncements of this dogma, had begun to write to their prescriptions. This short story is a very good example of what can happen to a writer when he simplifies his vision in an effort to satisfy the one, two, three requirements of a rather narrow-minded dogmatic group. So all he can write is about women rising up against their oppressor who is a monster, and this monster is described as somebody with a skin disease, some mysterious person, and in the end he is murdered by these women who are seeking their freedom. Now that's no story. I rather suspect that Omotoso could have done a much better story if he was not attempting to use this particular story to demonstrate the idea of liberation, the idea of the wicked oppressor. I will say that the writer who wants to deal with this kind of situation will see many more sides to the oppressor than this. Indeed he will not be doing justice to his vision as an artist if he eliminates certain perspectives of the person in order to create something that will satisfy a rigid orthodoxy.

J.O.J.N.: Our experience of the 2nd Republic in Nigeria no doubt leaves the signal that the Nangas and the Josiahs are still very much around. Do you foresee a time when we will outgrow these aberrations in our march towards nationhood?

Achebe: No, I don't see a time when the problem of society will be a thing of the past, as our newspapers are very fond of telling us. I don't think we'll ever have a situation where we'll not have these problems. It is possible, however, to have a situation where the problems will be manageable. Corruption there always will be, but you do not have to have corruption on a scale in which the economy of a whole country is destroyed and the life of the people threatened. Actually threatened, not metaphorically. The situation then was so grave that people were actually dying because they could not get the attention they were entitled to; they could not get attention in hospitals because there were no drugs; they could not obtain clean water because everything was broken down, because the wealth of the nation had been looted. Now if you have that kind of situation it is a different order of reality from what I have just said about societies, namely that societies will always have aberrations. In our own experience corruption then was like an epidemic situation which needed drastic steps in order to get the disease controlled. There are some diseases one may perhaps succeed in wiping out, which is good enough. Corruption is different. However, the thing to do is for everybody to be on the alert, and to make sure that the life of the nation is not threatened at any point.

J.O.J.N.: Do you consider Chinweizu and his collaborators—who call themselves "bolekaja" critics—fair to all those they attacked in their seminal poetics?

Achebe: Well, I don't think they themselves would particularly describe their behavior as fair. I think they were trying to draw attention to certain issues in a rather violent way because they felt perhaps we had become too cozy, too comfortable in our ways. The trend was becoming alarming to them, and so they expressed themselves. Again, as we were saying earlier on, it seems like one extreme and its opposite. At the same time I do think that a lot of good came out of their position, although a lot of it is exaggerated, a lot of it is provocative. I thought one of the unkindest cuts was to label the entire thing "Hopkins Disease." Hopkins was a very, very good poet. I am fond of some of his poems, and I haven't seen too much "disease" in his poetry. I think they were too sweeping in their dismissal of Okigbo, for instance. But as I have said, their kind of position can generate a lot of discussion which can help an evolving artistic cultural tradition. I think we can survive it. Some people may be offended here and there, but if they want to defend themselves, they can. I think by and large it was a good thing for them to have subjected what we were doing to this kind of severe criticism.

J.O.J.N.: Now that we have even mentioned "poetics," do you think that it is still early to have a poetics of African literature?

Achebe: I can't say it is early or it is late. What is important is for anybody who wants to demonstrate it to ground himself or herself on existing work. If somebody can demonstrate to us—by focusing on what has been produced in the oral literature, in the modern, written literature—that there is a poetics, I think we will be glad to be informed. This is not my field. There are certainly people whose interest runs in this direction; after all, Janheinz Jahn came all the way from Frankfurt in the fifties and was bold enough to postulate theories as important as an African poetics in his *Muntu.* Even though we were inclined to be somewhat skeptical—even dismissed it here—I was surprised when I went to teach in the United States how popular, how useful the Black Americans seemed to find this *Muntu.* It seemed they were looking for a crystallization of the ideas of their blackness, and this German seemed to have filled the gap. Therefore one can never rule out the usefulness of such an exercise as writing a poetics of African literature. But this must be done by those who are inclined that way, who are qualified to do that kind of thing. The danger is to create a poetics which is based on somebody's wishful thinking rather than on the poetry of Africa.

J.O.J.N.: Do you intend to write more sociological books or will you expand the themes in *The Trouble with Nigeria,* especially as the appraisers of the work, while commending its vivacity and vision, have described its size as being too slim to have contained much of the trouble with this African country?

Achebe: The size of a book, in my own view, has absolutely no significance in relation to its importance. If a page can do what you want it to do, then why increase it to two? This book came out the way I wanted it, the size I wanted it, the form I wanted it. It's better than to give more than anybody wants, which many books do. The book is an interesting one because it has caused more unhappiness in some quarters in this country than some people would admit. There are areas where the book is taboo; even among fellow writers they would not mention it. They may quote from it without the proper acknowledgement usually due to a title and its author. A very good example was an Ibadan newspaper—either *Sketch* or *Tribune*—which once quoted and boxed what I said about Shagari [Shehu Shagari was Nigeria's civilian president from 1979–1983] in *The Trouble with Nigeria* on the right hand corner of its front page without informing its readers it was in a book of mine. The paper simply said "Achebe said" so that nobody will go and look for the book and find out whether I said more than just attacking Shagari. If somebody knew it was a book and picked it up, then he would have discovered that I said something about Papa Awolowo [Obafemi Awolowo was one of the Presidential candidates during Nigeria's presidential elections of 1979 and 1983] as well. Again, I once picked up the Silver Jubilee (1985) anniversary of Nigerian Independence edition of *Newswatch* magazine and saw an article on the literary scene written by one of our writers in which he was quoting what I said in *The Trouble* about Jim Nwobodo [Jim Nwobodo was the civilian governor of Anambra State of Nigeria from 1979–1983]. This time it was not an editor with a political axe to grind but a fellow writer. He couldn't have got this particular information from anywhere else but from *The Trouble,* where I wrote that Nwobodo's photographs appeared ten times in one issue of *Daily Star* newspaper. Now this writer found it necessary to use what I said but he didn't want to mention the book where I said it. So that book in spite of its size is almost sacrilegious to some people; it touched the untouchable, it desecrated sacred cows. So they will find one reason or the other for putting it down. Unfortunately for them, the readers don't think so; I mean they will find it and read it; it will sell as many copies as Fourth Dimension Publishers are able to produce, and when they are not able to do so, book pirates will help them. It's good it's done its job and is still doing it and I intend to do things like it. I don't do anything twice because it's working. There will be other ideas. But it shows that apart from creative writing, a writer can also turn his hand to direct social criticism or whatever catches his fancy and imagination.

J.O.J.N.: In *Morning Yet on Creation Day* you took exception to Ayi Kwei Armah's scatological representation of Ghana when you accused him of imposing "so much foreign metaphor" on his literary landscape. Now, in a situation where the artist has access to neither the soap-box nor the armoury, what is wrong with imagery of angst?

Achebe: Nothing really, at least theoretically. At the time I was saying that I cared very much for Ayi Kwei Armah as an upcoming writer, as a writer with possibilities. This was why I spent my time on him. But he was so bitter and took such exception to what I said that he's never taken kindly to anything coming from me ever since. I only met him once. It was a very strange meeting in the home of J. P. Clark in Lagos. Before that he had written me a number of absolutely unbelievable and abusive letters, which I did not bother to answer. This is a kind of background. Definitely I was not trying to put Ayi Kwei Armah down. I was simply hoping he would not distort the talent which I thought I saw by his imitating the style and bias of some other people, imposing on his art what I have called the "foreign metaphor." At that point, you know, the Western world was so anti-Nkrumah. And I saw in Armah's book a number of flaws, including a sneaking attack on Nkrumah. I don't think I need to say any more about that because Ghanaians today now know whether Nkrumah was the villain that the West was so anxious to make him out to be. Now they have married more than one husband, as the proverb goes, and so they can tell what is what. Meanwhile Ayi Kwei Armah has gone on, as I feared, using his talent in rather unproductive ways. I still think so, I still think that he has not used his talents appropriately. This is my view of his writing. For instance, his *Two Thousand Seasons*—in which he is trying to re-create the history of Africa—I find unacceptable on the basis of fact, and on the basis of art. The work is ponderous and heavy and wooden, almost embarrassing in its heaviness. It doesn't have the air of epic authenticity which Ouologuem achieves in his *Bound to Violence,* controversial as it is for other reasons. I object to *Bound to Violence* because of this image of Africa as "bound to violence," which I don't accept. Yet as a strategy for re-interpreting African history it is two thousand times more successful than Ayi Kwei Armah's. You can see that Ouologuem's book moves; it has an epic scope and movement. Ayi Kwei Armah's has his scope and no movement; it is like a lump of concrete sitting in a place. Altogether those writers whose works I think are not going to advance the cause of African literature I don't talk about, since it is a waste of time to do so. I thought Ayi Kwei Armah had potential but unfortunately he got himself completely confused.

J.O.J.N.: Unoka, Okonkwo, Isaac Nwoye Okonkwo and Obi Okonkwo— offshoots of the same genealogical tree—are failures in their various degrees.

Is their systematic non-success a reflection of an aspect of Igbo world view on family inheritance or anything of the sort?

Achebe: We had been talking about poetics . . . I mean this is one area where you certainly can make your suggestions. I wasn't thinking about that. No. No, I wasn't thinking of that. Although, mark you, the cyclic idea, the cyclic metaphor in Igbo thought is never very far from one's mind if one is reared in the Igbo culture. The cyclic thought is that if something happened before, it will happen again; if one dies, one will return. If there's reincarnation and the grandfather comes back in the grandson, then you're likely to have certain events also, certain tendencies happening again and again. The world is not linear in the sense of wandering away in a straight trajectory; it is cyclic. Certainly such an interpretation in the works is possible, but really I wasn't consciously attempting to draw attention to that particular view of the world. However, it's something I'm aware of, something which may have come up subconsciously, if you like, in one's consideration of our history, of our events. But now I thought you were going to ask about my insisting that we as a nation fail! I've heard some people now say that I am responsible for our lack of success because I've always written about people who failed. Of all the superficial comments that one can make of literature I think that one is one of the most startling. It is saying that if you have heroes who are unsuccessful, then you are saying that there is no hope for the rest of us, that we are bound to that failure. And as I said, this is a new direction of criticism, and I've encountered it quite often lately. A reverend somebody from the North, I think from Abuja . . . Kuka, yes, Kuka is his name, has recently asserted that we are responsible for not giving Nigeria heroes. What a childish way to read a work of literature! What these critics are saying is that if I show you a tragedy, you're compelled immediately to repeat that tragedy. That's nonsense. If anything, if there were any kind of direct relationship in that way—I wish there were—if there were, then what it should really be doing is to caution you . . . yes, to warn you *away* from that tragedy. I don't see why it should lead you into it with your eyes wide open, opened by my cautionary tale. So even on the basis of fairly simple straightforward logic I don't think the inference holds. But there is a deeper psychological level at which it is absolute nonsense. If you go into the nature of reading and readers' response, which more and more people are now relating to psychoanalysis, you'll find that a lot of benefit can accrue to a perceptive reader from his reading somebody else's tragedy. Definitely some reformation of a kind can take place in one as a result of that experience. It's a kind of short-cut away from that experience in real life. The book makes it quicker and less painful and less time-consuming because one can go through a book in a period of days or even hours if one is a fast reader. On the other hand, a person who is left to encounter a similar experience in everyday life may require the rest of his life to be able to do so without, perhaps, having the opportunity to amend his life. So I think even that kind of criticism is really too naive for us to use.

J.O.J.N.: Professor Achebe, I'm afraid this is going to be a long one. I mean the next question. It has to do with the somewhat ambivalent presentation of Ezeulu in *Arrow of God*. At a point Ezeulu wants to deal with his people for letting him down but afterwards relents, especially after Ofoka's fearless and sincere remarks on the confusion of the elders of Umuaro. And at another point Ulu scolds his priest for coming between him and his enemies. At this stage one wants to exonerate the Chief Priest from any imminent mishap that might befall the people. Sir, is the portrayal of the chief character's terminal predicament aimed at showing that the Igbo pantheon is aimless and lacks poetic justice, or is it occasioned by the need to depict Ezeulu's inheritance of insanity, and perhaps further show that the "Ta! Nwanu" cry which the Chief Priest said he heard his god scream is after all mere hallucination?

Achebe: That's a long one indeed. Well, the book contains all the possibilities you are suggesting. I don't think that one should aim to read a character like Ezeulu in a simplistic manner. As an observer of society, I've always said that life and history are very complex. What we try to do when we encapsulate, perhaps, is merely to help us in our understanding of life; it is not to delude us into thinking that this is the final answer. I am fully convinced that Igbo tradition was very sophisticated in its appreciation of this complexity of life. It was in fact the Western, the Christian tradition which was more simplistic, more naive than what the Igbo were already practicing. The Igbo were practicing a complex view of the world which accepted diversity, which accepted the multiplicity of things, of gods even. For them, if the white man comes, well, he must have his own god just as they have their own. But the white man came, claiming to be the way, the light, the truth: nothing else works except him. Now this kind of thinking, this kind of simplicity and self-righteousness, wherever it is emanating from, is dangerous because it is one of the basic causes of distress to mankind today. Therefore, then, having accepted the complexity of reality, to attempt to interpret Ezeulu in a simplistic manner is bound to be problematic. My response to such questions as Oh, was he faking this situation? Was he really a victim of his god? Was he a victim of history? Was he taking revenge against his people?—is that he was doing all of these things. But in addition to that he was a very, very dedicated priest. He believed in his priesthood; he was not going to overthrow it in order to be considered advanced or in order to make things convenient for anybody. This is the whole point of being a priest. He swore to uphold his priesthood, its rites and rituals. And so for someone to come and tell him go and eat those yams because time is running out and so on is unrealistic. No priest worth his name will do that. In any religion the one who will do it is not really a priest. It is the kind of Moslem who will eat pork in order to avoid an argument! In short, not a proper priest or a genuine Moslem. This is the problem. There were too many things, too many possibilities going on in Umuaro at that time. Some people were exploiting the situation. And it was not Ezeulu's fault. True enough he was arrogant and obstinate, but that's how he was; that's how his grandfather was and yet his grandfather didn't face these problems. Ezeulu was caught at a time in history perhaps when it was inevitable that the Chief Priest of Ulu should be sacrificed so that his people could move into the modern world. There was a very, very perceptive critic of this book, an old lady—she's in her seventies now—an emeritus Professor of English at the University of Missouri, who saw Ezeulu's predicament in terms of the God of Isaiah, the God of the universe, taking over finally from the god of Ezeulu. In other words, it is not something which one should see in terms of Umuaro alone; it is something one ought to see in terms of the whole movement of world history. This is the point on which Europe was impinging on Africa beyond trade and politics. These were sacrifices which Africa was called upon to make, not in the sense of throwing out an excess baggage. In fact the sacrifices may have been the best things in the tradition, and yet Africa was called upon to make them. However, the problem that will come out of all these will be for Ezeulu's descendants to sort out. As far as he was concerned he stood his ground as much as he could and fought a good fight. Certainly we cannot impose our own facile, compromised judgments on him. So I think the importance of his stance is what we should be considering.

J.O.J.N.: Professor Obiechina, in an article entitled, "The Human Dimension of History in *Arrow of God*," contradicts Nwaka's position in the novel that "Igbo people knew no kings." He rests his argument on the works of

Jones, Nzimiro and Henderson on the Igbo country. Professor Ifemesia, another fellow Ogidi man, shares a view similar to Obiechina's. Would you want us to regard Nwaka's utterance as mere fictive ejaculation or are we to accept it as a faithful thesis on Igbo people?

Achebe: Again, as I was saying before, there are two views of the Igbo: do they have kings or do they not have kings? The answer is both. What I have to say in relation to this is completely outrageous because it is based on nothing at all except reading between the lines, and that is that the Igbo had kings before and had a bad experience somewhere along the line of their history and decided they were either not going to have kings again in the future or they were going to limit their powers severely. This is the only interpretation that seems to me to square with all the facts, because the Igbo have the name all right. This is one of Ifemesia's theses. *Eze, nze, ozo*—all these "Z" words have to do with nzele, title. They are obviously very old words; they are not like words borrowed yesterday. For sure, we have the name and we have kings appearing in our folk stories, in our legends and so on. Yet at the same time, when the Igbo were meeting with Europe, there were no kings in a vast majority of Igbo communities, at least not in the sense in which the word is understood elsewhere. Now the Igbo themselves say "Igbo enwegh eze" [The Igbo have no kings] as a proverb. Why do they say it? It must be because they know what "king" is and don't like it. A man like Nwaka can use a proverb like this to advance his position. At the same time somebody who wants to make himself a king in Igboland might say, as a certain professor once said at the crowning of his village king, that "Igbo enwegh eze" does not mean that "Igbo ama enwe eze" [The Igbo must never have kings]. In other words, that the Igbo don't have kings does not mean that they didn't have them. So it's all a matter of flexibility. If the Igbo want to have kings, they are obviously entitled to have them. We can only say that at the time we are talking about in *Arrow of God* most Igbo communities, with the exception of places like Onitsha, Oguta and the Igbo across the Niger, and perhaps a few other communities, had little or no place for kings.

J.O.J.N.: Finally, if you won the Nobel Prize for Literature, would it vitiate whatever misgivings you must have nurtured about the politics of the West, especially your criticism of what you once described as her "defect of self-centeredness?"

Achebe: Not at all. No, not at all. I don't think my views are negotiable. Many years ago I was in Stockholm along with some other writers. I think it

was to honour a Nobel Prize winner then, Heinrich Böll, a West German
writer who died in 1984. During a discussion with an audience, one of the
most powerful members of the Swedish Academy which normally picks the
winners said something which annoyed me and I told him off. And people
came to me later on and said the man was very powerful, that he was one of
those who decided on who won the prize. And I said, so what? As a matter
of fact, what I was saying about the West is in the interest of the West, in the
interest of the world. People have come to me in different parts of the world
and said, "Isn't it marvelous that we are reading your books here? I mean
you must be feeling very good about it." And I have replied that I don't feel
anything about it; I think rather that *you* should feel good that *you* have the
opportunity to read my books. I remember someone saying, "Aren't you
arrogant?" Maybe I am. I still insist that a Westerner reading my books is not
doing *me* a favour; he is instead doing himself a favor, widening his scope,
his awareness, his understanding of the world. I mean how can that be a
favour to me? It's not. So I think the West has got to learn that. They are not
going to learn it in a hurry because we are not even helping matters. I mean
we dash back and forth, between here and the U.S., Britain, France and so
on. We want to be recognized by them. And recognition by them carries a lot
of advantages which are tempting. But for me what we have to do is clear:
we have to stick to our vision, no matter what. As a matter of fact our vision
of the world, our vision of what is important, is not what is important to, say,
an American. Americans think that what is important to you is not important.
Therefore, the thing for us to do is to stick to our priorities. Unfortunately
there are too many writers and spokesmen acting against such a position. I
have mentioned Naipaul again and again and I'll mention him again here as
the case of a brilliant writer who sold himself to the West. And one day he'll
be "rewarded" with maybe a Nobel Prize or something. Meanwhile he is
getting a lot of attention. But I don't think I can get into that kind of act.

Interview with Chinua Achebe

Jane Wilkinson / 1987

From *Africa America Asia Australia* (Rome), 4 (1988), 69–82. Reprinted by permission of *Africa America Asia Australia* and Jane Wilkinson.

This interview was carried out shortly after the launching of Achebe's latest novel, London, 17 September 1987.

You said recently that the label "The Novelist as Teacher" has haunted you ever since you used it as the title of an essay in 1965. At the launching of *Anthills of the Savannah,* you seemed to be encouraging listeners to look upon the novelist rather as an explorer, or perhaps as a teacher who can be seen as an explorer. Could you enlarge on this?

You are right. I don't think I was completely aware how narrow people can be in their view of the teacher! I was never really thinking of the teacher in a narrow sense at all. I was thinking of the teacher in the sense of the great teachers, like Jesus Christ or Mohammed, Buddha or Plato. These were the people I had in mind, not some little fellow who is really oppressed by life and can't find any other job except to stand in front of people and punish them. This seems to me to be the problem. As there is this tendency to think in categories, perhaps I should have used some different kind of person rather than a teacher. Anyhow, I was not thinking of the kind of teacher who prescribes. A good teacher never prescribes; he *draws out.* Education is a drawing out of what is there, leading out, helping the pupil to discover . . . to explore.

The kind of relationship you want with your reader is presumably a very active one.

Yes, we are interacting: the teacher is learning from his pupils at the same time, so that he can sharpen his tools. I like your use of the explorer image, that's really what it is.

You seem in all five novels to be exploring the roles, responsibilities and limits of intellectuals in Africa. In *Things Fall Apart* there is a distinction between the man of action and the intellectual—Okonkwo and

his father—but the distinction tends to blur in your later novels, where the problem is rather how the two figures—the man of action and the artist/intellectual/creator—can combine.

That is a continuing problem. Even when I am not dealing with it specifically, it is always there. It is the man of action who is always at centre-stage: the political leader, or the priest who is also a political leader, the Minister, the Minister of Culture, these are all men of action. The way society is organized, they are the ones who make things *happen.* All we are saying really is that they should *listen,* they should listen to the voice of the artist even when the artist is not visible, for what he stands for. The artists are the other side of the truth, the side of gentleness where there is too much violence, humaneness where there is too much concentration on efficiency or strength, the voice of the mother who cares for life continuing. This side must not be suppressed. This is what I was really saying. But it was not clearly brought out again until *Anthills,* where I have an actual character who is an artist, maybe because I felt that what I was doing, leaving the voice of the artist hanging in the air, was not enough and that there should be somebody labelled 'artist' to take part in the action of the novel. I didn't think of it like this, but now that you raise the point I'm trying to understand what may have been going on in my mind.

These two roles, these two views of the world, are very much at the centre of my thinking: action and reflection. It is these two working together that can save the situation. In Ezeulu I tried to combine the two in one person. It had its interest, but it did not solve the problem. It's something I have to keep coming back to again and again, because it will never be really resolved. These are the two polarities of our reality and we must expect them sometimes even to be at loggerheads. There is certainly a lot of this conflict in the contemporary African situation, the artist and the regime, and this is a manifestation of the same thing. If we can create this consciousness that the two need to work out a way of surviving side by side, as I think our traditional societies tried to do, we would really be much better off.

This leads to the problem of commitment and "Non-Commitment," the title of one of your poems. Here you suggest that "wisdom" and "sensibleness" may be a bar to sight, a "diaphragm" against what you call "seminal rage." How do you view commitment as a writer?

It is at the root of the writer's being: his commitment to his vision of the world, to truth as he understands it, including the truth of fiction, which is a slightly different kind of truth from the truth you encounter when you are buying and selling; the commitment to the integrity of language, commitment to excellence in the use of your talent so that you don't tolerate from yourself, in your work, something that you know can be done better by a little more attention, by waiting, by some more patience. So it is commitment over a wide scope of things really. The writer, any artist, who defaults in this is betraying the nature of art. This is why it is so difficult for me to accept legislation from some kinds of people who cannot see the world in its complexity: the fanatics of all kinds, of right or left, the fundamentalists of all kinds. These people do not understand, they cannot possibly understand, the kind of commitment I'm talking about. They use the word "commitment" more frequently than artists do and they use it so frequently that the word has become debased and is now in the service of fanaticism. That is not what I had in mind. It is not what I mean by commitment: not commitment to a narrow definition of the world, to a narrow perception of reality, to a narrow view of politics or economics or anything, religion, race. One can become committed to any of these things, but that's not what I'm talking about. I'm talking about something quite different. When you are committed to your art, you are very different from the man who is committed, say, to his religion. I cannot see an artist being a fanatical person in terms of religion; it seems to me to be quite contradictory. You may have artists who are good churchmen, but if they are really good artists, you will soon discover that they cannot be fanatical in their religion. The same goes for politics. What they are committed to is bigger, something of infinitely greater value than what church you go to, what race you belong to, what language you speak.

There is a strong focus on the problem of communication in your books and on the possibilities and limits of language. You yourself use a very wide register of language, probably also because you are reflecting a multilingual situation. Could you discuss this?

The integrity I was talking about is also reflected in one's ability to listen, very carefully, to all these registers. If I'm going to explore a certain kind of character, I must *listen* to this character. Before I can understand how his or her mind operates I must also know how he or she uses words. This is the first and most obvious level of judging whether I am truly looking at this character or not: I must know what they sound like. I must know *how* they speak language. It's not simply a matter of making the novel sound like real life; it is really part of a wider integrity. This character deserves to be listened to seriously, so that when I introduce what he's saying, I'm doing this with integrity and you can recognize him through the way he uses language. Of course, if you have the kind of linguistic richness that we have in a place like Nigeria, it's an advantage to the writer. But you've got to learn to listen. Not everybody has learnt to listen; we all live in the same linguistic environment, but some writers bring their dialogue from I don't know where. This dialogue must come from the source, from the people. This is part of commitment to the people: I think it was Danquah who said we must pay one another's gods the compliment of calling them by their proper names. It is very, very important that you give people the respect that is due them by presenting them properly, not through some kind of travesty, jazzing it up to make it sound nice or because this is what is expected. Somebody was just telling me about a book written by an Englishman living in Lagos, where the Pidgin is a sort of *Uncle Tom's Cabin* dialect, rather than the real Nigerian Pidgin, which is a language in itself, not something you can just cook up. There are some people who are not bothering to listen, who are just using what you might call the "packaged" Pidgin: the "I love Massah too much" kind of thing, but that's not what people actually say. So the beginning of this kind of integrity and commitment is that we must listen carefully and learn how people speak and convey it carefully.

The style and structure of your two poems to Christopher Okigbo— one in Igbo and another, "Mango Seedling," in English—differ considerably. When you write poetry in Igbo do you tend to reproduce the traditional structures?

Sometimes. The Igbo poem on Christopher Okigbo is actually structured on a traditional dirge format, the song that people sing when one of their age-grade dies. The age-group goes around chanting. They don't accept that he is dead yet, so they are looking for him, wondering whether he has gone to the stream, or to the forest. It is a very old song, no doubt, and it's that form that I use in the Igbo poem, expanding it and asking more questions than the traditional song would ask.

In a 1970 interview at the University of Texas at Austin you explained that you were unwilling to write another novel because you were "not at ease." You felt that the novel was not appropriate for "creating in the context of our struggle." Judging by your essay in *The Trouble with Nigeria,* the past few years have been just as uneasy. Now, twenty years after

your last novel, you have published a new one. Is this made possible by a change in your view of the genre?

I've tried to answer this question a number of times already, but without complete satisfaction. I don't really know, as a matter of fact, why it is only now that I have succeeded in bringing the novel to fruition. I started writing it about fifteen years ago and put it away completely. When I picked it up again about five years ago, I had to read it carefully to see who and what were there and it still didn't advance at all, so I had to put it away again, thinking perhaps it was for good. I had the characters, these four people, who were there, but I hadn't got anything I considered adequate for them to do. But three years ago—I don't fully know why three years ago it was different—I picked the thing up again and reread it in order to get acquainted once more with the characters, and the story seemed to be there this time. So it is possible that I don't fully understand; perhaps the fact that I had rested and thought about our condition and written a rather angry essay about this, *The Trouble With Nigeria,* perhaps all that helped to ease the passage of the new story.

Do you see *Anthills* as being more related to your previous novels or to your other post-war writing?

I think they are all related. What I am trying to do is look at the story of Africa in the modern world, looking at it from different angles, according to what's happening at the time, according to what I've just been through, according to what I have just learned, or even just to be different from the way I looked at it previously. It's like the masquerade I talked about in *Arrow of God,* which is dancing. If you see the story of Africa in the modern age as that masquerade, you just have to keep circling the arena in order to catch the various glimpses which you need in order to approach anything like a complete image of its formidable presence. If you stand in one place, you see one view, and it's not enough. That's what I try to do: even the essays, even the poetry. I think they all come from the same concern, to tell as complete a story as possible. And of course our situation itself is not standing still; it's adding to itself all the time—and subtracting from it! The Civil War, for example, was not there, it had not happened, when I wrote the first four novels. Now it's a melancholy part of this dance, so what comes after it is going to be informed in one way or another by this tragedy. I'm not quite sure that I can say "This thing in this book has been caused by this specific experience," but I have had to assimilate the Civil War experience, and so it must be there, in this new book, which is the first since that horrendous event. So in a way perhaps it's going to be the first of a new generation of books.

***Anthills* seems to differ from your previous novels, which alternate between past and present, or in which past and present interrelate, in that it projects more explicitly into the future. Do you agree with this?**

Yes, I think it does, in the sense that it ends specifically with the birth of a new generation and with the possibility of some of the survivors picking up something from the wreck of their recent past that may help them as they make their way into the future. One of such gains being their awareness of the totality of the community as opposed to an elite sitting up there and not even knowing the names of the people they were dealing with or where they lived. Again, the same plea to respect the integrity of your fellows; to accord to everybody the respect that is due to them as people. They may be only labourers or taxi-drivers, but they are full people; they have total humanity which is no less than that of anybody else and has to be accorded full respect. The Igbo people say that when you appear in a crowd the greeting that you give is "Everybody and his own," because you can't go round shaking hands with 400 people or call each of them by his title; that would be impossible, so you say: "Everybody and his own," or "To every man his due." I think this is a new lesson that is insinuating itself into the consciousness of the survivors of *Anthills*. Beatrice particularly is aware of this and she is also aware that it is something new, something that even Chris did not know, or was just beginning to know at the moment of his death. So this is something that points to the possibility of better performance, to put it crudely, if they should have another chance. Now that kind of thought was actually present in my mind in *A Man of the People,* but I didn't dwell on it specifically. I just left it to my readers' imagination to understand, for instance, that if Odili were to have another chance to go through the same experience, he would do rather better, would be a better person than he was before. But clearly I seem to have once again overestimated the imagination some readers can bring to fiction!

Perhaps your irony in presenting the character was over-successful. The reader tends to view Odili as an unreliable narrator.

One thing that he wasn't unreliable about was his own feelings, and that saves him as a human being, as somebody who puts his own feelings under the microscope and analyses them honestly, seeing where he's behaving badly and so on. I think such a person is worthy of respect. Anyway, that was certainly in my mind there. But you are right, there's a more specific overtone in *Anthills* of what would happen in the future if the right lessons are learned. There's always a big "if," of course.

What about the youngest member of the new generation, the newly born baby, the girl who is given a boy's name?

Well, it's really a name that could belong to anybody. The fact that it was appropriated by men in the past was an indication of one of the flaws in the society. Amaechina is a real name and the implication of the "path," "May-the-path-never-close," is really that it is only a boy who can keep the family homestead alive, and the path they are talking about is the path that leads to the family's compound. Girls don't count because they go out, they marry elsewhere. It is only the boy who stays in the compound. If there is no boy, then the compound closes. This is why if you find a family that is having difficulty having a male issue, but finally succeeds, they are likely to call him Amaechina: their hope of immortality hangs on this one person. This is a masculine view of the world, so that to suggest that a girl can have this kind of name is of course saying that this arrangement in which only boys count in terms of maintaining the name of the family is really out-dated, because the family can survive also through the women. So it's more than just a name, it becomes something more complex than "My name is *A* so that if I have a son he will answer *A,* and *A* will always be answered by someone." It's something more important than that mechanical succession and survival through a specific name. It's something bigger. Even if Shakespeare didn't have children, he still survives as a name. That kind of awareness is important for people who are trapped in this notion that you are finished if you don't have a son, that your line will come to an end and you will come to nothing. It was very much the thinking in the past, not only in Africa but in Europe as well, certainly among the kings; if they didn't have a son, they would put away or even kill off their wife, or something! This is all a narrow view of survival, which the naming ceremony in *Anthills* is challenging and calling into question. The fact that the old man accepts it without too much difficulty is a very encouraging sign.

You've mentioned "surviving" several times. This is connected with the title of your novel as well, isn't it?

Well, it's simply that there is a proverb, or rather a saying (the word "prov-erb" does not quite cover all the oral sayings that we have in Igbo). The saying which I'm using for my title is really an observation of what happens after the dry season in the grasslands. Generally the grasslands tend to be burnt down during the dry season, before the next rains. Everything is burnt down and the only things that cannot be burnt are these structures of earth made by termites. If you go to the savannah country, after a fire you will see that this is really all that's left standing, these very interesting structures. So the people say these are the remnants, these are the survivors. When the rains come, the new grasses will grow—there's no problem there—but will they have a memory? There's no way they can know about the fire of last year because they were not there and they're likely to think that the world began with them, that the world is always green. So they need these experienced structures of indestructible earth that are standing in their midst and are very soon to be dwarfed, in fact, by the grass, which soon grows taller than they, but which are there as a memory: they know, they remember, and they will be there again when there is another fire and all the present grass is burnt. It's a very concise statement when it is said in Igbo, an effective image drawn from exact observation. You see, our people are very observant about nature, and all these proverbs, quite apart from how you can apply them as a metaphor and so on, are also very exact, actual observations of what goes on in nature and in society. This is what gives them their power, because they operate at different levels.

The setting of *Anthills* is an imaginary African country called Kangan, with its capital, Bassa, and a rebellious drought-stricken northern region, Abazon. But there are also many references to Nigeria, which the non-Nigerian reader may not be able to appreciate. Would you like to explain this double level?

Well, it is inevitable, it always happens. If the writer is using his own knowledge and experience, he is then located somewhere in space and time and the other people who occupy contiguous positions will see more than others further afield. But an important thing about stories is that they are also not *locked* in any particular place and time; a good writer tries to ensure this. This is one reason why I decided not to call the country Nigeria. I wanted it to have this possibility of application elsewhere, apart from wanting to avoid the possibility that someone will say "Oh, this is me here, this is my brother" or something like that, to give the story this air which a good story has of being anywhere. You actually lift it out of wherever it is and put it where it can stand for many things. This in itself becomes a metaphor on a big scale, not just for one country but for a whole continent. Having done that, I decided it wasn't perhaps necessary even to insist that everything here must be fictional. There are certain things which we now know which are common knowledge, certain names of real people, which I have deliberately left in: people like Nkrumah, Mazrui, names of Nigerian singers. It seemed to me that there is a value in doing that, making it both out there in space but also attached to events and people that the reader might recognize. If the reader doesn't know that there is somebody called Mazrui, it doesn't really matter very much, but if he does it adds to his understanding, I hope.

Is there any relationship between Beatrice and other female characters in previous novels, such as Eunice in _A Man of the People?_ Could you explain why you give Beatrice a double identity and why the relationship to the goddess Idemili?

Well, the Eunice connection you raise is interesting. I didn't think of it. What it means is that I have really been worried about the woman's role for some time, although I didn't have that scope for it in _A Man of the People._

There is an ambivalence to women in traditional society. There is a respect, a very deep respect, which is implied in such names as "Mother-is-supreme," which is quite a common name, and in certain customs like the burial of a woman: she has to be taken back and buried with her people, because in her husband's place she may just be treated like an outsider, but when she dies she must be taken back, because she belongs to her father's people, she is just like the men. So there are these attitudes that suggest that there are two streams in the minds of our people: one in which women are really oppressed and given very low status and one in which they are given very high honour, sometimes even greater honour than men, at least if not in fact, in language and metaphor. I think this suggests that in this situation the role of the woman has not yet been fully worked out, that we are still ambivalent about it. And then we find the situation where in actual life the men fail politically and the women are called upon to take over the running of things. We see that in the Senegalese filmmaker, Sembene Ousmane: there is a film in which this happens, in which the men give up the struggle against France and leave their spears where they staged their last dance and go away in disgrace and ignominy, and the women then arrive on the scene, take up the spears, have their own dance and take over the running of affairs. This is a very, very powerful metaphor. Now in real life, in my own society, there was a case where the women took over. It was when the British first came and began to tax the population. The men surrendered and allowed themselves to be taxed like slaves, but the women said no and came and took over and really caused the downfall of the system of colonial administration: the British had to think again. So I think we have this in our metaphors, in the names we call people and also in actual life, where situations can arise in which women are not the underdogs but can take over the affairs of society. I think we must re-examine this situation and find a way in which the modern woman in Africa will have a role which is not just something we refer to once in a while, but brings her talents and her special gifts to the running of affairs. This is one of the things that I was tentatively exploring in *Anthills*. I think that one of the ways we can do this is to allow the women to speak on this issue. It's not enough for men to work out what women should do now. I think women should organize themselves to speak, from a real understanding of our situation and not just from a copying of European fashions, women's lib and things like that, but out of our own traditions to work out a new role for themselves. This is the challenge I throw both to the men and to the women, but particularly to the women.

You say that Beatrice does not actually know the legends but that she has an inheritance. Is Idemili a very well-known figure in Nigeria?

In my own part of Igboland, yes. She is the daughter of God and there is a river of that name—Idemili—from which my local government area is named. It goes back to the idea that the Almighty has a daughter.

Is the legend also behind some of the imagery connected with Beatrice, the water imagery, for example?

Yes, "Idemili" actually means the "pillar of water," literally. The source of Idemili River is a lake. It runs through a territory throughout which the python is held sacred, and flows into the River Niger.

At the end of the novel you refer to Mazisi Kunene's epic poem *Emperor Shaka the Great* and to Shaka's "smiling" and "beautiful" death. Were you also thinking of how Kunene's "Palm Race" sing of how Shaka's children shall "rise, scatter the dust of our enemies and make our earth free for the Palm Race"?

Well, I was trying to invoke that particular incident and other incidents like it in our literature and also to suggest that in our literature and in our lives as Africans today we should make a habit of invoking these powerful images from our history, legend and art. Because this is really what history and literature are about: that we can use them as a shorthand to say things which then start off resonances in the minds of everybody who has this kind of experience and history and is aware of it. You don't have to repeat everything that Kunene said, but just mention the keyword, the password, and the whole image is called up in the imagination of those who know, who are aware, who are literate in our traditions. I think this is very important. It's like a sort of short cut, saving a lot of time and energy, and in its result way beyond the size of the effort you make. But also I think that as writers we have tended to imitate the politicians who do not invoke the men before them. Even great politicians like Nkrumah: if you lived in Nkrumah's Ghana, for instance, you did not hear a lot about the people who laboured twenty or thirty years before: names like Aggrey, perhaps because they were too moderate for the taste of later times and we therefore forget that no matter how moderate they may have been they were actually in the field before us and made a significant contribution. And I think the same thing can be said in the literary area, for the negritude/tigritude argument, for instance. By renouncing that whole movement we were really cutting ourselves off from a source that could have helped us. I am saying that we should not behave like politicians who think that the good things, the revolution, the change only began when *they* arrived on the scene. We must recognize that there has been a ferment in Africa for a long time and that different people through the ages played a role according to their light and their ability and perhaps according to the constraints of the time. We must make use of all this to give us momentum. If you don't have a long history, you won't have any momentum, you'll be starting again every day, you'll be a new man in the world every day and this is terrible.

I also wondered if in the emphasis on beauty there was not a veiled allusion to Ayi Kwei Armah's *The Beautyful Ones Are Not Yet Born.*

I don't know, but it's quite possible. I believe that Ayi Kwei Armah's title is a very powerful image. It's a book that I taught for years when I was in the United States. Perhaps it was from teaching it that I was able to see some fundamental flaws that I then pointed out, causing a kind of rupture in our relationship, so I don't want to get involved in his work again! But I think it is possible. The image of the beautiful ones waiting to be born is a very good one and a very powerful one.

A consciously intended allusion is surely made to Christopher Okigbo when you speak of the "complex and paradoxical cavern of Mother Idoto." To what extent is Okigbo present in *Anthills*?

I don't recall having him clearly in front of me as a model, but I would like to say that his presence as a friend, when he was alive, and his presence as a poet have been so powerful in my experience and in the experience of my generation that it is inconceivable that I would be creating a poet without somehow having reference to my experience of Okigbo as *the* poet. Now you mention it, thinking back on some of the actions of Ikem, the poet in *Anthills,* I think some of the things he gets into could easily have been got into by Okigbo. So you are probably right, to that extent. He was probably there, at the back of my mind.

As to the reference to the paradoxical cavern of Mother Idoto—which comes straight out of Okigbo's poetry—it is the end of the journey of the prodigal, who is the poet, who is Okigbo, who is ourselves, discovering the roots again, searching and finally, after a long search, being accepted by the goddess Idoto into her paradise, a paradise, in my view, that is the paradise of artists and poets. It is paradoxical, it is complex, it cannot be described in one word. There is a very detailed description of the passageway, for instance: all this phosphorescence and these geometrical forms and figures appearing. It is something beyond words, and Okigbo simply *hints* at it. For me, this is where we are all headed, all artists, all those who work with words, all those who create stories. To be accepted here is to have one's work endorsed by the Owner of stories, this goddess . . . It is a *complex* place and I repeat that it is not a place for fanatics. Okigbo was the very opposite of fanatical. He wanted to experience everything. He wanted to get to London through Barcelona one day and through Rome the next, as he said. He was striving to discover the secret of his ancestors, but he had also read the Latin and Greek classics and he wasn't going to renounce those. That was the kind of person he was. The kind of paradise where he was going to be would be a paradise where this kind of openness was possible, not a paradise where narrow visions, *one* vision of the way and the truth and the light would dominate, but where everything is possible. This is one of the things I was trying to say in this passage. Of course, if you hadn't read Okigbo, you might say "Oh, this is very nice" and that would be that, but if you had, then all kinds of bonuses in echoes and resonances would be yours.

Could you tell me something about your teaching experience, how you present African literature and what African literature you present?

Teaching African literature in America and teaching it in Nigeria are very different things. Students in Nigeria are having more and more trouble simply being literate, being able to read extensively. To many students coming to the University, reading a novel is a huge chore. To plough through a novel is intimidating to many of them. Some will even run away and do linguistics because they imagine there is very little reading required there. So you have to coax them into literature. Many of them had never read before, except for what they had to read for their School Certificate. What I did was to introduce short stories, African short stories, that anybody could manage: the scope is small, the time required is small, and there are some stories that can really trigger off discussion and interest. People could really come alive in discussing what happens in this story in a way that they would never have imagined before they had thought of these stories as something dead, that you had to struggle to master. Once this was done with the shorter things, then they were readier to tackle a longer novel.

In America the problem is different. Here you are dealing with students who are coming out of a tradition where Africa is not really like anywhere else they know: Africa in literature, Africa in the newspapers, Africa in the sermons preached in the churches is really the Other Place. It is the Africa of *Heart of Darkness:* there are no real people in the Dark Continent, only *forces* operating; and people don't speak any language you can understand, they just grunt, too busy jumping up and down in frenzy. This is what is in the minds of these students as they come to African literature. So I find that the first thing is to familiarize them with Africa, make them think that this is a place of *people;* it's not the Other Place, the opposite of Europe or America. This is quite a task. But once you've done it—going into the history of Africa, showing how this is something that could have happened to anybody— the reaction is often quite interesting. I remember a white American boy who came to me very tense, after reading *Things Fall Apart,* and saying "This Okonkwo is my father!" Now I'd never in my wildest dreams thought of Okonkwo as a White Anglo-Saxon Protestant! But this is what literature is about and why it's worth doing. Otherwise why go to America to teach African literature?

Do you connect the written literature with the oral tradition?
The oral tradition is dealt with extensively in the introduction. I begin with issues, all kinds of issues, in African literature: the history, philosophy, negritude, African personality, issues like racism, like African language, before we begin to deal with the texts. And the oral tradition plays a very important part here, and also in actual handling of the texts, like for instance in Amos

Tutuola, *The Palm-Wine Drinkard,* which I always teach. This is quite a
useful peg on which to hang a discussion of the oral tradition.

As for the people I teach, Amos Tutuola; Cheikh Hamidou Kane, *Ambiguous Adventure;* Camara Laye, *The Dark Child* and sometimes *The Radiance
of the King* as well; Ferdinand Oyono, *Houseboy;* Mongo Beti, *Mission to
Kala;* Alex La Guma's stories and his short novel *A Walk in the Night,* which
is very effective: he says more about the South African situation than anyone
else; I always teach him. This time I'm including two women, writing out of
the Islamic tradition: an Egyptian, Alifa Rifaat, whose collection of short
stories, *A View from the Minaret,* is absolutely stunning, and Mariama Bâ,
So Long a Letter.

**You have also been working on the collection of oral literature in
Nigeria . . .**

This is really a matter of life and death. You see, there are some elements
of tradition that will keep struggling on for some time, but there are some
that will not. Where the environment no longer exists for a particular art
form, then that art form will disappear. Epic poems and poets flourished in a
village society in which there was a planting season, then a harvest season,
and then a time of rest after the harvest, and the way they used this time was
for the village to come and listen for a whole night, sometimes for five nights
in a row, to the poets reciting the stories of the heroes. Sometimes there
would be a contest between two poets and the village would be the audience.
Now the form I have been studying, which has been going on through the
millennia, no longer has a viable audience, because these communities are
dispersing and the people are no longer handing down the art to anybody
because the children have gone to school and gone on to the towns. The men
are all very old, in their seventies, in fact one of them started off his recital
for us but couldn't continue from physical exhaustion, and said we must
come back another time. So it's a life and death thing. We were able to put
as much as we could on video-tape so that we will be publishing extracts
with translations. We have in fact started a new journal, *Uwa ndi Igbo* ("The
World of the Igbo") in which the first extracts from these recordings were
published side by side in Igbo and in English.

Achebe and the Bruised Heart of Africa

Chris Searle / 1987

From *Wasafiri,* 14 (1991), 12–16. Reprinted by permission of *Wasafiri.*

Searle: From *Things Fall Apart* to *Anthills of the Savannah* is nearly 30 years, and your setting has changed from an African village to the highest echelons of State power. What has caused you to shift your setting in this way?

Achebe: I suppose one really ought to touch as many areas as possible. My understanding of the need of African literature is to see the story from as many points of view as possible. I don't believe in one view of anything. The same story told by two different people will be almost two different stories. So, having done the rural aspect and also the urban—although not at the level at which *Anthills* is done—this is the first time I am looking at the leaders, the elite, those who make things happen. I think that before in my writing I was preparing myself for this because I believe that this is where the key problem is. I have argued in my little book of essays, *The Trouble with Nigeria,* that our problem is really a problem of leadership. That doesn't mean this is the only problem, but it's one we should really aim to solve first and then it will be easier to deal with the multitude of other problems.

Searle: It is over 20 years since your previous novel, *A Man of the People* was published. Why has there been such a long period of gestation for *Anthills of the Savannah?*

Achebe: I am only speculating because in this area nobody really knows. I think that one of the reasons could have been the civil war in Nigeria, the Biafran War. This was such a cataclysmic experience that for me it virtually changed the history of Africa and the history of Nigeria. Everything I had known before, all the optimism had to be re-thought. I had to get used to a very new situation. I had found myself writing poetry and short stories, and writing for children in between, as it were writing, and trying to get acquainted with this new reality. The other factor was that I have never felt I *had* to write a book. I began this book 15 years ago. I had the characters but I didn't have a story. So I put it away and five years later I took it up again

155

and still wasn't ready. So I simply let it stay, until three years ago when I began again and this time it worked. At that time the situation in Nigeria was deteriorating again very fast, particularly at the level of the leadership. The second civilian republic had failed and the army had returned. Things were seeming to get totally out of hand again, and worry was being created in all our minds.

Searle: How do you see *Anthills of the Savannah* in comparison to *A Man of the People,* which was also about the qualities and failings of leadership?

Achebe: The writer is extending the story all the time. *Anthills* goes into more detail about the kind of people involved in leadership and I go from that to consider the kind of education for leadership such people need to acquire in order to be fit for its tasks. This education has to do with our leaders re-connecting themselves with the people and not living up there, unaware of their reality. Our leaders do not realise how quickly they become completely cut off. It doesn't take a year! You move in cars with sirens and everybody clears the route for you—they even pave the road for you before you make a visit. They paint everything before you see it. And if you are not careful you quickly lose touch. This is one of the key problems. So I'm making this point specifically. That this leadership has to connect itself with the source of its legitimacy: the peasantry, the workers, the women—the people. At the end of *Anthills of the Savannah* there is a kind of groping towards this reality.

Searle: How do you think that the major themes of your writing have changed since you wrote *Things Fall Apart?*

Achebe: The changes are really in the direction that I've indicated. It has been a filling out of the story. It is the same story, the story of Africa in the modern world and our problem with Europe, our problems with modernisation, the story of Africa in our time. What I'm doing is trying to see it from different angles like in the proverb about the masquerade. Africa is the masquerade and you don't stand in one place to see it, you move around the arena and take different perspectives. I'm against those who see Africa as a one-issue case. That is not true. It's a case of a multiplicity of issues, and you can take them one at a time, like the urgent issue of leadership. But that is not the only one. So to get it right you have to circulate the arena and take your shots like a photographer from different positions.

Searle: Are you saying then that your whole life of writing is really one novel that includes all those perspectives?

Achebe: It is; that's what I'm saying. It's like four synoptic gospels, I think that's what it is.

Searle: In *Anthills of the Savannah* you refer to the "Bruised Heart" of Africa. Could you explain this a little?

Achebe: What happened to Africa in its meeting with Europe was devastating. It was our people losing grip on their history, being swept out of the current of their history into somebody else's history, becoming a footnote. So the history of Africa became the history of alien races in Africa, and the real history that had been going on since the millennia was virtually forgotten—especially because it was not written down. As a result of this, many of us lost our knowledge, our memory of Africa. I can't think of anything more grave happening to a people than this. Then you get into the details and humiliations of colonialism. Then independence came and we assumed that we would immediately take up the story as if nothing had happened and, of course, this has proved to be impossible. So the source of the bruise is a long one, and it has been compounded lately by the brutality of the kind of leadership we have had. So the people have lost their sense of person, their sense of worth. Yet the romantic would suggest that the people are okay, that all you need to do is get the people and they would already know what to do. But this is not true and this is why I talk of this bruise. Our people need to be healed. They are the owners of the land, and we, the elite—and among them I count the writers too and we too are bruised in our own way—we must connect with them and we must also expect some disappointments. We must not be so romantic as to think otherwise, or think that once we call upon the people all our problems will be solved.

Searle: A number of prominent African writers, like Ngugi and Sembene Ousmane, are using their novels to explain and contest the force of neo-colonialism in Africa, and its local leaders. *Anthills of the Savannah* seems to have a similar preoccupation. Would you see this concern with neo-colonialism as a highly important theme, perhaps the most important, for the African novelists?

Achebe: This is a very, very important theme. But I hesitate to prescribe or to say "this is it" or to be obsessed with either the one problem or the one answer. Some writers, for example, say that the only problem is imperialism. I don't think this is true. There are other issues in Africa beyond imperialism. Nkrumah used to say that if you seek the political kingdom, everything else will be added unto you. But we pursued the political kingdom and found that everything was not added to us. So we must learn to live and write on a broad front. Neo-colonialism is a portmanteau word for all kinds of illnesses; it's a real thing, it's colonialism re-grouping and coming back using local jokers as leaders. This is very important, but there are other ways of looking at our problems and we must not get trapped in only looking at them through one vision. This leads to the using of more slogans and the oversimplifying of the problem. This then leads to further disappointment because you have not faced the complexities of the issue. We are lazy-minded; we want to know the answers quickly. "Cut out this long thing," we say, "tell me what to do to be saved." But our problems have been there for hundreds of years and they vary from place to place, country to country. So we must be prepared to face this complexity, as untidy as it may seem, because this is the only way we shall make progress.

Searle: A number of younger Nigerian writers—Festus Iyayi, for example—are concentrating their settings around urban and working-class life, rather than rural settings. What do you see as the significance of this?

Achebe: I approve of this development completely. Every writer needs to pick upon a different aspect of this single story and reflect upon it. Therefore a new writer will be ill-advised to start treading the same path as older writers. In addition, some of these writers writing about urban life and working-class Nigerians, do not know very much about the rural situation. So as a writer you use the strength of knowledge that you have and you write about what you know. However, what I do not approve of is sometimes the feeling that you come across that this concern for the urban, for the worker in the city, is the *real* story and the other, rural one, is not real. This, of course, is falsifying the story, for with regard to numbers the urban population is still the minority, so their story can only be *one* of the stories.

This new culture of the cities is emerging and growing but it hasn't developed overnight, and it isn't growing in isolation from the villages. These are village people living in the cities and the vitality of the villages still survives with them, even in huge cities like Lagos. So you have a large number of village communities operating, often through the town unions who organize the people from the various upcountry locations. So it is a complex combination of city and village and, again, we stand to weaken our potential for dealing with our problems if we try to oversimplify the situation.

Searle: In *Anthills of the Savannah* you describe the writer as the people's "escort." What do you see as the role of the novelist in Africa and how has it changed since you first started writing?

Achebe: A little correction, it is the *story* that is the escort. The *story* is more important than the writer, although they are related, naturally. If you look at the things that are happening in the society: the struggle itself, the inspirer to struggle, the story of the struggle; when you put all these things together and say what is the most important, then the choice falls upon the *story*. It is the story that conveys all our gains, all our failures, all we hold dear and all we condemn. To convey this to the next generation is the only way we can keep going and keep alive as a people. Therefore the story is like the genes that are transferred to create the new being. It is far more important than anything else.

It has been the same right through my period of writing. I have been using different words, a new metaphor for expressing it. But I don't think that any change has happened to the truth that the *story* is crucial to the survival of a people. This is why those who say that the past is no longer useful to us are so mistaken. You cannot have a present if you do not have a past. The past is all we have. All we can call our own is what has happened—that is, our history. It is so very vital to us and our survival, so we cannot treat it like jokers. If we consider the folktales which our ancestors crafted with such care, we must strive to do the same thing and communicate to the next generations what is important, what is of value, what must be preserved. If they decide to alter this and that, then that's fine, but they will be doing it in the full knowledge of what has gone on before. So, above all, I too am a story-teller—not as good as our ancestors, but trying my best!

Searle: You clearly have a belief in the power of the African storyteller and the integrity of his words. In *Anthills of the Savannah* the most commendable characters are those concerned with the making of words. Your character, Beatrice, at the end of the novel also invokes the promise and hope of "people and ideas." In what ways does your faith in the storyteller, ideas and the people point towards an Africa where the bruises are healed?

Achebe: This is my belief and hope. I shall do my best to bring this about. But I say this knowing there are still dangers on the way, there is still a lot of work ahead of us before we arrive at this ideal state where the storyteller, the people and the force of ideas are working together in harmony. This is a great future, but it may never come fully, because our human condition is that we shall always struggle, struggle to achieve our utmost. Even if we shall never see it, our lives would be incredibly reduced if we were not to struggle. I don't know whether what I've done will bear any fruit, but whether it does or not, I like to feel that when I go, then those who come behind will say that although I may have failed, I struggled.

It is like the tortoise and the leopard and the way the tortoise put up a fake impression of struggle. You remember in the Ibo folk story the leopard caught up with the tortoise. He had been trying to catch him for a long time. He wanted to kill him. So, when he finally caught him, he said, 'Aha, now prepare yourself to die.' So the tortoise began to scatter and push sand all around him on the road, to create the impression of a struggle. The leopard was mystified. He thought the tortoise would simply want to stand still and contemplate his death, rather than get involved in this frantic action. So he said, "why are you doing that?" And the tortoise told him, "When I'm dead, I want people who pass by to say that here a man met his match." In other words, that there was a struggle, that he did not go meekly. That is the metaphor of a writer.

Searle: Why is the writing in English that is emerging from Africa and the Caribbean so much more powerful and positive than that coming from the imperialist and old colonising powers like Britain and the US?

Achebe: It comes from that same source of struggle. The writer is involved far more in the world of struggle in our countries, real life-and-death struggle. We are not playing games. We are dealing with serious issues. I remember in Stockholm, at a conference, a European writer once saying: "You know, I envy you people. Here nothing I do will ever put me in prison!" We have the advantage that we can be locked up—that is what he was saying! But in a way he was acknowledging that what we are doing is more serious, more fundamental. But in addition, we have the advantage of our largely unrecognised huge oral tradition. This is a vital source for us. We are now in a position to be able to use it and call upon it in our literature.

We have a massive diversity within our struggle in Africa. Wherever we are there is struggle and we must struggle ourselves to see the whole picture. This is again why we must not fall into the narrow view that we are a one-issue continent. And one place again where we must begin is in the area of leadership. Africa must link up, for we are all in this struggle, whether it is the elemental struggle against famine and hunger and Ethiopia having to appeal to the world for grain, or the struggle in South Africa against Apartheid. In Nigeria we do not have Apartheid but the fact that the South African people are locked in this struggle diminishes us and diminishes our own potential for solving our problems in Nigeria. For ultimately it is a struggle about the great wealth of South Africa and its economy and the way this wealth is *not used* for the benefit of Africa and its people. And, of course, the disruption it causes to other states in Africa, like Mozambique for example. Mozambique cannot face its own problems of development because it has to constantly fight off the agents of South Africa. So the whole continent is one war front, for anything that reduces an African in Ethiopia or South Africa reduces *all* Africans anywhere.

So our writing *must be* political and must carry the vigour of these fundamental issues into it. There is not writing in Africa that can fail to be political. Whereas in the West, if a novel is said to be "political," it means that it is not very good, it's used as a criticism. Or the critics say "although it is political, it is a good novel," which is in itself a very political thing to say. For it means "the world is okay; we don't need to drag in any of these extraneous factors. Let's talk about Art, about style, about the use of language. Things are okay!" So there are two positions. One is conservative, the other one is not—because it doesn't have anything to conserve, it wants a re-sharing of things. So this must be reflected in the difference between the writers of Europe and Africa and the work they produce.

Searle: You talked earlier about how the civil war in your country had shattered the optimism of your writers, particularly with regard to African political leadership. But don't Africa's great leaders like Machel, Cabral, Nkrumah or Nyerere give you cause for some optimism?

Achebe: In 1983, in Nigeria, I wrote a little political book out of some desperation before the election called *The Trouble with Nigeria.* I was concerned with the question of leadership. I did point to a few great leaders by name. This was not exhaustive. But I did talk about the late Aminu Kano in Nigeria itself, who at least had this record of going through all the offices of state and still coming out a very poor man. I also gave the example of Julius Nyerere, a legendary figure. Today there will be those who say he failed, that the Tanzanian economy crumbled in his hands, but that's not true. But even if he did, he was a man who was not helping himself to the treasury, which has been very common behaviour in our continent. So we have had our exemplary leaders, and we should talk about them, understand that it has never been one grim story of failure all the way. In fact, there is a need to get away from the pessimism and change our words and imagery and not harp on about failure. But it must not be simple-minded; it must concentrate intelligently upon the examples and signs that have been positive and successful.

For example, despite the immense difficulties that Mozambique faces, these would have been infinitely worse without a leader like Machel, or the same with Tanzania without a Nyerere. These are desperately poor countries, yet they have never made a fiasco with independence. They have free education, for example, which we don't have in Nigeria, even though they don't have oil. Failure is not simply that the man died, as in my novels. But these characters in the story of Africa did not fail. Okonkwo in *Things Fall Apart* or Ezeulu in *Arrow of God* did not fail. We are still talking about them. The example of their struggle has been lodged in our consciousness, and we can use the example of their courage and energy they brought to their lives for making our conditions better. It is the same with these great leaders. Machel is dead, but actually he is not yet dead, and the same with Lumumba, Neto, Cabral and the others. They stay in the memory of Africa. That is their greatest contribution: that we remember them and their struggle. And now we also have the written word to keep their work and example in our minds.

Searle: What can the Nigerian writer do to show solidarity with the South African people in their struggle against Apartheid?

Achebe: When I was President of the Nigerian Association of Writers, our congress discussed Apartheid as one of the key issues. We tried to convey to the Nigerian Government that it is not enough to say we are against Apartheid or we are giving money and so on—when we are known to have a very cosy relationship with those countries which make Apartheid possible, like America, West Germany and Britain. We need to demonstrate our displeasure in our economic relationship with these countries, for this is where the struggle is.

Searle: In *Anthills* one of your characters condemns very forcefully the impact in Africa of US imperial culture. What kind of damage do you see it causing in Nigeria?

Achebe: US culture itself is a strong force of debilitation, not just against Nigerian or African culture, but almost all other cultures around the world. It is difficult to stand up, to be yourself as you ought to, because the West, and America in particular, has so much power and influence. The music that my children listen to now is the same that American children listen to. The Nigerian high-life is virtually dead because of this. In dancing too. We are the great dancers, but our own youth now shuffle like the Americans. This has been a very serious penetration of our life and culture. It is where everything is coming from and the world is imperilled by its influence. So, again, we need to insist upon the multiplicity of cultures to combat this and stand up also for the way in which our own ancestors did things, in order to give ourselves more confidence. In writing too, we have a group of writers who create totally un-African settings and try to copy the fast-car, fast-murder kind of story that comes from America and the West. Again, it shows us that all of us, including our writers, must educate ourselves about our own culture in order to be strong enough to withstand this force. It is not easy to resist because it requires no effort or energy to accept it, no thought; it is so well-packaged, so seemingly attractive and, of course, it accompanies the economic penetration of the wealth of our country and our people.

Searle: How do you find that the particular qualities and strengths of your first language, Ibo, have become a part of the English that you write. Do you think they have given it a particular African quality?

Achebe: I think it has done that, certainly. I don't know how, and it would be difficult to explain in detail unless we are students of linguistics, tinkering with the forms and structures of language. But I'm not very interested in that. There is a way in which the vigour of one language, its imagery and metaphors, can be transferred across. And there is a certain irreducibility in human language anyway, which is what makes translation possible, even though we are not always satisfied with the result and we keep striving. And, if one has this respect of the integrity of language, you make this extra effort to get as close as possible to what you have in your mind. And that may not be what you actually manage to get down on paper. But you worry about it, work at it and try to get something better.

But the other vital question is what happens to the African languages in the situation where we are writing our books in English, French or Portuguese? What happens to Swahili, or Gikuyu, or Yoruba? As you know, there is a very strong lobby for abandoning the European languages. This is a very understandable passion, to move away from the metropolitan languages and to revive the African languages. We must respect this. But we can also get trapped in this one-issue mentality. "If only we abandoned the European languages, our problems would be solved!" But this is not true at all. Our problems would not be solved by this. We have got a very, very complicated situation in Africa, including the survival of the nation states. It is not for nothing that the most radical countries in Africa like Mozambique, Angola, Burkina Faso have chosen the metropolitan European languages as national languages and have more or less foreclosed the argument. They are the ones

who are the most forthright in saying "we cannot be without these languages." The Minister of Culture of Burkina Faso was saying not so long
ago, almost with a shudder that was coming across, that if the 60 languages
of his country were to be officially used, the one state would disintegrate into
60 states. So it doesn't do us any good to belittle this danger which the
political leaders of all modern African states must be aware of, this peril of
disintegration. So writers who are not responsible for keeping their country
together must not talk or behave as if there is no real problem, as if you can
simply go back to a pre-Treaty of Berlin situation. As an African and a nationalist looking at the situation now, there is a real value in keeping our
countries together using a language that has been imposed upon us. It may
not last for all time, but writers are not only there for all time; they're here
for now as well.

An Interview with Chinua Achebe

Charles H. Rowell / 1989

From *Callaloo,* 13 (1990), 86–101. © 1990. Reprinted by permission of *Callaloo.*

This interview was conducted in Mr. Achebe's quarters at the International House in New York City on Sunday, May 28, 1989.

Rowell: Mr. Achebe, here in the United States, those of us who read twentieth-century world literature think of you as one of the most important writers in this era. We view you as an artist—and for us the word *artist* has a certain kind of meaning. In the African world, does *artist* have the same meaning as that conceptualized in the Western world? Or, more specifically, what do Nigerians conceive the writer to be?

Is he or she thought of as an artist, a creator of the kind that we think of here in the United States when we speak about writers?

Achebe: Well, I think that there are obviously certain common factors when anybody talks about an artist, whether in America or in Africa. I think there are certain factors which would apply to either place—and so we can leave those aside, if you like. But there are differences definitely, in emphasis if not absolute, and it is these that one should draw attention to. The artist has always existed in Africa in the form of the sculptor, the painter, or the storyteller, the poet. And I suppose the role of the writer, the modern writer, is closer to that of the *griot,* the historian and poet, than to any other practitioner of the arts. But I think one can find, even from the other forms of art, fundamental statements, cultural statements, made about art in general which seem to me to be peculiarly African in their emphasis.

What I mean, for instance, is this. The ceremony, which is called *"Mbari"* among the Igbo people, is a festival of art, a celebration of humanity. It is not a festival of oral arts; it is more a festival of the visual arts, the plastic arts, though drama and songs are presented there as well. There you will find, I think, what our people thought of art—and that's the reason I am referring to it. Some of the statements made by *Mbari* are very profound. One is that art is in the service of the community. There is no apology at all about that. Art is invented to make the life of the community easier, not to make it more

165

difficult. Artists are people who live in society. The professional artist, the master artist and craftsman, is a special kind of person, but he is not the only person who is expected to practice art.

For this celebration, this *Mbari* celebration, ordinary people are brought in to work under the supervision of professional artists, because we assume that everybody has art in themselves. So ordinary people are brought in, and they are secluded with the professionals for a period—months and sometimes even years—to create this celebration of life through art. So what this says to me is that art is not something up there in the rarified reaches of the upper atmosphere but something which is down here where we live. Art is not something which is beyond the comprehension of ordinary people. It is something which ordinary people not only can understand and use, but even take part in making. So these are ideas which I don't find very much in the West, you see. These are some of the ideas we have that one should specify and draw attention to. If one looked at what we do and compared it with what our contemporaries do in the West, these ideas would explain some of the differences and some of the puzzlement that certain Western critics have, for instance, when they encounter African literature and say: "Why do they do that? Why are they so political?" And they ask these questions to the point of irritation. If only they understood where we were coming from, then perhaps they would not be so puzzled. Perhaps they would even be open to persuasion on this score.

Rowell: At the University of Virginia, last April [19, 1989], you responded to a question from the audience which I think describes further what you have just said or is related to it. I can't quote you directly. However, I do remember that you implied that art, in Nigeria, is intimately linked to social responsibility and that it is connected to that which is moral, that which is ethical, that which is right, or that which is good. I think you made that statement in response to a question about Joseph Conrad—and I'm not trying to get into a Joseph Conrad discussion here. Will you say more about art?

Achebe: Yes. The festival which I have just been talking about, the *Mbari* festival, is commanded from time to time by the goddess of creativity, the earth goddess, called *Ala* or *Ani* by the Igbo people. This goddess is not only responsible for creativity in the world; she is also responsible for morality. So that an abomination is described as taboo to her, as *nso-ani*. That's the word for something which is not supposed to be done—not just a wrongdoing—but an abomination, something which is forbidden by this goddess.

So obviously by putting the two portfolios, if you like, of art and morality in her domain, a statement is being made about the meaning of art. Art cannot be in the service of destruction, cannot be in the service of oppression, cannot be in the service of evil. We tend to be a little apologetic about that. You know, if you talk about "good," people will get uneasy. They become uneasy. I don't know why that should be so, but we work ourselves into all kinds of corners from which we then become uneasy when certain words are mentioned. That's not the fault of the words; there is perhaps something wrong with us.

So there is no question at all, in the view of my people, that art cannot serve immorality. And morality here doesn't mean "be good and go to church." That's not what I'm talking about. I'm talking about manifest wickedness like murder. There is no art that can say that it is right to commit murder. I remember, I think it was Yevtushenko who once said that "You cannot be a poet and a slave trader." It seems to me fairly obvious that you cannot combine those particular professions, because they are antithetical. And this is not something which only the Africans or the Igbo people know. I think it is there, embedded also, in the minds of other people. The difference is that our culture makes no bones about it, and I think this comes through too in our writing. It does not mean that our heroes have to be angels. Of course not. It means, in fact, that heroes will be as human as anybody else; and yet the frontier between good and evil must not be blurred; it means that somewhere, no matter how fuzzy it may be to us, there is still a distinction between what is permissible and what is not permissible. One thing which is not permissible is to stereotype and dehumanize your fellows. That is not permissible in our art. You celebrate them, their good and their bad. You celebrate even rascals, because they abound in the world and are part of its richness.

Rowell: You just said that this conceptualization of art comes through "in our writing." Will you talk about how this is exemplified in your own work or that of other African writers, either consciously or unconsciously?

Achebe: Well, I think if you took a tape recorder and went around African writers, I bet you will find them making rather large statements for what they do. You'll find them saying, for instance, "I am writing so that the life of my people will be better." I even found a modern story in Hausa which ended: "And so they married and they produced many sons and daughters who helped to raise the standard of education in the country." That's the way the story ends, imitating the format of the folk story but obviously turning it into something very practical for today, you see. And I said elsewhere, if anybody reads this story and says "oh now, this is an anticlimax," he could not possibly know anything about Africa, because the story of today has to do with raising the standards of education of the country, you see. We are engaged in a great mission, and we attempt to bring this into our storytelling. It is this mission that our storyteller brings into his tale without the slightest inclination to discuss it self-consciously in the way we are doing now. He instinctively felt a need for his story and supplied it. This is why we get letters saying, to me for instance, "Why did you let Okonkwo fail in *Things Fall Apart?* Why did you let a good man or a good cause stumble and fall?" At another time, I remember a letter from a woman in Ghana saying, "Why did Obi, in *No Longer at Ease,* not have the courage to marry the girl he loved instead of crumbling?" People are expecting from literature serious comment on their lives. They are not expecting frivolity. They are expecting literature to say something important to help them in their struggle with life.

That is what literature, what art, was supposed to do: to give us a second handle on reality so that when it becomes necessary to do so, we can turn to art and find a way out. So it is a serious matter. That's what I'm saying, and I think every African writer you talk to will say something approaching what I have just said—in different forms of words, except those who have too much of the West in them, and there are some people, of course, who are that way. But the writer I am referring to is the real and serious African writer. I think you will find them saying something which sounds as serious, as austere, or as earnest as what I have just said.

Rowell: You've mentioned the *griot.* I have read many things about what a *griot* is. And sometimes these texts seem to contradict each other. What is a *griot?* The word itself sounds Francophone.

Achebe: It's a word that comes from somewhere; I don't even know where it comes from. I know it certainly is not a Nigerian word. It's not an Igbo word. But it is a word which concerns us, because we know roughly what kind of person we are talking about. We are talking about the traditional poet and historian. The function of this person would not be exactly the same thing in all cultures. Where you have a monarchical system, for instance, the chances are that the *griot* or the poet, this historian, would be connected with the history of the dynasty. This is supposedly where problems immediately arise, you know. How reliable, then, is this poet, who resides in the court of the emperor, reciting the history? There are problems there. And the greatest *griots,* I think, have managed to find a way around those problems. How they do it we cannot go into here. It suffices to remind us that 700 years after the life and death of Sundiata, the first emperor of Mali, the *griots* in West Africa were still reciting the story of his birth and life and death. It was only in the fifties, the 1950s, that this story was finally put down in writing. And the person who put it down in writing went to different and widely separated places and compared the versions given by various *griots* and discovered that the core of the story remained the same, you see. This is quite remarkable: over a period of 700 years . . . because we tend to think that unless something is scribbled down on some piece of paper it cannot be true. I don't know who told us that. And we have come to believe it ourselves, that our history should be measured in terms of paper. So whenever you don't have a piece of paper, somebody says there is no history. And we seem to be quite ready to accept it. So you would find our historians going to archives in Portugal, for instance, to see what some sailor from Portugal had said when he came to Benin in the fifteenth century. We don't ask the condition of this sailor when he was making his entry, whether he was drunk or sober. He is on a piece of paper and therefore reliable—and more reliable than what you might gather in the field by asking people: "What do you remember? What do your people remember about this?"

Anyway, I think we are learning. We know a little better now than we used to. Thanks to the work of people like the late Professor Dike, who helped to create a new historiography of Africa using the oral tradition. We know now that we can find some of the truth in oral traditions. Now, to get back to the problem of the *griot,* let me tell the story of one short fable in Hausa, which I think exemplifies the way a *griot* might approach his problem obliquely, because if you are dealing with the emperor who is so much more powerful than yourself, you have to have your wits around you. If you start telling a story which puts him in a bad light or a bad mood, your career will be very short indeed! So you have to find a way of getting around this problem.

Now this is a story, a very simple animal story, from the Hausa language, which I encountered years ago. And I have used it again and again because I think it is a marvelous little story. In my own words, it goes something like this: The snake was riding his horse, coiled up in his saddle. That's the way the snake rode his horse. And he came down the road and met the toad walking by the roadside. And the toad said to him, "Excuse me, sir, but that's not how to ride a horse." And the snake said, "No? Can you show me then?"

And the toad said, "Yes, if you would step down, sir." So the snake came down. The toad jumped into the saddle and sat bolt upright and galloped most elegantly up and down the road. When he came back he said, "That's how to ride a horse." And the snake said, "Excellent. Very good. Very good, indeed. Thank you. Come down, if you don't mind." So the toad came down, and the snake went up and coiled himself in the saddle as he was used to doing and then said to the toad, "It is very good to know, but it is even better to have. What good does excellent horsemanship do to a man without a horse?" And with that he rode away.

Now, the Hausa, who made this story, are a monarchical people. They have classes: the emir, the upper class, the nobility, etc., down to the bottom, the ordinary people, the *talakawa*. As you can see, the snake in this story is an aristocrat, and the toad a commoner. The statement, even the rebuke, which the snake issues is, in fact, saying: "Keep where you belong. You see, people like me are entitled to horses, and we don't have to know how to ride. There's no point in being an expert. That's not going to help you." Now that's very nice in that kind of political situation. And we can visualize the emir and his court enjoying this kind of story and laughing their heads off—because, you see, it's putting the commoner in his place. But also if you think deeply about this story, it's a two-edged sword. I think that's the excellence of the *griot* who fashioned it. To put this other edge to it, which is not noticed at first . . . this other side is that the snake is incompetent, the snake is complacent, the snake is even unattractive. It's all there in the story, you see, and the time will come in this political system when all this will be questioned. Why is it that a snake is entitled to a horse? Why is it that the man who knows how to ride does not have a horse to ride? You see. This questioning will come in a revolutionary time, and when it comes you don't need another story. It is the same story that will stand ready to be used; and this to me is the excellence of the *griot* in creating laughter and hiding what you might call the glint of steel. In the voluminous folds of this laughter, you can catch the hint of a concealed weapon which will be used when the time comes. Now this is one way in which the *griot* gets around the problem of telling the emperor the truth, you see. That is very, very important. Of course, if the *griot* is strong enough to say this to the emperor in his face, he will do it. But if he is not, he will find a way to conceal his weapon. Of course, there will be *griots* who sell out, but we're not talking about those, those who sing for their dinner.

Rowell: After your reading-lecture at the University of Virginia last April, one of my graduate students, a native of Mauritania, said to me: "In this culture, meaning the Western culture, you meet knowledge, you meet erudition, you meet expertise, but not wisdom. Mr. Achebe speaks and writes wisdom." That was what the student, Mohamed B. Taleb-Khyar, said, and I quote him directly.

Achebe: That was very kind of him.

Rowell: What I would like to ask of you is this: Does this speaking wisdom characterize, in any way, the sensibility of the African artist?

Achebe: Yes, I think it does. Wisdom is as good a word to use, I think, in describing the seriousness I was talking about, this *gravitas* that I'm talking about which informs our art. We can be as jovial, as lighthearted, even as frivolous as anybody else. But everything has its place and its measure. When you are dealing with art of the level at which we are dealing with it, it's a serious matter, a matter of clarification and wisdom.

Rowell: You are a teacher—in the United States we would say that you are a professor—of literature. What is the status of teaching literature in Africa? That's to say, does the teaching of literature contribute positively or negatively in the development, for example, of the new Nigeria? In other words, what is the role of the humanities in the African context?

Achebe: Well, we as writers and artists have or should have a central role in the society. We are not necessarily carrying the day in that way of thinking. For instance, when I gave the National Lecture in Nigeria (which you give if you win the Nigerian National Merit Award which is our highest honor for intellectual achievement), the lecture I gave recently in Nigeria was entitled "What Has Literature Got To Do With It?" It was about the problem of development which concerns all of us. How do we develop, how do we raise our standard of living, how do we improve the life of our people, how do we modernize, and all of that which we aspire to like anybody else? How do we even raise the income per capita? All of these things are important. What I'm asking is: What has literature got to do with them? Has literature any relevance to all this or is it simply something we can perhaps forget for the time being? Are we to concentrate on the hard sciences, and then perhaps when we have become developed we can afford the luxury of literature. Is that what we want? There will be people who say so. There are attempts, for instance, to shift the emphasis in the universities in Nigeria from the humanities to the sciences, to limit the admissions for the humanities and increase the admissions for the sciences. Now all that, of course, may be necessary. I really don't know, but I think any people who neglect the importance of addressing the minds and hearts and the spirit of the people will find that they will be really getting nowhere at all in their development. One of the examples I gave was a story told us in Japan.

Some years ago I was taking part in a symposium in Japan. The Japanese would bring two foreign experts to Japan to meet with about half a dozen local experts in similar disciplines. They would talk and discuss for three or four days. On this occasion, the subject was culture and development. I remember the story which a Japanese professor told. His grandfather went to the University of Tokyo and graduated, he said, I think, about 1900. All of his notes, the notes he wrote in the university as a student, were written in English. His own father graduated about 1920. Half of his notes were written in English and half in Japanese. Then he, the man who was telling us the story, graduated in 1950 or thereabouts, from the same university. All his notes were written in Japanese. Now this profile is very interesting. The Japanese were becoming giants in the modern world, in technology and so on, surpassing those who began the industrial revolution. They were also, as it were, travelling back to regain their own culture through their language, you see. This is very important; I think this is an extremely important story. It says something about the relationship between technology and the humanities.

How far can you develop without dealing with certain humanistic problems, such as who am I, why am I here, what is the meaning of life, what is my culture? I believe that the relationship is close, important and crucial.

Rowell: You teach literature courses. You told me that you teach African literature frequently. But when you teach a literature course that does not include an African literary text, what are some of the creative works or texts you select?

Achebe: No, I have never taught anything but African literatures, and I'm not really a professional literature teacher. The only reason I got into teaching at all is that I wanted to teach African literature. So I taught African literature from the start. I guess I've not done anything else in my teaching career.

Rowell: If you were teaching a course in twentieth-century literature, what are some of the texts you'd use? And why would you select them? I guess, ultimately, I'm asking this: What are some of the twentieth-century texts you consider to be important? For example, I couldn't imagine teaching a course in twentieth-century American literature without including Ralph Ellison's *Invisible Man* or William Faulkner's *Absalom, Absalom!* or Toni Morrison's *Sula.* In other words, what do you consider some of the most important texts for teaching twentieth-century world literature?

Achebe: Well, it's not really a question I can answer satisfactorily. The texts you mention are all very important—and there are other important ones as well. I wouldn't really be able to or want to rattle off a list just like that, but I would certainly try to cover the world. I would attempt to cover those writers who have written what you call "the landmarks" of the twentieth century. And I guess that would include people like T. S. Eliot, would include Ezra Pound, would include Faulkner, would include Hemingway. Then if you come nearer to our time . . . yes, yes, *Invisible Man* is an outstanding novel by any stretch of the imagination—and I would include it for that reason and also for the reason that Ellison is writing from a history and a tradition which have a unique message for us. I would include one—at least one—Baldwin text. From African literature I would include *Ambiguous Adventure* by Cheikh Hamidou Kane, I would include Camara Laye and Amos Tutuola, I would include Alex La Guma and Nadine Gordimer. Then I would attempt to find, even in translation, some Arabic writers from Egypt, Naguib Mahfouz and Alifa Rifaat, for example. Then I would attempt to include writers from India, Raja Rao for example. That doesn't cover the whole world. Then I would move to Latin America, you see. I would include Neruda and Marquez. Actually, some of the most interesting writing is taking place there. I would also go to the Caribbean which, for its size, is perhaps the most dynamic literary environment in the world in our time. There is a legion of people there I would want to include. So you see I would have really to end up with a very long list and then begin to pare it down. But the important thing I would attempt to do is not to limit myself to anybody's "Great Tradition," because that sort of thing limits you and blinds you to what is going on in the real world.

Rowell: Are there other reasons that you would not include "anybody's 'Great Tradition' "?

Achebe: No, no, I said I would go beyond anyone's "Great Tradition." Why? Because it is not the "Great Tradition." It cannot be. No way. One small corner of the world cannot wake up one morning and call its artifact the "Great Tradition," you see. Our people have a saying that the man who's never traveled thinks that his mother makes the best soup. Now we need to travel—with all due respect to our mothers—we need to travel. So the question of a "Great Tradition" makes sense only if you're not aware of other people's traditions.

I had a very curious experience in Holland, where I was put up to run as president of International PEN. An older, much older, man, a Frenchman, was put up also—or he put himself up after he saw my name. And he won. But the interesting thing is that he had no conception—and didn't want to have any conception—of the literature of Africa. He kept quite clearly and studiously avoiding any mention of African literature, and at some point he said something like this: "How can we expect the Third World, with all of their problems, to produce great art?" Do you see what I mean? Now this is the kind of mind or mentality I'm talking about. It remains alien to me though I encounter it frequently. It is alien to me because my whole life has been ordered in such a way that I have to know about other people. This is one of the penalties of being an underdog: that you have to know about the overdog, you see. The overdog doesn't need to know about the underdog; therefore, he suffers severe limitations, and the underdog ends up being wiser because he knows about himself and knows about the overdog. So my reading list would be really catholic, would be catholic in every sense of the word. I haven't talked about the Far East, because I don't know enough, but I will try and find, for example, some good writers from Japan. One must read the Japanese novelists. Their own contribution to the consciousness of the twentieth century is unique.

Rowell: Is the Third World writer presently participating in the ongoing revision of what one calls "the literary canon"?

Achebe: Oh yes, yes. By just being there. He/she is, in fact, the reason for the revision. He/she is the very reason for the revision.

Rowell: Isn't the Third World writer something else other than what we just said? The matter I'm thinking of here is linguistic. Let us assume for a moment that Percy Shelley was correct when he said that "the poet is the legislator of the world." The poet is indeed a person who shapes our vision of the world; he or she does that and provides us with a vocabulary, or new vocabulary, to describe it. I'm thinking of you and what you do for the English-speaking world as a writer, and what Jorges Luis Borges does, or did, for the Spanish-speaking world, and what Aimé Césaire does linguistically, for example, for the French-speaking world. In other words, does the Third World writer alter or adapt the medium and, through a destruction of what is out there as—I'll call it this—"the parent language or dialect" itself, revise or reinvest the medium?

Achebe: Well, yes. My answer to the previous question was rather brief, but it was really intended to contain all of this. This Third World creature comes with an experience which is peculiar, including the linguistic experience. The use of French, in the case of Césaire, is the use of a French that has been in dialogue with other languages, you see. In my case, it is an English which has been in dialogue with a very rich alien linguistic milieu— that is, you have African languages strong in their own right, and an African history and experience. An English which has had this particular encounter cannot be the same as the English of Kingsley Amis writing in London. So this is something which the members of the metropolis have to deal with, and they don't always like it. But it is not really something for me to worry about. I know some people who are worried, and they say, "Look what they are doing to my language!" They are horrified.

We come with this particular preparation which, as it happens, actually enriches the metropolitan languages. But that's not why we do it; we're not doing it in order to enrich the metropolitan language. We're doing it because this is the only way we can convey the story of ourselves, the way we can celebrate ourselves in our new history and the new experience of colonialism, and all the other things. We have had to fashion a language that can carry the story we are about to tell.

It's not all so new, even though, perhaps, it's happening now on such a wide scale that we are paying more attention to it than before. But if you think, for instance, of all the great writers in English in our century, they are virtually all Irish. Why is that so? This is very important, and I think it is the same situation. James Joyce, of course, addresses it directly and talks about it in that famous passage in which Stephen Daedalus is talking about what the English language means to him and to his teacher who is English. He muses on the fact that every word he says means something different to each of them—any word, "ale" or "Christ"; no word can mean the same thing to me as it does to him. Why? Because we colonials and excolonials come to the English language with a whole baggage of peculiar experiences which the English person doesn't have. This is what has made the English language, in our time, such a powerful force in literature. This is why we're talking about the Caribbean literature and about African literature.

Rowell: Will you elaborate on a statement you just made about using a new form of English? You said that it (the new form of the medium) was the only "way we can convey the history of ourselves." You said we use the language in the way we do because this is the only way we can convey the history or the story of ourselves. Apparently, you are talking about the nature of that revised form, or the new fabric, of English.

Achebe: Well, take Nigeria. Nigeria is a vibrant cultural environment. It has been for a long time. It has, literally, two hundred languages—not all of them important, but some quite big. The three main Nigerian languages are spoken by at least ten million people each, and some of them, like Hausa, cross beyond Nigeria's borders to other places. The English language arrives in Nigeria, then, and is thrown into this very active linguistic environment. Of course, it has the special privilege of being the language of administration, the language of higher education—the *lingua franca,* in fact, the language in which the various indigenous political and linguistic entities can communicate among themselves. Unless he learns the Igbo language, the Hausa man will communicate with the Igbo man in English. A Yoruba man communicates with a Hausa man in English. We're talking about Nigeria. And this has gone on for a number of generations. English, then, acquires a particular position of importance. You must recognize this, unless, of course, you agree with some of my friends who have said that we should ignore this history and ignore this reality and ignore whatever advantage of mutual communication English has brought to our very complex situation. Unless you were to accept that extreme position, you would have to say, "What will we do with this English language that's been knocking around here now for so long? Our people don't allow anything as powerful as that to keep knocking around without having a job to do, because it would cause trouble.

This is the whole point of that *Mbari* phenomenon that I was describing earlier, in which anything which is new and powerful, which appears in the horizon, is brought in and domesticated in the *Mbari* house with all the other things that have been around, so that it doesn't have the opportunity to stay out of sight and scheme to overthrow the environment. This is what art does. Something comes along and you bring it in—and even if you don't yet fully understand it, you give it a place to stand. This is the way in which we have been using the English language to tell our story. It's not the only way we can tell our story, of course. I can tell our story in the Igbo language. It would be different in many ways. It would also not be available to as many people, even within the Nigerian environment. So this is the reality: this English, then, which I am using, has witnessed peculiar events in my land that it has never experienced anywhere else. The English language has never been close to Igbo, Hausa, or Yoruba anywhere else in the world. So it has to be different, because these other languages and their environment are not inert. They are active, and they are acting on this language which has invaded their territory. And the result of all this complex series of actions and reactions is the language we use. The language I write in. And, therefore, it comes empowered by its experience of the encounter with me. One advantage it has is this: Although it is thus different, it is not so different that you would have to go to school to learn it in America or in India or Kenya or anywhere English is already spoken. So it definitely has certain advantages which we can only ignore to our own disadvantage. It is a world language in a way that Hausa, Yoruba, Igbo are not. There is no way we can change that. Now that is not to say that we should therefore send these other languages to sleep. That's not what I'm saying. I am saying that we have a very, very complex and dynamic multilingual situation, which we cannot run away from but contain and control.

Rowell: *No Longer at Ease* addresses the problem of communication in particular terms. There are moments in the novel when there's a lack of communication. This problem revolves around Obi, your central character. Will you comment on the issues related to language and its failure as a medium in modern society?

Achebe: Well, yes, language is of course a marvelous tool of communication. This is what makes us different from cattle, that we have language and we are able to communicate with the precision that language brings. But even this is not enough. We all know that. Sometimes we say, "I know what I want to say, but I just can't find the words to say it." In other words, language is not absolutely perfect; there are still things we struggle to express. Sometimes we approach fairly close to what we feel, what we want to say, but at other times no. So it's not surprising that there should be problems in communication, even though we've got language in the technical sense of just using words. But, of course, you can be using the same words and still not communicate, because of other blocks, of other factors. People can refuse to listen. People can for all kinds of reasons not want to accept the message.

That failure of communication, for instance, between Obi and Clara is interesting. They speak the same language but there is a communication breakdown. Obi is saying "just give me a little more time, my mother is sick, let's wait, we'll get married later on." Now, Clara cannot understand that, you see, and it's not because she's unreasonable. She's very reasonable.

She's so reasonable that she had foreseen this problem before, and warned Obi about it, you see. She is not going to allow herself to be brutalized over and over again; this is why she'd taken the humiliating pains to say: "Do you know that you're not supposed to marry someone like me?" Obi says, "Nonsense, we're beyond that, we're civilized people." And now that Clara has invested her life in this civilization she's being told: "Let's wait a minute." So this is an example of my own view of the breakdown in communication because it's not that either party does not understand the words being used, it's just that no words can solve their predicament. There's no way you can resolve this particular problem in any kind of language; we are at an impasse, and it's now beyond language. But we have no better tool than language to communicate with one another. So when language fails, what do we do? We resort to fighting, but that, of course, is destructive. So language is very important, it is a hallmark of our humanity, one of the hallmarks of our humanity, but it is never enough, even that is not enough. We work at it, we give it all the patience we have, but we must expect that even when all is said and done there will always remain those areas, those instances when we are unable to get across.

Rowell: What about Obi and communication with his family?

Achebe: Well, the same kind of thing is happening but not to the same degree, obviously. Between him and his mother there is a very peculiar relationship that has been built up from birth, which he's in no position to deal with at all. He can deal with his father quite abruptly, in fact, and overwhelm him, but he doesn't even try with his mother. This is a relationship we may not comprehend unless we come from a culture like his. There's no way he can argue with his mother when she says, "well, if you're going to marry that girl, wait until I'm dead. You won't have very long to wait." In some cultures they say "to hell with that, she's had her own life, this is my life." That's not the Igbo people, you know. There's no way Obi can respond like that. So that's communication again. One part of Obi knows that he can say "mother, I can't wait." Another part of him says "you can't say that to your mother."

Rowell: Critics have often described Okonkwo in *Things Fall Apart* as representative of a kind of Aristotelian tragic hero. How do you respond to critics reading Okonkwo as a hero in terms of Aristotle's concept of tragedy?

Achebe: No. I don't think I was responding to that particular format. This is not, of course, to say that there is no relationship between these. If we are to believe what we are hearing these days, the Greeks did not drop from the sky. They evolved in a certain place which was very close to Africa. Very close to Egypt which in itself was also very close to the Sudan and Nubia which was very close to West Africa. So it may well turn out, believe it or not, that some of the things Aristotle was saying about tragedy were not really unheard of in other cultures. It's just that we are not yet ready to make these quantum leaps! For instance, it has been shown that one-third of the entire vocabulary of ancient Greek came from Egypt and the Middle East. And so obviously there were links with us which the Greeks themselves apparently had no problem acknowledging. It was only late, from the eighteenth century, that the Europeans began to find it difficult to accept that they owed anything to Africa. In any event, I think a lot of what Aristotle says makes sense. Putting it in a neat, schematic way may be peculiar to the Greek way of thinking about the hero. But that idea is not necessarily foreign to other people: the man who's larger than life, who exemplifies virtues that are admired by the community, but also a man who for all that is still human. He can have flaws, you see; all that seems to me to be very elegantly underlined in Aristotle's work. I think they are there in human nature itself, and would be found in other traditions even if they were not spelled out in the same exact way.

Rowell: Would you agree that there are patterns of irony or an extensive use of irony in all of your first four novels, from *Things Fall Apart* all the way down to *No Longer at Ease?* If there are ironic situations or ironic characters, will you talk about that irony? I really don't like to ask writers to talk about their own work.

Achebe: I think irony is one of the most powerful (how does one say it?) . . . one of the most powerful conditions in human experience. And anybody who is a storyteller—I see myself as a storyteller—will sooner or later come to the realization that ironies are among the most potent devices available to them. Irony can raise a humdrum story to a totally new level of power and significance simply by the fact of its presence, the presence of ironic juxtaposition. That's really all I can say. Your question seems to me almost like asking what do I think about metaphors. Well, you can't even begin to tell a story without saying *this thing* is like *that thing.* Or even *this thing* is *that thing.* Or, as in an almost grotesque proverb of Igbo, *the corpse of another person is a log of wood.* Of course, we know that somebody else's body is not a log of wood; but it could be so for all we care. We don't seem to be able to put ourselves inside that box. We do not say "there go I but for the grace of God." We lack the imagination to leap into that box. And if we didn't the world would have been a much more wholesome place. The oppression in the world would not be as great as it is. The inhumanity we practice would be greatly reduced. But because we lack the metaphoric imagination we are unable to make that imaginative leap from out of our own skin into somebody else's. And so our storytellers jolt us with metaphor and irony, and remind us that "there but for the grace of God go I." Without metaphor and irony things would be white or black, and not very interesting. It's only when you show that this white is also black that something very interesting and important begins to happen.

Rowell: In this interview, you have, I've noticed, in more than one instance, used a tale to illustrate your point. You have also used the proverb. I suddenly remember the narrator of *Things Fall Apart* talking about the importance of proverbs in Igbo conversation.

Achebe: Proverbs are miniature tales; they are the building blocks, if you like, of tales. They are tales refined to their simplest form, because a good proverb is a short story. It is very short indeed. What it demonstrates, first of all—before we go on to the why—is the clarity with which those who made these proverbs had observed their reality. A proverb is a very careful observation of reality and the world, and then a distillation into the wisdom of an elegant statement so that it sticks in the mind. You see it, you know it's true, you tell yourself, "this is actually true, why hadn't I thought of it," and you remember it. And there is a whole repertory of these statements made by my people across the millennia. Some must have fallen out of use, others have remained and have been passed on from one generation to the next. And part of the training, of socialization of young people in this society, is to become familiar with these statements from our immemorial past. So that when we are dealing with a contemporary situation, when we are dealing with here and now, we have the opportunity to draw from the proverbial repertory to support or refute what is said. It's like citing the precedents in law. This case before us is what we are talking about. But similar things have happened before; look at the way our ancestors dealt with them down the ages. So it gives one a certain stability, it gives one a certain connectedness; it banishes, it helps to banish the sense of loneliness, the cry of desolation: why is this happening to me, what have I done, woe is me! The proverb is saying no, it's tough, but our ancestors made this proverb about this kind of situation, so it must have happened to someone else before you, possibly even to a whole lot of other people before. Therefore, take heart, people survived in the face of this kind of situation before. So proverbs do many kinds of things. They are, just for their elegance as literary forms, interesting and satisfying; then they ground us in our "Great Tradition"; they tell us something about the importance of observing our reality carefully, very carefully.

Rowell: We know you in the United States as a novelist mainly. But you're also a poet, a critic, and a short story writer. Does the poem, or the essay, or the short story do something for you that the novel cannot do?

Achebe: Yes, I think so, I think so. Though, I hope you won't ask me what it is, because that would be more difficult. But suddenly I have not been writing short stories for some time; there was a period in my life when I wrote a lot of short stories. At that point I was not writing novels. There was also a period when I wrote much poetry, much for me; now I rarely write poetry and so it must mean these forms serve me at particular times or have served me at particular times. If I may be more specific, during the Biafran war, the civil war in Nigeria, I was not writing novels for years and years and years; after that I was not in a mood to write novels. I wrote most of my poetry at that period, many of the short stories. So without saying categorically that I only write poetry in times of war, I think that there is some connection between the particular distress of war, the particular tension of war, and the kind of literary response, the genres that I have employed in that period. I remember in particular one poem, "Christmas in Biafra," which actually came out of the kind of desperation which you felt hearing carols on short-wave radio and being reminded that there were places in the world where people were singing about the birth of the Prince of Peace and you were trapped in this incredible tragedy. Now it's a very powerful feeling, a very powerful feeling indeed. It is analogous to that scene in *Things Fall Apart* just before those men kill Ikemefuna and they hear in the air the sound of music from a distant clan. I don't know how those men felt hearing it: the sounds of peace and celebration in the world and a horrendous event at home. So what I'm feeling at any particular time and what the world is doing impinge on the kind of writing I do, obviously.

Rowell: Earlier you said, "I see myself as a storyteller." What do you mean?

Achebe: Well, that's just a manner of speaking, of again relating myself in the manner of the proverbs we are talking about to something that had happened before. So even though I don't think I'll ever be in the court of the emperor, telling stories to him and his courtiers, still I am in that tradition, you see. The story has always been with us, it is a very old thing, it is not new; it may take new forms, but it is the same old story. That's mostly what I'm saying, and we mustn't forget that we have a certain link of apostolic succession, if you like, to the old *Griots* and storytellers and poets. It helps me anyway; it gives me that sense of connectedness, of being part of things that are eternal like the rivers, the mountains, and the sky, and creation myths about man and the world. The beginning was a story, it is the story that creates man, then man makes other stories, you see. And for me this is almost like Ezeulu in *Arrow of God* who before he performs important functions in his community has to go to the beginning and tell how his priesthood came into existence. He has to recite that story to his community to validate his priestly rites. They know it already but cannot hear it too often. This is how stories came into being, and this is what they did for our ancestors and we hope that they will continue to serve our generations, not in the same form necessarily, but the same spirit.

Rowell: What is the role of the literary critic in the new Nigerian society?

Achebe: Well, that's a good question. I didn't want to speak for critics, but I dare say that there were ancestors of literary critics in the past; I mean spectators who might get up and say: I don't like that stuff! Obviously modern critics could claim a certain apostolic succession but quite frankly I don't think the role of their ancestors was as elevated as that of the original creators. Today when the thing is down in print on paper, I think the role of the critic has become a lot more complex and thus a lot more important. It is important because there is need for mediation. Since I'm not going to go around and meet the people and answer their questions as a storyteller would do in the past, actually meet them face to face and experience their support or disagreement, somebody else is called into existence to perhaps explain difficult parts, or perform all kinds of functions of a mediating nature. Also, there is so much which is produced, there is so much that is written, all of it is not of the same quality and a certain amount of discrimination is necessary just to survive the barrage of production in the modern world, the sheer number of books. I think therefore the role of the critic is important. Also, I think the critic is there to draw attention to this continuity that I was talking about, to the tradition. How does this new work relate to what has happened before, how does it relate to writers who were here before, how does it even relate to those who did not write their stories but told them? So I think there is a new and necessary and important role for the critic.

Rowell: I'm going to ask one more question about art and literature. Then I want to turn to a handful of questions about your background. If you had to look back on your works and judge them, is there one text or one genre which allowed you to speak or write the best way you wanted to? Or is there one of them which is more representative of the kind of expression you wanted to make?

Achebe: Well, I think I can only talk about the genre, and the only reason I can talk about it is that I can lean on the simple fact of numbers. I've written more novels than I've done any other thing, and therefore that must be the one that as of now seems most congenial. But I really don't even try to think about that and even if I were tempted I would resist the thought. I would go out of my way to stop it because, as I've said, everything I have written has been useful to me at the time when I needed to write it, and I wouldn't want to say that this time is more important than that time. So apart from being able to say that obviously I have written more novels, I would not bother to rank my texts and genres, or award distinctions, even secretly.

Rowell: Did your education at the University of Ibadan direct you in any way toward a career in creative writing? I guess what I'm ultimately asking is how did you come to write?

Achebe: Yes, well, I think I grew up in Ibadan in a way that pointed clearly in the direction of writing. That was the period when I was able to reassess what I had read and all I had to go by at that point was the colonial novel written by white people about us. And so it was a very, very crucial moment in my career, that moment when I was reading these things again with a new awareness of what was going on, the subtle denigration, and sometimes not so subtle, that I had missed before. So in that sense it's at Ibadan that I grew up, and growing up is part of the decision to write. It did not give me the taste for writing; it was always there. Even in high school and before that, because the taste for stories was always there. I think it's simply encountering myself in literature and becoming aware that that's not me, you see. A number of texts helped; one of them was Joyce Cary's *Mister Johnson,* and I suppose one of them was Conrad's *Heart of Darkness.* There were a lot of other books not so well known and not worth remembering. But what I'm talking about is encountering the colonial ideology, for the first time in fiction, as something sinister and unacceptable. So if you add to this the weakness to stories anyway, you have the possibilities, even the incitement to become a writer, somebody who will attempt to tell his own story. Because we all have a story in us, at least one story, I believe. So in my case Ibadan was the watershed, a turning point.

Rowell: At the present time we have only a bit of biographical or autobiographical public information about you, the man and the writer, and I've always wondered whether or not the Christian component of your background (your father was a mission teacher) extracted you from Igbo culture in any way?

Achebe: I think it intended to, but I don't think it succeeded. Certainly it had its moments of success. But with my curiosity, my natural curiosity, I didn't allow it to succeed completely. And so there I was between two competing claims but not aware of any discomfort as a child. I was certainly aware of curiosity about the non-Christian things that were going on in my community, and I was not really convinced that because they were non-Christian they were therefore bad, or evil. And even though I met a lot of Christians who seemed to operate on the basis that everything in the traditional society was bad or evil or should be suppressed, I think that slowly, little by little, they realized too that that was really a lost hope, a wrong kind of attitude to adopt. I could see that a bit in my father. I know that he became less rigid as he grew older. The things he would not tolerate, when I was very little, I saw him not pay too much attention to later on—like traditional dancing and singing, you know. I never had any problem with those things. I was in a peculiar and an interesting position of seeing two worlds at once and finding them both interesting in their way. I mean I was moved by the Christian message. I was moved by hymns in the church. I was moved by the poetry of Christianity. I was also moved by the thing that Christianity was attempting to suppress: the traditional religion, about which at the beginning I didn't know very much. But I was going to make it my business to listen and learn and go out of my way to find out more about the religion. This is how it happened. So I was not distressed at all by being born in that kind of crossroads. On the contrary, I thought it was one of the major advantages I had as a writer.

Interview with Chinua Achebe

Gordon Lewis / 1995

Published by permission of Gordon Lewis.

Here's the information I have so far: your father's name was Isaiah Okafo Achebe, your mother was Janet N. Iloegbunam Achebe, and you were born in Ogidi on November 16, 1930, the fifth of six children. You were named Albert Chinualumogu Achebe, but you later dropped the name Albert. I read that you considered it too much of a concession to British colonization. I understand completely. As nearly as you can translate it, what would be the meaning of your name?

It means, "May chi fight for me." Chi is my personal divinity. A central concept of Ibo religion is that every individual, every single individual in the world, has his or her own particular chi. No two people have the same. This is an aspect of God, assigned to each person by God himself at the very beginning, so it's a pretty strong entity.

I understand your father was a Christian missionary. He gave you a Christian name, but I assume he was also aware of the meaning of the Ibo name he gave you.

Yes. At the time the missionaries arrived, one of the things they attempted to do was to Christianize the Ibo pantheon so that the Ibo Chukwu became Jehovah, so chi in fact was taken as an aspect of God himself. There was nothing unChristian about it.

Concerning your family, could you tell me the names of your five brothers and sisters? What careers or activities did they pursue?

One is dead now, the eldest brother. I'll give you their Christian names. The eldest was Frank, the next John, then my eldest sister Zinobia, then Augustine, then myself, and the youngest Grace. Frank went into government service after his secondary education. In those days there was no university in Nigeria, so he went to the Posts and Telegraphs Department, the wireless section, and worked there until his retirement, when he came home and occupied our father's home, because that was his right. John went into teaching at the encouragement of my father, ostensibly to take his place. Then he moved on into publishing and finally ended up where my father would have loved to, which was in the ministry; he's now a pastor in the Anglican Church. Zinobia taught for a short while, then married a teacher who also became a pastor, so the Christian presence in my family remained very strong. Augustine is a structural engineer who studied both in Nigeria and in England. Grace did a spot of teaching before she married. Both sisters are now widows.

Which of your siblings would you say had the greatest influence on you when you were growing up?

It's difficult to say because there are different kinds of influences. I grew up with Grace because we were the youngest, and there was a big gap between us and the rest. At the time we were growing up, my eldest brother Frank was already working in Lagos, and he had taken my immediate senior brother Augustine with him to go to school there. Our sister Zinobia was more like a surrogate mother to Grace and me; she took care of us when our mother was out, and she was the one who told us stories. Grace and I were the closest in age. We started school the same day, the reason being that while I was old enough to go to school, she wasn't, but what would she be doing if she stayed at home? The two of us were very close in that way. John also had a lot of influence on me because in my final year in elementary school, when he was teaching elsewhere, he took me with him to look after me and to make sure that I got a sound education that would enable me to enter a good secondary school. That was a critical moment in my educational career. I lived with him for one year and was able to get into Umuahia, probably the best secondary school in Eastern Nigeria. He was a kind of model for me, and I still think that he was probably the most talented of all of us. He and Frank simply didn't have the opportunity we younger kids had, but they took as much as was available in their time. By my time things had changed. A brand new university was built just as I was finishing secondary school, so I just walked in. It wasn't because I was spectacular or anything like that, in relation to my siblings.

What influence would you say your father had on you? Could you describe his personality?

He was a great disciplinarian. He didn't talk very much. Both my parents were very quiet people. My father was very serious and had a very exceptional career himself. He was an orphan very early and was brought up in the home of his uncle on his mother's side. His mother had died giving birth to the next child, who did not live. His father died soon after that, so he was reared not by his parents but by his uncle and his mother's family. He was the first one in the family, and one of the first in town, who converted, and he became a very enthusiastic evangelist. He was already well-known in the community as a wrestler, and he would have had his future cut out for him in traditional society, but he decided to switch when Christianity arrived, so he turned away from traditional ways. He even tried to convert his uncle, a very powerful man who had taken some of the highest titles in the community. His uncle said no, no, no, but didn't discourage him from pursuing Christianity.

In 1904 my father went to the first teachers college established by the Church Missionary Society and met my mother there. He eventually sent her to be trained by the mission in the first girls' school in the vicinity. Thereafter they began missionary work—teaching, preaching, going from place to place throughout our area.

My parents knew that education was important. To my father it was almost a religion. He wanted us to have as much education as possible, as much as he could afford. He spent everything he had sending one child after another to school. It was fairly expensive to do so in those days, for there were no free schools to begin with. For a long time church schools were the primary source of education, but eventually the colonial government set up a few schools. I went to one of them. The government had resources that made them good schools in terms of facilities, books, and so forth, but it was the missionary societies, first the Anglicans and then the Roman Catholics, who provided the bulk of education.

Within your community was your father of high standing because of his status as a teacher?

Yes. He was a real pioneer. The first church in our part of Ogidi was created by him. He was the first teacher there, before he was hired by the mission to go on their behalf to teach in other places. From 1904 to 1935 he was teaching. He was in the first generation that became Christians, so he was a man of considerable importance in our town. Even though his salary was miserable by today's standards, we were well-off compared with other families. How my parents managed to exist on such a small income is a miracle, but as their children we were better off than those who had nothing as they grew up.

What about your mother? What was her role?

The wife of an evangelist was also an evangelist. There was really no division, no separation, between them; they were the teacher and the teacher's wife. Just as my father looked after the church, my mother would look after the women of the church. In addition, women always had more roles than men, especially in providing food for the family in the traditional Ibo way. The man planted one crop, which he said was the king of the crops, the yam. But the yam was so regal that it was only eaten once in the day, in the afternoon. So the woman had to find breakfast and dinner, and this made her work actually quite heavy. Being a teacher's wife did not spare you from this; you still had to provide for your family. My mother grew cocoyams and vegetables, and she also did a certain amount of petty trading to supplement all this, so she had a very, very full life. She was a very strong and solid influence on us.

Did your sisters help out too?

In certain ways. It was Zinobia, the elder of my sisters, who sort of acted as an assistant to our mother. She was five or so classes ahead of me. I remember that when I first went to school, I just didn't like it. I used to skip my class and go to Zinobia's class and sit with her. They let me do that for a few days, and then they kicked me out. She was a support to my mother in the home.

I gather that your parents were very hardworking people. Is it fair to say that in your family environment there was an emphasis on hard work, order and stability?

Yes, the environment was structured, the family was structured, and this was typical of our situation. Child-rearing practices were clear and direct. Your parents knew the world, and you didn't, so what they told you was right. No parent tells his or her child a falsehood; this is a kind of feeling that's implanted in our culture. A man could stand up and swear an oath simply on the basis of what his father told him. If there was a quarrel about a boundary between this man's land and that man's, and my father told me that the line was between this tree and that tree, I was ready to swear the most frightful oath if necessary, because a father doesn't tell a lie. So it was a very ordered society in that sense. Whether you were Christian or non-Christian, it was the same.

Could you comment on your early schooling?

From fairly early in my schooling my teachers thought I was going to go far. I remember one headmaster coming to visit my father, telling him this boy is going very far, so you better find money for his education. My results were very good, generally. The teachers said I was very lazy, but that's really because I didn't like physical education. I didn't care for games, sports. If I put my mind to it, I could do as well as the average athlete, but I was not interested in physical exertion, in competition.

Academic competition was a different matter, but at first I didn't really see that as competition. I just enjoyed what I was doing, and if we were tested, I would do well. I didn't see myself in competition with anybody, until later on.

After my elementary education there were two schools available to me, the top schools. One was a missionary secondary school called Dennis Memorial, a grammar school. That was famous in my area and very popular. The students wore a red blazer and red cap, and that was really where I wanted to go. But there was another school that had been built by the colonial government, a college called Umuahia. It was really as good as the public schools in England. The British colonial government tried to create what they considered the best secondary schools in the colony, but not too many of them. They were elitists by nature, so they built just four government colleges in the whole country. I took the entrance exams for both Dennis Memorial Grammar School and Government College Umuahia and was accepted by both. I was awarded a scholarship by DMGS and I thought that settled the matter, but my brother John said, "You are going to Umuahia, even if you don't get a scholarship." In the end I got a scholarship to Umuahia as well. And that feat, of winning scholarships to DMGS and Umuahia, made me a celebrity at home. Senior teachers would come to visit our house to shake hands with me.

After four years at Umuahia, I took the school leaving certificate exam, which was set in England, and not just passed it but came out top in the school. University College Ibadan had just opened its doors, so I took their entrance exam at that time and had one of the two best results in the whole country. I was awarded a major scholarship for my undergraduate studies. I went to Ibadan to study science—in fact, medicine—because my performance in the entrance examination was stronger in the sciences than it was in the arts. The difference wasn't that much, but it was certainly stronger, so the scholarship was awarded for study in the sciences. But after one year I said I don't want to go on with this, I want to change. I wasn't doing well because I just wasn't interested in physics and chemistry and biology. But the university said you can't switch, for we don't know how well you will do in the arts. It was difficult for me to persuade them to let me make the change, but in the end they allowed me to do so. However, it meant that I lost my scholarship. Eventually my brothers John and Augustine came in and said you must go on; we'll find the fees. And this is what happened. I was able to continue, and the second year after this fiasco I was able to get a government scholarship to see me through. I then went into English, history and religion, which were my three main subjects.

I think the department that influenced me more than any of the others was the Department of Religion. English was always my favorite subject through thick and thin. History I had come to enjoy, but religion was something new, especially since it was comparative religion. That I found extraordinarily interesting because for the first time I was able to see the Ibo system of beliefs set beside other systems. For instance, I discovered that the Yoruba and even the Ashanti in Ghana had a pantheon of gods and various gradations of divinity that resembled those of the Ibo. To study this seriously was something quite new to me.

Throughout the colonial period education was very much tailored by the British. You didn't really study too much of your own things. Your own things were more or less not fit for education. If you read poetry, you read Wordsworth, Keats and other British poets. You even did the geography of England, even though it was thousands of miles away, and most students were never going to be there. You knew all kinds of things about other people but very little about yourself. Religious studies was different in that it set out to examine indigenous religious beliefs seriously and to look at them alongside Christian religion and theology. Ultimately other departments began to do the same. History began to take a lot more interest in the history of Nigeria itself, the history of our peoples. This was one of the major contributions of a new institution of higher learning.

Was there a moment or period of time when you began to find the beginnings of your own path?

Yes, I suppose, though I don't think I could tell you specifically when or how. I think there was the notion that what was happening to us was important and that we were a very, very fortunate generation, for everybody was saying that we were the future leaders of Nigeria. You even said that yourself. And everything went to support you. Things simply happened in your favor all along. But finding my path in the sense of deciding that literature was going to be the way, that took a long time. It was rather nebulous. Apart from my interest in reading literature, it goes back to the stories I heard told in my home, the stories told in my village. Discovering written literature was amazing, and being able to get into it was like having a new window on the world. The more you read, the more you enjoyed it. I read whatever I could find, as well as the required texts in the heavily British curriculum.

I think it was all part of the revolution that was going on not just in my own life but in the life of my country. The transformation of a colonial people into a people agitating for independence introduced something in the air that was not there before—a rebelliousness. Everyone was questioning everything. This is the feature of the 1950s when I was going to the university—that everything was up for questioning, including the church, including the faith, including Christianity, and that was the stage when I dropped my Christian name. That was simply one little token from one person in a movement that was universal in Nigeria and in Africa.

Index

Aborigines, 83
Abraham, William E., *The Mind of Africa*, 14
Abuja, Nigeria, 136
Achebe, Augustine (elder brother), 102, 185, 190
Achebe, Chinelo (elder daughter), 60
Achebe, Chinua: academic life, sterilizing effect of, 10; Akan religion, 104; American culture, 79, 162–63; black power, 37; British people, 66; British taxation, 149–50; children, learning from, 85–87; Christianity, 5, 18, 30–31, 48–50, 69, 79, 80–81, 85, 104, 107, 113–14, 137, 184, 185–87, 191; colonialism, 50, 89, 129, 175, 183, 185; Commonwealth, concept of, 92–93; cruelty and injustice as failures of imagination, 119; cultural revolution in Africa, 27–28; disenchantment with political independence, 39; dogmatism, 24, 38, 42, 68; education, 129, 167–68; English tradition, 51; Europeans in Africa, 29–30; fanaticism, 143, 152; films, 10, 15, 19, 26; God, 83, 84, 107, 117, 138; griots, 165, 168–70, 182; human condition, 159–60; Ijo people, 87; imperialism, 157; infant mortality, 85–86; Marxism, 36–37; multinational companies, 85; Neocolonialism, 32–33, 37, 157–58; next generation, 44; radio, 10, 121; revolution, 70–71; struggle for survival, 147–48, 159–60; television, 10, 59, 82, 121, 128; tribalism, 22, 23, 33; universities, 44; university professors, 10, 44; violence, 70–71; Western culture, 82; women in traditional society, 149–50; **Autobiographical:** broadcasting work, 5, 10, 18, 21, 62, 114–16; brothers, 102, 107, 185–86, 190; children, 79, 82; Christian influences, 5, 18, 58, 107, 113–14, 184, 185–87, 191; collecting oral literature, 154; contacts with other writers, 4–5, 9, 77–78, 79–80, 107, 115, 120; dancing, 106–07, 162; daughters, 60, 82; desire to study Ibo culture, 52, 54; early development as a writer, 3–4; early life, 5, 12–13, 18, 58, 113, 185–89; editing work, 97, 103, 111, 120, 124–29; euphoria at independence, 116; father, 5, 8, 18, 49, 58, 79, 100, 107, 113–14, 184, 185–88; first cousins, 50; getting started as a writer, 20, 103, 190–91; grandfather, 14, 58, 186; grandmother, 186;

granduncle, 187; inability to write novels during civil war, 34, 39, 53; living at crossroads, 5, 13, 76, 79, 80, 85, 184; meeting African-American writers, 15–16; mother, 76, 81–82, 100, 185, 187–88; plans for publishing house, 40; reading, identification with European characters in, 112–13; returning to Nigeria, 52; schooling, 99–101, 188–89; sisters, 76, 81–82, 185–86, 188; teachers, 99–109, 111; teaching, 10, 62, 73–74, 105, 141, 152–53, 171, 172–73; uncles, 50, 76; university experience, 4, 10, 13, 102–13, 183–84, 189–91; visiting America, 15–16; wife, 84, 85, 107; **On Ibo Life and Culture:** ancestors, 14, 69, 76, 86–87, 159, 180; artists, 165; ceremonies, 68; chi (personal divinity), 66, 83–84, 185; conversation, 9, 13; costumes, 67–68; culture, 52, 65–67, 77–79, 82, 88–89, 114, 136, 184; cyclic world view, 136; democracy, 66–67; duality principle, 42, 65, 87, 121, 155, 161; egwugwu (masked spirits), 67–68; elders, 70; family life, 69–70; gods, 90, 125, 150, 185; Iboland, 29, 52, 125, 150; Ibo people, 8, 52, 64, 66, 77, 137, 165–67, 178; Ibo society, 9, 11–12, 64, 88–89, 118; Ikenga carving, 11; kingship, 31, 47–48, 77–78, 138–39; manliness, 11–12, 46–47; new yam festival, 68, 90; ogbanje (spirit) children, 85; reincarnation, 86–87; religion, 30–31, 48, 68, 69, 185, 190; ritual, 90; social change, 88–90; spiritual world, 78–80, 84, 86–87, 126; suicide, 49; title-taking, 47–48; values, 11; village life, 18; **On Language and Style:** African languages, 59, 95, 97–98, 175; choice of language, 14; English, 9, 51, 54–56, 59–60, 74, 91, 95, 98, 144, 154, 163, 172, 175–77; French, 8–9, 163, 174, 175; Gikuyu (*see* Kikuyu); Ibo, 54–56, 57, 59–60, 74, 79, 82, 84, 144, 147–48, 154, 163, 168, 176–77; imagery, 67; Kikuyu, 59, 163; language registers, 143–44; linguistic complexity in Africa, 163; metaphors, 58, 135; names in Ibo, 84; pidgin, 9, 74, 144; Portuguese, 163; respect for language, 83; styles, 8–9, 12, 25, 29, 91, 117–18; Swahili, 59, 163; symbols, 57–58; translations, 10, 21, 59, 154; **On Other Literatures, Other Literary**